TEACHER'S BOOK

Language

for Key Stages 3 and 4

with
David
Crystal

cartoons by
Edward McLachan

LONGMAN

Longman Group UK Limited,
*Longman House, Burnt Mill, Harlow,
Essex, CM20 2JE, England
and Associated Companies throughout the World.*

First published 1991

ISBN 0 582 07562 9

set in 10/11pt Palatino

Printed in Great Britain by
BPCC Hazell Books, Aylesbury

Introduction

It was the best of times. It was the worst of times. It was 1990.

It was the best of times because of the remarkable amount of attention which had been devoted to the English language in the late 1980s, relating to the publication of the Kingman and Cox Reports, and the development of the National Curriculum. English language scholars, teachers and students were impressed. Those with an awareness of the recent history of ideas in language work also noted the way, for the first time in educational linguistic practice, concepts of language structure and concepts of language use were being brought together into a single programme. No one had ever seen anything quite like it before.

But it was also the worst of times, because nobody had any clear idea what to do about it. Proper emphasis was being paid to the view that teachers should develop their awareness of language, their knowledge about language, their metalanguage. Yet there was a simultaneous awareness of the gap which existed between the theoretical framework which underlay the National Curriculum and the demands of daily classroom practice. The initial impression of specificity and precision which came from reading the Curriculum documents dissipated as people realised how far away from the actual task of teaching were the statements of attainment at the different levels. They were left with the question: how could a teaching syllabus be devised, based on such crude introductory material? How many possible syllabuses were there? And how should one evaluate the proliferation of terminology? There were glorious mountains glittering in the distance, but no one had any definite plan for reaching them.

In theory, it could be done. Language researchers could collaborate with teachers in observing classroom practice, discuss new terms and concepts, judge their relevance to the kinds of activity taking place there, and work out successful ways of teaching them, at the various chronological and conceptual levels. They could develop a sense of which language concepts are easy (from the child's point of view) and which are difficult, and devise ways of helping students around the difficult concepts. They could provide a syllabus which would be carefully graded, comprehensive, and a solid foundation for advanced work. It would take five years or so.

As we all know, none of this has happened. The people charged with developing the links between theory and practice were placed under great pressure of time, and very little applied language research ever took place. They were fortunate in having the assistance of many hundreds of teachers who cooperated in the provision of trial materials, and the results speak for themselves. But a great deal remains to be done.

The present series

The present series of books aims to make a small but precise contribution to the task facing language teachers in school in the 1990s. It came about like this. I began by reading through all the recent government reports about language, along with the National Curriculum proposals, and pulled out everything that was a language term. I disregarded those which seemed to have a common-sense application (such as *clarity*, *accuracy*, *speaking*), and concentrated on the remainder. There were over 200 of them. It was quickly apparent that the list was by no means systematic. The published guidelines were notoriously anecdotal and selective in their coverage, and might mention a term X without making any reference to the related term Y. I therefore systematised the list, following the guidelines, and adding only those terms which related to the ones already mentioned in the documentation. That made over 400. I then looked at the total list, noticed several areas of omission, added the relevant terms, and reached the final total of 445 – a total eventually split between the KS 3 book (217, including 59 cross-references), and the KS 4 (228, including 56 cross-references).

The next step was the tricky one. It would be impracticable to publish all the entries in a single book. They would need to be divided into levels. The decision was made to focus on Key Stages 3 and 4, these being the stages at which teachers seemed to be most in need of material. The resulting two books are thus the result of my attempt to divide the 445 terms in a sensible way. In the absence of any agreed language syllabus, it was inevitably an arbitrary process. There are obviously some concepts which should be introduced earlier than others. Some indeed are dependent on others (especially in the field of grammar). But there are many terms which could be introduced at either level, and in some cases the question arose as to whether certain terminological areas should be introduced at all. A good example is the basic terminology of phonetics. After some heart-searching, and discussion with teacher colleagues, I decided to include it, largely at KS 4, on the grounds that unless students are given some systematic training in listening to the sounds of speech, their work on spoken language is likely to remain vague and waffly. At all times, I tried to bring to bear my own experiences of teaching language notions to undergraduates and to various groups of professionals over the years, which has given me a sense of where some of the difficulties lie. But writing for children of 11 to 15 is a different ball-game from writing for undergraduates and in-service professionals.

Having drawn up my head-word list, therefore, the next task was to write the entries at an appropriate level. Here, I have tried to devise an expository style which will appeal, as far as the students are concerned. I have used wherever possible the kind of language which motivates students at these ages. This has made my entries somewhat unconventional, and I hope the style works. I was fortunate in having two secondary-school students available to read through all the entries and howl whenever they met something which they found boring or unintelligible. I have no doubt that, if I've got it wrong, other students will let me know it.

The teaching book

The same point applies to this teacher's book. I have tried to incorporate various kinds of information. Some of my comments are simply further clarifications of terms, indications of connections between terms, and suggestions for further lines of enquiry. I always give the answers to any questions posed or tasks set in the entries. I have thought hard about real and motivating activities which might be introduced into the class. I have been particularly anxious to build bridges between the study of language and the study of literature. However, I know that I have only scratched the surface of what can be done. I very much hope that teachers will let me know when they have better ideas about how to teach a particular point. If they do, the second edition of this book will be considerably better than the first.

The teacher's book, then, contains comments on all the entries in the two student books, plus a few extra entries thrown in for good measure. These last (39 in all, including 9 cross-references) are general linguistic terms which I think are likely to be encountered nowadays, though I doubt whether they have very much immediate pedagogical application. I may be wrong. I have also given some suggestions for follow-up reading, both within several entries, and at the end of almost every entry. As I am unable to anticipate the level of linguistic awareness of readers of this book, I have used a range of sources written at different levels, in the hope that teachers will be able to find their individual level among them. Lastly, I have added an Appendix in which the terms are grouped into broad thematic categories.

Having said all this, I am not entirely clear about how these books can best be employed. Are they best used as reference works to be dipped into whenever an unfamiliar term comes up? Or are they best used as a source of ideas for lesson topics and activities? How practical and motivating and relevant are the study tasks? I very much look forward to hearing whether, from the student's point of view, working with *Language A to Z* proves to be the best, or the worst, of times.

Further Reading

Most entries end with a reference to a chapter or section in one or more of the following books, where further information about the topic can be obtained. In the case of grammatical entries, three references are given, corresponding to three levels of awareness: RG – introductory; SGE – intermediate; CGEL – advanced.

CEL David Crystal, *The Cambridge Encyclopedia of Language* (CUP, 1987)

CGEL Randolph Quirk, Sidney Greenbaum, Geoffrey Leech, and Jan Svartvik, *A Comprehensive Grammar of the English Language* (Longman, 1985)

EL David Crystal, *The English Language* (Penguin, 1988)

EPP Peter Roach, *English Phonetics and Phonology* (CUP, 1983)

ET *English Today* (CUP, quarterly)

IPE A C Gimson, *An Introduction to the Pronunciation of English* (Edward Arnold, 1989, 4th edn)

LG Geoffrey Leech, *A Linguistic Guide to English Poetry* (Longman, 1969)

RG David Crystal, *Rediscover Grammar* (Longman, 1988)

SGE Sidney Greenbaum and Randolph Quirk, *A Student's Grammar of the English Language* (Longman, 1990)

Further terminological information can be found in:

David Crystal, *A Dictionary of Linguistics and Phonetics* (Blackwell, 1991, 3rd edn)

abbreviation (KS 3)

• This is a very general term, and several types can be distinguished: see separate entries on **acronym**, **blend** and **clipping**. There are also various ways of classifying them, such as whether their pronunciation is letter-by-letter (*RIP*) or syllabic (*ad*), and whether they are used only in writing (*Mr, St, Stn, Res Inst*) or in both writing and speech (*Fred, NATO, eg*). Notice which words are omitted from the full version (*PhD* – no *of*). *PhD* is read back-to-front (as is *MD*). Note also the problems of usage sometimes encountered. If we read *MP* as letters, we must precede it by *an*; if we read it 'in full', we must precede it by *a*. The full form of a word is often unacceptable – illustrated in the sample sentence by 'telephone-in'. If we expand *NATO*, we have to insert *the*. Some abbreviations can combine with affixes (*ex-POW, ICBMs*). There is considerable usage variation over whether written abbreviations should contain full stops: the older practice is to use the punctuation; modern practice increasingly avoids it.

• All uses of English seem to make use of abbreviations, so starting a collection is not difficult. Students could look out for instances where there is frequent use of abbreviations, and evaluate the questions of overuse and intelligibility. Specialist magazines are a good place to look – a computer magazine should generate a sample very quickly. What charities does the student know (*NSPCC, RSPCA*)? For spoken language, official spokespersons (government, trade union) can be a good source. There could also be a collection of the abbreviations used in school. Many dictionaries and encyclopedias contain a collection of abbreviations. Other sources: the list of abbreviations often given at the front of a published work, such as a reference book. The large collection referred to is the *Acronyms, Initialisms and Abbreviations Dictionary* (Gale, 1987, 11th edn).

• Some other tasks: making up facetious abbreviations (*SAPS* – 'School Abbreviation Protection Society') – compare well-known ones such as *TGIF* ('Thank God It's Friday'), *CMG* ('Call Me God', properly 'Commander of St Michael and St George'); collecting abbreviations which are more well known than their full forms (*AIDS*); finding abbreviation sequences (*IBM PC*); looking for variation among newspapers, especially tabloid vs quality press; comparing types of abbreviation in different subject areas (eg history, chemistry); for students studying a foreign language, how many foreign abbreviations do they know?

CGEL App I.73–6; ET 15

abstract noun and concrete noun (KS 4)

• This distinction has been around a very long time, and you'll often find the terms used in impressionistic studies of style; but you won't always find it a very easy distinction to work with in a systematic way. The trouble is, there are many uncertain cases where you just can't be sure whether the noun is abstract or concrete. Go through some pages of a dictionary, and you'll find several cases. Different senses can confuse the issue (as in the *music* and *smell* examples), but even in cases where the sense is clear, there can be problems (is *guideline* abstract or concrete? is *neighbourhood*? is *Spanish*?). The traditional definition focuses on the visual and the tactile senses as the criteria for concreteness, leaving nouns for sound, smell, and taste in a somewhat uncertain state (how would you rate *remark*, for instance?). Metaphorical uses also complicate the issue (*That place is a dump*), as do idioms (*on guard*).

• Having said all that, there are nonetheless many clear cases. Look out especially for the use of suffixes which form abstract or concrete nouns. Abstract suffixes include *-age (mileage), -al (refusal), -(a)tion (foundation), -dom (kingdom), -(e)ry (slavery), -ful (glassful), -hood (boyhood), -ing (farming), -ism (idealism), -ity (rapidity), -ment (amazement), -ness (kindness), -ocracy (democracy), -ship (friendship)*. There are fewer concrete suffixes, and only *-er* is really creative: *-ant (contestant), -ee (payee), -eer (profiteer), -er (singer), -ess (waitress), -ette (kitchinette), -let (piglet), -ling (duckling), -ster (gangster)*.

• An interesting exercise is to try identifying 'abstract' and 'concrete' styles in uses of language. There are very few contexts which are just one or the other. Most uses are mixed, and we can at best talk about a 'predominantly abstract' style. What actually happens in newspapers, magazines, radio talks, TV news, and so on? How abstract (concrete) are school textbooks, for instance? What happens in a political speech, or on a record or CD cover? How do *Radio Times* and *TV Times* compare? Ask students what their expectations are (there won't always be agreement), and then investigate.

RG 30; SGE 5.1; CGEL 5.3, App I.32–7

accent (KS 3)

• It's important to ensure that the difference between accent and dialect is understood. **Accent** refers only to features of pronunciation, whereas **dialect** includes distinctive grammar and vocabulary. Some dialects (notably, standard English) are spoken with many accents.

• It's very difficult to write accents down. There have been many attempts to do this in literature, such as Emily Brontë's version of Joseph's accent in *Wuthering Heights*: 'Nelly, we's hae a Crahnr's quest enah, at ahr folks . . .'. Dickens, George Eliot, and Thomas Hardy are other authors who often work with accent conventions, and there are many examples in Shakespeare (notably Fluellen in *Henry V – pridge, prains, falorous, aggriefed*, etc). A useful book for further examples is Norman Blake's *Non-standard Language in English Literature* (Blackwell, 1981). The main problem for an author is how to reconcile the need for accuracy and identity with that for consistency and intelligibility. Students should experience the difficulty of trying to write down a local accent, or the accent of a well-known person, in such a way that other people can guess who it is.

• Some people are extremely good at mimicking accents, and if you have some 'naturals' in the class, role-play activities can be helpful. Note that such accents are likely to be stereotypes – somewhat artificial versions of the reality, but sufficiently close to be recognisable. Some students may already have noticed themselves being influenced by the accent of the person they are talking to: they start talking more like the other person (a phenomenon called **accommodation** – one **accommodates** to the other speaker). Is anyone in the class currently under pressure to change their accent – from parents, friends, the school? Would anyone *like* to change their accent? Is anyone self-conscious about their accent?

• A discussion of accent will raise several issues (see also Peter Trudgill, *Accent, Dialect and the School*, Edward Arnold, 1975). What is meant by a 'good' accent or the 'best' accent? Cross-reference will be necessary to the notion of **standard**, and it always helps to know something about the historical situation which has led one accent to become prestigious (see **Received Pronunciation**). What is the value of a standard accent? Consider the importance of being intelligible to all in such contexts as teaching English to foreigners, the 'talking clock' on the telephone, or the BBC. Is intelligibility the only issue? Why do accents exist at all? What local or national identities do they express? What about other aspects of social identity, such as occupational accents (policeman, clergyman, lawyer) or ethnic accents? Are there any occupations or contexts where one accent would be appropriate and another would not?

• More advanced students might carry out an accent survey: what regional and social accents can be heard in school, or in the community around the school? Stress the non-judgmental nature of the exercise: the emphasis isn't on whether the accents are 'nice' or not, but on the existence of variety and why it is there. (A tape recorder is an essential piece of equipment for this kind of work.) A similar exercise can be carried out using a period of television viewing. You could also try an accent attitude survey, asking people why they like or dislike certain accents.

CEL 8, 10; IPE 6.3, App; EL 4

accents (KS 3)

• There's further illustration in the entries on **alphabet** and **diacritic** (which is a more general notion). Examples of accents in English can be easily tracked down from a dictionary of foreign words in English, such as John Ayto, *Making Sense of Foreign Words in English* (Chambers, 1991), but I imagine most of these words and phrases are too difficult for younger students. It can be interesting to go out looking for accents (in posters, shop signs, product labels, ads, newspapers, comics). Other aspects: pick out cases where the accent is really needed to distinguish words (*résumé* vs *resume*, *learnèd* vs *learned*); work out which sounds are signalled by an accent, in a language; look at the range of accents in familiar foreign languages (anyone brought a foreign paper or magazine back from abroad?); look out for idiosyncratic uses of accents, such as the metrical marks on lines of poetry.

• Incidentally, the mnemonic on grave and acute only works because we read English from left to right. In a language where the direction was the other way (eg Arabic), the impression would be the reverse.

CEL 33

accidence

• This term isn't one which pupils are likely to need, because it belongs to an earlier era of language study when Latin and Greek were widely taught. It refers to the changes in the form of a word which alter the word's grammatical function in a sentence – for example, *walk*, *walking*, *walked*, *walks*. In Latin, there were many word endings (see **inflection**) which were studied under this heading. However, the notion is of limited relevance for work on English, where there are few such word endings. These days, the term has been largely replaced by a more general conception of word structure: see **morphology**.

RG 74

accusative

• I haven't introduced students to this term, in these books, or to the other case-ending terms from Latin grammar which aren't relevant for English, such as **nominative** and **ablative**. English doesn't make much use of case endings; word order and prepositions express the grammatical notions which were conveyed by cases in Latin. The chief exception is the **genitive**, which *is* used in modern English: this is dealt with under **case**. The other exception is the object form of some pronouns (eg *he*/*him*): this too is described in the entry on **case**. There's nothing wrong with using **nominative** and **accusative** for the subject and object pronoun forms, but I prefer to use **subjective** and **objective**, which clearly relate to subject and object. I find these terms to be less off-putting than the Latinate labels from the former tradition of grammatical study.

acronym (KS 3)

• Several of the points raised under **abbreviation** apply to acronyms as well. Note that acronyms can be classified in several ways. Some are pronounced letter by letter (*GCSE*, *EEC*, *AA*, *RAC*); some can be pronounced as a whole syllable or word (*NATO*, *UNESCO*, *NALGO*). Some are written in capitals (all the above) and some in small letters (*eg*, *c/o*, *ie*). Some letters represent full words (all the above) and some represent parts of words (*ID* for 'identification'). Some acronyms have become conventional words in the language (such as *laser* – 'light amplification by

stimulated emission of radiation'). Note the existence of a usage problem over the term **acronym**: some people think that a word is an acronym *only* if it can be pronounced as a word, thus excluding the letter-by-letter category. I adopt the broader view in my entry.

• An interesting angle is the way new organisations often try to invent a name which makes a good pronounceable acronym: some genuine examples include *CACTUS* ('Campaign Against Cable Television Under Swindon') and *MADD* ('Mothers Against Drunken Drivers'). Sometimes, the rules are broken, in the interests of ending up with a memorable name: *GASP* ('Group Against Smoking'). A good class competition is to think up the best acronyms for a given task, society, invention, etc, such as a device for picking up litter in playgrounds, or a society for protecting poodles.

CGEL App I.73–6; ET 15

acrostic (KS 3)

• Acrostics have an ancient history: the name ultimately comes from the Greek, *akron* 'end' and *stikhos* 'verse line'. Authors would often put the letters of their name into the lines; riddles in verse form would be answered using an acrostic (both these techniques are found in Old English). Poets would flatter their patrons by including the patron's name as an acrostic in their poems – a practice which sometimes aroused the scorn of other writers. Dryden gives advice to a poor playwright (in 'Mac Flecknoe', 1682):

Leave writing plays, and choose for thy command
Some peaceful province in Acrostick Land.

Tony Augarde gives some of this historical background in *The Oxford Guide to Word Games* (Oxford, 1984), Chapter 4.

• Acrostic poem puzzles seem simple, but they are quite tricky to construct, and thus provide a good topic for class competitions. The solution is chosen in advance (say, EGGS), and the winner is the one who writes the most ingenious four-line verse. Each line needs to be semantically appropriate horizontally and relevant vertically. You will need to lay down the rules for the poetic part of the task – whether the lines need to be metrically regular, and whether they need to rhyme.

EL 7

active voice (KS 4) see **voice** (in grammar)

adjective (KS 3)

• The point about there being different kinds of adjectives is important, but it's also important to get across the fact that the vast majority of adjectives satisfy the four criteria in the entry (these are usually called the **central** class of adjectives). To instil a sense of which words are central and which are **peripheral**, you can use an adjective matrix, with the four criteria across the top, and candidate adjectives down the side.

	can use before noun	can use after *is/are*	can use with *very*	can use with *-er/more*
big	yes	yes	yes	yes
afraid	no	yes	yes	yes
six	yes	yes	no	no
side (road)	yes	no	no	no

Cases like *side* have so little grammatically in common with central adjectives that some grammarians don't call them adjectives at all, but talk instead of 'adjective-like words', 'adjectivals', or the like. On the other hand, these words do play a similar role to central adjectives, from the point of view of meaning. The words are different because they usually play a different role in the language – for example, *side* is usually a noun, *inside* is usually an adverb, *scraping* is usually a verb. When such words are made to serve as adjectives, they take up their new role somewhat uneasily.

• Note that adjectives (and adjective-like words) express various types of meaning: 'describe' in the definition is rather vague, as it stands. For example, adjectives can be used to express a distinguishing attribute of a noun (*a red apple* as opposed to *a green apple*), to express a quality (*the hot sun* – which incidentally isn't opposed to *the cold sun*), to express intensity (*a perfect gentleman*), and to express a quantity (*the three bears*).

• Students may be confused by the cases where an adjective is used as the head of a noun phrase; these cases refer to well-established classes of people (eg *the poor*, *the English*) and abstract notions (eg *the unknown*, *the supernatural*). This usage is really midway between adjective and noun: the words don't function as adjectives (for example, they don't inflect), nor do they function as nouns (for example, they don't have a plural). Grammars vary in what to call them: 'nominals', 'nominal adjectives', 'adjectival nouns'. The point to stress is that these items shouldn't be called adjectives, because they are no longer functioning as adjectives in the sentence; they are best seen as a rather unusual type of noun.

• For more advanced students, you can experiment with adjective order. We prefer to say *lovely green car* to *green lovely car*; *small round table* to *round small table*. The rules are not clear-cut, but there are definite tendencies: we like to put intensifying adjectives at the beginning of a string; noun-like adjectives tend to go at the end, nearest the noun; and there are restrictions governing where we put adjectives of size, length, height, and colour. Make up a sequence such as *those five superb comfortable new red English wooden garden chairs*, and see what options there are for changing the order.

RG 48–51; SGE 7.1–25, 17.41; CGEL 7.1–45, 17.113–18

adjective phrase (KS 3)

• All the examples in the entry have the modifying words occurring *before* the adjective. There are also adjective phrases in English where the modifying words go after the noun, but these can be more difficult to analyse, as they may involve a subordinate clause – for example, *I was happy to go*, *She was fond of him*, *That's subject to confirmation*, *He was aware of what was said*. Notice how the words following the adjective (the **complementation**) are optional in some cases (*happy*, *aware*) and obligatory in others (*fond*, *subject*).

• Adjective phrases can be usefully compared to adverb phrases: *very quick*, *very quickly*, etc. Note the usage problem: standard English requires *They ran very quickly* whereas non-standard English allows *They ran very quick*. But this point also applies to adjectives standing alone (*They did great*).

RG 49; SGE 7.22, 7.32, 16.38–41; CGEL 7.22, 7.27, 16.68–83

adjunct

• This is a term with widely varying modern use, so I haven't introduced it here. In its broadest sense, it refers to an element which plays a less important role in a construction – such as a connecting adverb (*however*) or a vocative (*Mary*, . . .). However, some grammarians use it in a narrower sense, meaning any kind of adverbial. Some (such as the Quirk team) use it even more narrowly, for a particular kind of adverbial (the most familiar kind, such as *quickly* and *in the garden*, which work closely with the other elements of clause structure). They then distinguish adjuncts from other terms ending in **-unct** – **conjunct**, **disjunct** and **subjunct**. I didn't feel that this level of sub-classification was appropriate for either KS 3 or 4. The distinctions are important, but the criteria are quite difficult to follow. I suggest they are left until a later stage of language study. But you might find it useful to keep the term on stand-by, ready for whenever you need a general term meaning an 'extra' or 'optional' element in a sentence.

RG 55

adverb (KS 3)

- The adverb is the most heterogeneous of all the word classes, and it is not possible to make simple generalisations which apply to all the words that have been called an adverb by grammarians. The uses mentioned in the entry are the main ones, but there are several other words that have been placed within the class, such as *not*, and the category of connectives can be broken down into many sub-types. It's important to focus on the main function of adverbs, to modify verbs, but it's also important not to concentrate on these to the exclusion of other functions. Apart from modifying verbs, adverbs can also modify adjectives (*very quick*), other adverbs (*very quickly*), nouns (*nearly 100, my trip abroad*), and certain other word classes.

- The entry lists the three main semantic classes of adverb, but there are several other types, such as frequency (*often*), emphasis (*certainly*), and approximation (*probably*). Point out the important connection with question forms: How? Manner. When? Time. Where? Place. As all adverb meanings are more fully expressed by larger constructions, these are discussed further under **adverbial**.

- The ending *-ly* isn't the only way of forming an adverb. Other ways include the use of *-wise* (*clockwise*), *-wards* (*southwards*), *-ways* (*sideways*), and *-style* (*boxer-style*). These are much less common, and some British people don't like to use *-wise*, usually on the grounds that it sounds too American. Also, note that there are several adjectives where you can't add *-ly* – if there's a *-ly* there already, for instance (*ugly, silly*) – and the adjective-like words don't (*inside, three*). Interesting idiosyncrasies include *good/goodly* (stays an adjective) and *hard/hardly* (changes meaning).

- Several of the factors that affect adjectives also affect adverbs – in particular, the ability to express comparison (eg *soon – sooner – soonest; quickly – more quickly – most quickly*). Some of these forms are irregular (notably *well – better – best; badly – worse – worst*), and give rise to alternative usages in non-standard English (such as *They did good, That was worser*).

RG 52; SGE 7.27–44; CGEL 7.46–90

adverbial (KS 3)

• It's important to see why this term was invented: it was primarily to get round the limitations of **adverb**, which refers only to a particular part of speech. The term **adverb phrase** is ambiguous: it can mean either 'a phrase which can replace an adverb, and which has an adverb in it' (*very slowly*) or 'a phrase which can replace an adverb, but which doesn't have an adverb in it' (*in the garden*). (I use **adverb phrase** only in the former sense, in these books, to preserve the parallelism with **noun phrase**, and the others.) An **adverb clause**, similarly, doesn't necessarily have an adverb inside it. The term **adverbial** gets round these problems – but there's no need to penalise anyone for using 'adverb' instead, as long as they've grasped this next point.

• The chief purpose of the term is to name an element of clause structure, and not a part of speech. The adverbial is one of the five main elements of clause structure in English. It's quite an important concept, therefore, and best introduced along with the other high-ranking elements – subject, object, verb, and complement. It's essential to see the functional parallelism between the three types of adverbial in the diagram. Despite the differences in the 'look' of the constructions, ranging from single words to long clauses, they all do the same job in a sentence. Simple substitution games usually make this point clear.

• Most adverbials are optionally present in a clause; if you leave them out, you still have a respectable sentence (*Ermintrude dropped the book on the floor – Ermintrude dropped the book*). But some verbs require an adverbial for the sentence to be acceptable: *put* is one of these – *Ermintrude put the book on the table*, but not **Ermintrude put the book*. You have to say where. Other such verbs include *lie* (somewhere) and *stay* (somewhere).

RG 12, 53–4; SGE 2.3, 8.1–11; CGEL 2.13–15, 8.1–24, 10.10

adverb phrase (KS 3)

• The only point to remember here is that some people do use this term in a more general sense, to include all phrases with an adverbial function, whether they have an adverb in them or not – such as *on Thursday* and *in the garden*. I find it more useful, though – especially when teaching about grammar – to use terms which reflect as closely as possible the structure of the phrase. So, a noun phrase has a noun in it, a verb phrase has a verb in it – and, likewise, an adverb phrase has an adverb in it. Phrases such as *on Thursday* are called **prepositional phrases** in this book, for the same reason.

• Of course, to recognise an adverb phrase, it helps if you can recognise the adverb. This won't be a problem with *quickly*, *happily*, and others where the *-ly* ending gives a nice clue; but students do have trouble remembering *there*, *soon*, *now*, and a few others. Also, in non-standard speech, the *-ly* ending may be dropped (*they ran quick down the street*). Focusing on the meaning can help: adverbials express time (ask *when?*), place (ask *where?*), and so on.

RG 52; SGE 2.4; CGEL 2.28

affirmative (KS 3)

• Many grammar books prefer the term **positive**, and don't use **affirmative** at all, other than in the general sense of an 'affirming' response (the entry on **negative** has further examples). When **affirmative** *is* used as a grammatical term, it usually refers to a whole sentence. Grammarians talk about clauses, utterances, sentences, statements, questions, and so on as being affirmative or negative. The terms aren't usually applied to individual word classes – 'affirmative adjective' or 'affirmative noun', for example.

• The affirmative/negative contrast focuses on the word *not* in relation to the verb. Be careful when you see *not* attached to other words than the verb: *Six not very happy people stood on the doorstep*. This is still an affirmative sentence. You are affirming that 'six people stood on the doorstep', even though they weren't very happy people. The negative sentence corresponding to this would be: *Six not very happy people weren't standing on the doorstep*. Similarly, if a verb is negative in meaning, the sentence can still be an affirmative one. Compare these sentences:

She said she wasn't married. (affirmative first clause, negative second clause)
She denied that she was married. (affirmative first clause, affirmative second clause)

Draw attention to the problems which can come when a sentence has more than one shift from affirmative to negative. It can be very difficult to follow the meaning: *I can't believe that John is uneasy or that he isn't interested in saying that he will be present*. Is he going or isn't he? I haven't the energy to work it out.

RG 5; SGE 10.33–41; CGEL 10.54–70

affix (KS 3)

• In this entry, I've dealt only with the affixes which form ('derive') a new word from an old one by changing its dictionary meaning, and often its part of speech – the **derivational** prefixes and suffixes. I've not illustrated the other type of affix – the **inflectional** affixes, which change the grammatical role a word has in a sentence without altering its part of speech. There's more on these in the entry on **inflection**. It is of course possible to have both types of affix in the same word: for example, from the verb *build* we can derive the noun *building*, and then this can be made plural – *buildings*. Notice that the inflectional affix is the one which goes at the very end – so the plural of the long word at the beginning of the entry is: *antidisestablishmentarianism-s*.

• Many affixes can be grouped together on the basis of their meaning. The prefixes express such meanings as negation (*un-*, *non-*, *in-*, *dis-*, *a-*); degree or size (*arch-*, *hyper-*, *mini-*, *mega-*, *super-*, *ultra-*); oppositeness (*anti-*, *contra-*, *counter-*); time (*ex-*, *post-*, *pre-*), and number (*bi-*, *di-*, *poly-*, *semi-*, *mono-*). The suffixes can be grouped in terms of which parts of speech they form: for example, abstract nouns from adjectives (*falsity*, *sadness*), adjectives from nouns (*foolish*, *homeless*), adjectives from verbs (*drinkable*, *talkative*), and adverbs from adjectives (*quickly*). In cases like *mileage* and *friendship*, there's no new part of speech: the words stay nouns, but become abstract.

• There are several interesting points about affixes which could be investigated. Which affixes are used to form many words (*-tion*, *-er* . . .); which are used for only a few words (*-ette*, *-let* . . .)? Which affixes are currently fashionable (*bio-*, *Euro-*, *mega-*, *techno-*, *tele-*, *-athon*, *-gate*, *-ist* . . .)? Look in *The Longman Register of New Words* (Longman, 1989, but published at regular intervals). For instance, recent coinages using *super-* include *superbug*, *supercentre*, *superchip*, *supercomputer*, *supercop*, *supergran*, and *superyob*. An interesting angle is to coin words which don't exist yet. What would *Birminghamgate* be? Could there be a *homeworkaholic*?

CGEL App I.20–42

affricate (KS 4)

• Any combination of a plosive and a fricative is an affricate, as long as it is used as a single sound unit in a language. [ʧ] and [ʤ] are clear examples in English, as they occur at the beginning of a word, in the middle, and at the end (see below). They are technically called **palato-alveolar fricatives**: the alveolar plosive leads to a palatal glide (see the entries on **alveolar** and **palate**). People 'feel' them to be single sounds, and not a sequence of two sounds. Other possible affricates in English include [tr] and [dr], but these aren't so clear, as they occur only at the beginning and in the middle of words, and not at the end (*tram*, *mattress*, *dry*, *tawdry*). [ts] and [dz] occur in the middle and at the end of words in English, but not at the beginning (*cats*, *roads*, *curtsey*). People don't feel these to be single sounds: [ts], for example, is felt to be [t] + [s].

• A good task for focusing the ear on affricates is to find contrasts (see **minimal pair**) between [ʧ] and [ʤ], as in *chin/gin*, *chest/jest*, *choke/joke*, *catches/cadges*, *riches/ridges*, *larch/large*, *beseech/besiege*; also, draw attention to contrasts between the affricates and their component parts: *chin*, *tin*, *shin*. It's also interesting to compare what happens in English with what happens in other languages. German, for example, has [pf] and [ts] at the beginnings of words, which isn't possible in English. And – if you need to fill a few spare minutes – no words ending in [tr] or [dr] in English? Give them a dictionary, and let them find it out the hard way.

IPE 8.3; EPP 6.3

agent (KS 4)

- Some approaches give this term a broader sense than the one I outline in the entry. They use it to mean not only *who* carried out an action but also *what* carried it out – what instrument or means. For example, in *He broke the window with a stone*, *stone* could be called the agent. This broader idea of agency is useful, but there are important differences between the animate and the inanimate agents. An interesting test is to see what happens when we put pairs of agents together. Let's imagine a scenario where Horace and Fred have been jointly trying to loosen a stiff nut using a spanner and a wrench. We can put the two animate agents together without difficulty: *The stiff nut was loosened by Horace and Fred*. We can put two inanimate agents together without difficulty: *The stiff nut was loosened by the spanner and the wrench*. But we can't easily put an animate and an inanimate agent together, without attracting criticism: it sounds unusual to say *The stiff nut was loosened by Horace and the spanner* (though you'll find this usage in jocular and literary style). So it rather looks as if these two types of agency are not identical in usage. If you take this view, reserving **agent** for the animate cases, you'll need a term for the inanimate ones: several authors talk about the **instrument**, in such cases.

- The usual prepositions to express agency are *by* and *with* – but students will need warning that not all uses of these prepositions are agentive. In *We went out by the back door*, *by* expresses the meaning 'by means of'. In *We put it by the car*, *by* expresses nearness. Be prepared to find sentences where it's very difficult to disentangle the meanings of 'means' and 'agent'.

RG 61; SGE 9.13; CGEL 9.50

agreement (KS 3) see **concord**

alliteration (KS 4)

- The quotations are from Shakespeare's *Antony and Cleopatra* (II.2), Milton's *Paradise Lost*, and G K Chesterton's *Lepanto*.

- I've restricted the entry to cases of alliteration at the beginning of a word, as these are the clearest instances. It would be more precise to say that sounds alliterate at the beginning of stressed syllables, wherever in a word these occur (for example, the [l] sounds alliterate in *unlikely love*).

- It's important for students to note the functions of alliteration (as for other sound effects involving repetition – see **assonance** and **rhyme**). It isn't enough to say gleefully, 'There's an example of alliteration in line 1'! The question is: what is it doing there? What would be the difference if it *weren't* there? There are two functions. Traditionally, people recognise its *phonetic* function: the repetition of consonants is thought to 'sound effective', or to symbolise some aspect of the real world (eg the 'hissing' quality of the [s] sounds in the Milton example). More recently, critics have emphasised the idea that alliteration also has a structural (or *phonological*) function – as William Empson pointed out, a similarity of sound makes one think of possible connections of sense (see **phonology**). So, for example, in the Chesterton quotation, the repeated [g] sounds bring the meanings of *gongs* and *groaning* together in a way which would be less striking if the line had been, say, 'Strong gongs moaning . . .'. (Students should not take such assertions on trust, of course, but check them out against their own intuitions. Altering texts in this way can be a useful exercise as a means of drawing attention to specific stylistic features.) The effect has the ability to cross intervening words, as in 'Thus conscience does make cowards of us all' (*Hamlet*, III.1).

• The repeated sounds need to be fairly close together to be sensed as alliteration. If I now include a word beginning with [s] in the present sentence, no one will feel that it alliterates with *sounds* in the previous sentence. The distance is too great. (However, stylisticians have not yet worked out how far apart words can be before we cease to feel any sound link between them.)

• A good exercise is to compile a collection of alliterative texts. Students need to appreciate that alliteration isn't restricted to poetry. They will find it in slogans, adverts, newspaper headlines, sports commentaries, speeches, sermons, and many other contexts.

CEL 12; LG 6.2

allophone (KS 4)

• The differences in the /t/ example are as follows:

- in *tea*, the blade of the tongue is against the alveolar ridge and the lips are spread; as the tongue leaves the ridge, it's followed by a puff of air (see **aspiration** – get them to use the backs of their hands);
- in *too*, the articulation is the same, except that the lips are rounded;
- in *pot* (in such phrases as *pot black*), the tongue doesn't come away from the alveolar ridge, so there's no aspiration (check with the back of the hand again);
- in *eighth*, the tip of the tongue presses against the teeth (you should be able to see it), anticipating the following *th* sound;
- in *stop*, the articulation is the same as that in *tea* or *too*, but there isn't any aspiration when the sound is released (check with the back of the hand again), because the preceding [s] inhibits it.

• The allophone concept is very important in phonology, but I wouldn't recommend that you draw attention to it until students have had a fair amount of practice listening to the sounds of speech. Some of the phonetic distinctions are quite subtle. For another reasonably clear example, point to the different sounds of /l/, as in *leap* and *pool* (see the Government Sound Warning under **lateral**).

• There are several other **allo-** terms in language study, all expressing the same basic idea of 'variant of'. For instance, if students have difficulty grasping the concept of 'variant', introduce the analogous concept of letter variants (**allographs**) – such as the different ways of writing *a* or *g* (see the entry on **grapheme** for more about this). In the study of grammar, the term **allomorph** is used for a variant of a morpheme (see **morphology**): for example, the morpheme 'plural' in English is shown by such allomorphs as the /s/ of *cats*, the /z/ of *dogs*, and the /iz/ of *horses*.

• Note that this entry is one of the two places in this book where it is important to use / / brackets instead of [ ]: this point is discussed under **phoneme**.

IPE 5.3, 8.2; EPP 5.2

alphabet (KS 3)

• It's worth noting that the 44 shapes referred to relate to a single typeface. There are of course thousands of different typefaces available for English, several of which employ markedly different letter shapes (eg Gothic print). It can be an interesting exercise trying to decode some of the more obscure symbols, and working out what the distinctive or contrasting features are.

• There are 26 written units (see **grapheme**) but over 40 spoken units (see **phoneme**) in English – the exact number depends on your accent. It would be useful at this point to draw attention to the inevitable problems this imbalance will cause for spelling, and perhaps to speculate about possible ways of making 26 letters carry 40-odd distinctions (see further, **orthography**).

• The few cases of change in the alphabet inventory of English are interesting to note. In Old English, there were distinct symbols for the two *th* sounds (þ 'thorn' and ð 'eth', the *th* here pronounced as in *the*), a *w* sound (ƿ 'wyn'), a *g* sound (ʒ 'yogh'), and a front vowel sound between *e* and *a* (æ 'ash'). Some of these symbols lasted until early Middle English, and then were gradually replaced. Accented letters (*é*, etc) are particularly subject to change. Conservative styles tend to keep them; innovative styles will drop them. A study of who uses accents (which newspapers, which shops, which products) can bring interesting results. Is *café* used in your town? Is *CAFÉ*?

• According to one frequency count (of the letters in US newspapers), the frequency order of letters is: ETAONISRHLDCMUFPGWYBVKJXQZ. The order in the Morse Code, which was based on the quantities of type found in a printer's office, is slightly different: ETAINOSHRDLUCMFWYGPBV KQJXZ. Changes in subject-matter do affect frequency counts, so be prepared for certain minor changes if pupils do experiments from different kinds of materials (eg scientific text, newspapers). See what happens to *J* in the New Testament, for example.

• Collect some children's alphabet books, and see how they differ. Discuss the problem of the 'A is for apple' formula (eg 'X is for?'). Would 'A is in apple' be better (cf 'X is in fox')? Try out the idea of comic alphabets ('A is for 'orses'): an excellent collection is in Eric Partridge's *Comic Alphabets* (Routledge & Kegan Paul, 1961).

EL 5; CEL 33

alveolar (KS 4)

• This term has an alternative pronunciation, (al-**vee**-uh-luh).

• There's a little test built into the sentence *Len sat . . .*, where 'every' consonant is an alveolar. The sentence includes [l], but [l] isn't mentioned in the entry as a consonant with alveolar articulation. This is because [l] is usually described in different terms, its most noticeable feature being the way the air moves round the sides of the tongue (see **lateral**). The point of contact at the front of the tongue, though, is at the alveolar ridge.

IPE 8; EPP 4, 6, 7

ambiguous (KS 3)

• There are two main types of ambiguity illustrated in this entry. When the grammatical construction is ambiguous, it's called **structural ambiguity** (or **grammatical ambiguity**). When the ambiguity resides in a single word, it's called **lexical ambiguity**. Some further cases of the first include *old men and women* and *visiting snakes can be dangerous*. For lexical examples, look in a dictionary, and see the range of meanings for an individual word (such as *That's an interesting table* – furniture? statistics?), any of which could be the source of an ambiguity.

• If words have so many meanings, why isn't ambiguity more common? Draw attention to the importance of **context**. A sentence like *I only eat blue cheese* is theoretically ambiguous: it could mean 'I eat only blue cheese' (and no other kind) or 'I only eat blue cheese' (I don't smell it, or sell it, or jump on it). In practice, the context makes it perfectly clear which meaning is required (as I've just had to do, in fact, in order to demonstrate what the two meanings are).

• It's important to distinguish between ambiguity and vagueness. The problem of ambiguity is the choice between two or more clear alternative readings of a sentence. Vagueness, however, is when a reading is unclear. *I bought lots* is vague, not ambiguous.

• The implications of the last sentence in the entry could be explored. In speech, ambiguity is less worrying because there is usually the opportunity for the listener to ask the speaker what was meant; also, intonation and stress often help to sort out a problem (as in 'I only *eat* blue cheese' above).

But in the written language, the possibility of reader feedback is remote, and rarely immediate.

CEL 16–17

amplifier see **degree**

anacoluthon (KS 4)

• Students' writing often displays anacolutha, especially when they're attempting to use the more advanced syntactic constructions. Sentences start in one way and finish in another. Instilling the practice of reading through the work can help, or getting the student to read the problem sentence aloud, but it won't solve all problems, as in some cases there is a genuine lack of awareness as to what the problem is. In such cases, it will be necessary to tease apart the contributing structures, to show what went wrong. For example, a DES report on the writing of 15-year-olds (1983) includes the sentence *Does it not worry you that the man to whom you will marry might be cruel to you?* The extra *to* could be here for either (or both) of two reasons: the student could have been uncertain about how to use the *whom* construction, or was planning to write *the man to whom you will be married*, and changed her mind half way through. This approach is well illustrated in Katharine Perera's work, such as her *Children's Writing and Reading* (Blackwell, 1984; see especially Chapter 5). As she points out, it is very important to appreciate that errors such as these are signs of growth, not of carelessness. To criticise an attempt at a complex construction may lead to the student avoiding it, and staying with the safer, simpler constructions.

• Any tape recording of informal conversation will bring to light dozens of examples of anacolutha, and they'll be found in sports commentary and other occasions where pressure is on the speaker, and changes of mind are routine. Also, as emotions rise, anacolutha increase. It's important to stress that anacoluthon isn't anything to feel guilty about, in such circumstances, but is a natural consequence of the dynamics of the speech situation. However, in formal circumstances, and of course in writing, rather different criteria apply.

anagram (KS 3)

• The answers to the anagram tasks are: *lager*, *glare*, *large* and *danger*, *gander*. For thousands of other examples, look up all the common possibilities in the language, for words of 5 to 15 letters, in Chambers's *Anagrams* (1985). That's where you'll find, quickly, that *panel*, *penal* and *plane* are anagrams, as are *archaism* and *charisma*, and *gramophonic* and *monographic*. Here are some other clever anagrams: *Clint Eastwood* (= 'old

West action'); *HMS Pinafore* (= 'name for ship'); *conversation* (= 'voices rant on'); *desperation* (= 'a rope ends it'); *the eyes* (= 'they see').

• There are several famous anagrams, such as Samuel Butler's *Erewhon* (Nowhere), and Jonathan Swift's *Tribnia* (Britain – in *Gulliver's Travels*). A useful historical perspective, with many examples, is given in Tony Augarde's *The Oxford Guide to Word Games* (OUP, 1984, Chapter 8). Anagrams were once considered a serious occupation, with mystical power attributed to the letters, and people employed to interpret the significance of rearrangements. Louis XIII of France, for example, employed the services of a Royal Anagrammatist.

CEL 11

analogy (KS 4)

• A good exercise is to explore what makes a good analogy and what makes a bad one. The test is simple: does the analogy help? Start with a familiar concept, and imagine it has to be explained to a younger child or to a Martian. Teachers draw analogies all the time, especially in the sciences when they are trying to instil understanding of abstract concepts or unobservable processes. Students might be asked to keep their ears open for analogies that are used in other classes or in their textbooks. They should look critically at commonly used analogies – for example, is the earth's 'greenhouse effect' really like what happens inside a greenhouse? Or look at the analogies I use myself in these books, such as the clothing analogy in the entry on **appropriate**.

• Analogy often makes use of figures of speech (see **metaphor**, **simile**), but an analogy is much greater than a figure of speech – it's a whole chain of reasoning, and it may not make formal use of figures of speech at all. Compare *A disk is a cake* (metaphor), *A disk is like a cake* (simile), and *Imagine a cake* . . . (analogy).

anapaest (KS 4) see **foot**

anaphora (uh-**na**-fuh-ruh)

• This term is quite often used in modern approaches to grammar for the situation where a word refers back to something expressed in a previous sentence; the reference is said to be **anaphoric**. For instance, if you read *She pulled it over* in the middle of a paragraph, the words *she* and *it* make sense only if you look back to a preceding sentence. Words which refer you in a forward direction are also sometimes called anaphoric (for example, *this* in *John said this: . . .*), but some writers talk about forward reference under the heading of **cataphora** (kuh-**ta**-fuh-ruh). I haven't introduced either of these terms in the present books; if you felt it appropriate, they could be brought in during the discussion of **antecedent**, which is a similar term used in traditional grammar.

RG 36, 62; SGE 5.14, 6.8, 12.18; CGEL 5.30–2, 6.19, 12.12

animate and inanimate (KS 4)

• This distinction essentially applies to nouns; it's less usual to talk of animate verbs, adjectives, or adverbs (incidentally, adverbs – such as *busily* and *foolishly* – aren't referred to in the entry). Also, the entry talks only of words, whereas you can also talk about the whole of a noun phrase or adjective phrase in this way (as in *wet to the skin* below).

• A good source of animate and inanimate words is a thesaurus (such as Roget's). For example, under *sobriety* we're given such animate adjectives as *sober*, *abstinent*, and *teetotal*, and there are similar lists for verbs and adverbs. Under *moisture*, we have *humid*, *moist*, *undrained*, and so on. An enjoyable exercise is to go through a list and see which items are typically animates and which inanimates. Try these (from Roget's entry for *moisture*): *drizzling*, *dripping*, *dank*, *muggy*, *steaming*, *oozy*, *slushy*, *squelchy*, *seeping*, *soaked*, *drenched*, *sopping*, *irrigated*, *waterlogged*. Some are never animate (*irrigated*); some are never inanimate (*wet to the skin*); some can be both (*wet*); and some can be both with humorous or other connotations (*my waterlogged uncle*).

• In one interesting classroom exercise, the verbs *eat* and *sleep* were put up on the board, and students suggested likely (eg *man*) and unlikely (eg *stone*) words to act as subjects. Rather more difficult to contextualise were *house*, *factory*, *town* and *planet* (*The town lay sleeping*, *This house eats electricity*). Idioms also came to light: thus we can say *The hotel sleeps 30 people* but not *The restaurant eats 30 people*!

RG 33; SGE 5.45–7; CGEL 5.104–11

antecedent (KS 4)

• It's important to note the point (especially if you are familiar with this term from traditional grammar) that **antecedent** can be used to refer both backwards and forwards in a sentence. Don't be fooled by the etymology, which suggests that the word has only backwards reference. Examples such as the *Angelina* one should help to make this point. (Having said this, be prepared for arguments from people who insist that the meaning of a word should follow its etymology. *Ante-* meant 'before' in Latin, they will say, therefore **antecedent** should be restricted to backwards reference. See **etymology** for an answer to this criticism.)

• The various substitute words are usually called **pro-forms** in modern approaches to grammar (on analogy with **pronouns**). The more general term is used in order to include words which cross-refer to other units than

nouns – for example, *do* refers back to a verb or a clause in *Miranda washed the dishes, and so did Sam* (ie wash the dishes).

• An antecedent may be earlier in the same sentence, or come in the immediately preceding sentence, or even before that. However, the greater the distance the antecedent from its substitute word, the more likely intervening nouns will cause ambiguity. This is a common source of error in students' written work, so it shouldn't be too difficult to find examples. 'Dangling pronouns' are especially troublesome.

RG 62; SGE 12.2–13; CGEL 12.10

antonyms (KS 3)

• Not everyone agrees on the best way to use the term **antonym**. I use it here to refer to both gradable and ungradable opposites; but some writers use it to mean only the former, the latter being called **complementary** terms. More examples of the ungradable type? *Boy/girl, catch/drop* (a ball), *bachelor/spinster*.

• There are other kinds of oppositeness of meaning. For example, there are pairs of words where one term presupposes another: *husband/wife, employer/employee, buy/sell*. These are often called **converse** terms.

• Note that many words in the language don't have 'natural' opposites at all – *bus, bell, February* . . . It doesn't make sense to ask 'What's the opposite of *bus*?' You have to discover which words have opposites and which don't. Several words have more than one possible opposite: for example, the opposite of *crafty* could be *stupid, dull, dense, crass, dumb, obtuse*.

Students will also discover that you can set up words as temporary opposites, depending on the context. For example, *walk* can be opposed to *crawl* (*My baby doesn't crawl any more – he walks*), *ride* (*She rode but I had to walk*), *run*, *swim*, and so on. A good source of examples is *Webster's Dictionary of Synonyms* (Merriam, 1951), which also contains lists of antonyms.

CEL 17

aphorism (KS 4)

• The crucial feature of an aphorism is that it expresses an insight of some kind in a condensed, pithy manner. My examples are all very short. An example of a longer aphorism is Johnson's *Patriotism is the last refuge of a scoundrel* or *Example is always more efficacious than precept*. Any book of quotations will provide dozens of examples.

• Here are some further examples of aphoristic sentences using a balanced structure:

The sooner, the better.	So far, so good.
First come, first served.	Like father, like son.
Waste not, want not.	No homework, no TV.

Notice that the amount and kind of 'wisdom' contained varies greatly.

RG 2; SGE 11.21; CGEL 11.43

apostrophe (KS 3)

• I've compressed a lot of information into a short space, in this entry. It's important to get across the fact that there are two main uses for the apostrophe, which shouldn't be mixed up.

1 The apostrophe marks that something has been omitted. These cases include contractions (*there's*, *she'll*, *n't*, *e'er*), certain abbreviations in conservative writing style (*'cello*, *'phone*), and transcriptions of words in vernacular speech (*goin'*, *'cos*). Note that sometimes an apostrophe may mark a shortened form in writing which does not correspond to anything in speech, as when in casual note-taking we might write *quot'n* for *quotation*.

2 The apostrophe also indicates a grammatical contrast – mainly, the singular/plural contrast in the genitive construction (see **case**), as in *girl's* and *girls'*, where nothing has been omitted. (Having said this, it should be noted that the origins of this use may indeed reflect the omission of a sound. Opinions vary, but the genitive apostrophe may derive from the shortening of an Early Modern English construction (as in *Henry his name*), or possibly it may be a remnant of the vowel formerly present in the genitive ending of Old English.) Another grammatical use is where the apostrophe shows an unusual grammatical form – for example, plurals

such as *1890's*, *if's and but's*, and *i's and t's*, or past tenses such as *macro'd*.

- There is a great deal of uncertainty these days over the use of the apostrophe. Students will regularly see such shop notices as *tomato's* and *butchers shop*. With large businesses, for example, an *-s* ending is sometimes interpreted as a plural and sometimes as a genitive, so we find both *Woolworths* and *Woolworth's*, *Barclays* and *Barclay's*. The trend to drop the apostrophe from business names began around the turn of the century, and today it is almost always omitted in shop signs, placards, posters, and the like (for instance, the London tube stations are *St Pauls* and *Earls Court*). Modern typographical designers often think that the apostrophe is fussy and old-fashioned, and most publishing house styles now do not use it in such contexts as *ifs and buts* or *1990s*. People with a strongly conservative or purist streak will be horrified by this, but we have to remember that the history of the apostrophe in English is hardly 400 years old. The mark was introduced in the sixteenth century, and took a century to become widespread, often being used in ways which seem alien now (for instance, it marked the plural of words ending in a vowel, so that we find such forms as *comma's*). The uncertainty steadily grew until, in the middle of the nineteenth century, grammarians and printers laid down rules as to how the apostrophe was to be used. Several arbitrary decisions were made, and within a few years their validity came to be disputed. It's not surprising, therefore, that only a century later people are still uncertain about its use.

- The moral of all this is plain. If students have trouble learning the modern conventions governing the use of the apostrophe, this is understandable, and teaching policy over corrections should recognise different levels of seriousness in the errors, and the need for different kinds of explanation. Cases where the distinction is critical in writing (such as *girl's* and *girls'*) need to be distinguished from cases where no contrast (and thus no ambiguity) is involved (Shaw, for example, wrote such forms as *havnt*, in his later plays), and both of these from cases where there is wide variation in adult usage (as in *Mans/Man's Shop* or *Teachers/Teacher's Teachers' College*). Send everyone out on an apostrophe hunt, and see what they bring back.

RG 34; CGEL III.27; ET 8, 19

apposition (KS 4)

- It's important to make students see the difference between coordination and apposition. Use such pairs of sentences as *John and the butcher arrived* vs *John, the butcher, arrived*. Note also another way of describing appositional constructions: one says that the two phrases are **in apposition**.

- Ask students to think about the different kinds of meaning expressed by apposition. For example, in some cases, the second noun phrase adds a more specific meaning to the first (*my neighbour, Mr Smith*); in others, the second phrase provides a rewording (*linguistics, the science of language*); in others it adds extra attributes (*a library book, a rather tattered edition*).

• Other interesting examples of apposition are *the word 'happy', the play 'Macbeth'*. Some grammarians analyse proper names containing two nouns (such as *Farmer Brown, Oxford Street*, and *Mount Everest*) as examples of apposition. On this analysis, *Mount Everest*, say, would be 'the Mountain which is Everest' (compare 'John, who is the butcher'). It's also worth noting that an appositional relationship can exist between other parts of speech than nouns – *The bomb destroyed, devastated, the building; Thirdly, finally, I want to say this . . .*

RG 42; SGE 17.27; CGEL 17.65–93

appropriate (KS 3)

• This is a fundamental notion in language awareness. It was introduced to avoid the black-and-white approach to language encapsulated in the term **correctness**, and that entry should be read in relation to this one. It's important to stress that to talk in terms of appropriateness is not at all to diminish the notion of standards, or standard English. The clothes analogy should illustrate this point: by recognising the distinct and appropriate role of, say, a swimming costume, one does not thereby discount the distinct and appropriate role of a suit. Focusing on appropriateness should, rather, increase a student's sense of stylistic occasion, and promote a more responsible attitude towards language in use. The approach which said simply that 'X is correct and Y incorrect' fostered an unrealistic and lazy approach to language, and hindered the development of a critical sense of style.

• Exercises to develop a sense of linguistic appropriateness can involve all kinds of techniques. A piece of writing can be rewritten to make it appropriate to some other context (eg instructions about how to find a location in the school written for a school-friend and then for an outsider). Students can role-play parts in a dialogue, using language appropriate to their roles (eg an account of a traffic incident from the driver's, witness's, and policeman's point of view). Comparisons can be made between articles on the same topic in the tabloid and quality press. The language of presenters on different radio channels can be compared. Students can record samples of classroom and playground language, or look at the language of different kinds of subject texts used in class. More specific examples include investigations of how people name each other (first names, second names, nickname, use of *Sir, Miss*); of where and when people swear; of the use of pet names for members of the family at home; of the 'with it' language in programmes such as *Top of the Pops*; and of the way language is matched to a product in a TV ad.

EL 2,13,14; SGE 1; CGEL 1

approximant (KS 4)

• In some books, there is yet another term used for talking about these sounds – **frictionless continuant**. This term quite nicely describes two characteristics of these consonants: they involve a continuous sound (unlike, say, the plosive sounds, such as [p], which are short and sharp), and they don't produce any audible friction (unlike the fricative sounds, such as [f]).

- Note the text says 'many people', in talking about *r*. The pronunciation of *r* varies greatly from one part of the country to another. Some people make a trilled sound here (see **trill**), as you can hear in several accents of Scots and Welsh, for example. Some make a **retroflex** sound, where the tip of the tongue is curled back towards the palate, as you can hear in the way many speakers of Indian or American English say *r*. In Received Pronunciation, the *r* is an approximant (more precisely, a 'post-alveolar' approximant, to show where the tongue approaches the top of the mouth – just behind the alveolar ridge). Note also a simplification I've introduced into the transcription. Strictly speaking, in a phonetic transcription, the symbol for the *r* approximant is an upside-down *r* [ɹ]; the familiar [r] symbol is reserved for the trilled sound, heard in some Welsh and Scots accents, for example (see **trill**). Rather than bring in yet another unfamiliar symbol, at this stage, I've opted for the straightforward [r], which is also the one used in a phonemic transcription,/r/ (see **phoneme**).

- The use of [j] instead of [y] as a symbol here will make more sense to students if you point out that the [y] symbol is used in phonetics for something else – a front rounded vowel, as in French *tu* [ty].

IPE 8.8–9; EPP 7.3–4

archaism (KS 3)

- Hunting archaisms can be an interesting task. Point students in the direction of historical novels, plays, and films, including children's literature (such as the *Narnia* stories). Really old comics (kept from one's (grand)parents' days) will have some. Novelists who have used archaic language in a careful way include Scott in *Ivanhoe* and Thackeray in *Esmond*. In poetry, Spenser and Milton were influential in maintaining an archaic tradition of usage. Collections of nursery rhymes and fairy tales (such as Grimm's) will be useful references. The language of law and religion will also provide material, though the subject-matter is often difficult. The Authorised Version of the Bible is a good source. Look out for people deliberately being archaic (as in *Ye olde tea shoppe*). Rural dialects also often retain words which have gone out of use in the standard language. And don't forget local place names, which can preserve an earlier word.

- Some examples of archaic vocabulary: *behold*, *damsel*, *ere*, *fain*, *hither*, *oft*, *quoth*, *smite*, *unto*, *wight*, *wot*, *yonder*. In grammar, apart from the *-est*, *-eth* endings, there are such forms as *'tis*, *'twas*, *'gainst*, *ne'er*, *e'en*, *o'er*. Some older forms of verbs will be found, such as *spake* and *clothèd*. And don't forget old-fashioned spellings, such as Eliot's *daunsinge, signifying matrimonie . . . holding eche other by the hand . . .* ('East Coker', *Four Quartets*).

• This topic raises many interesting functional issues. What makes people use archaisms? Why would a lawyer use archaisms? or a priest? What's the difference between a *Tea Shop* and a *Tea Shoppe*? Would you expect to find archaisms in a TV ad? When is archaism desirable and when undesirable? The value of the stylistic effect needs to be set against the risk of unintelligibility. Archaic grammar, vocabulary and spelling are easy to spot – but what about archaic pronunciations (eg *wind* rhyming with *find*). And don't forget 'recent' archaisms, such as an old-fashioned word or phrase used by a grandparent, or a word no longer in use (such as the vocabulary and slang of the First World War).

LG 1.2.1

argot (KS 4)

• Excellent source-books exist on this topic, notably Eric Partridge's *A Dictionary of the Underworld, British and American* (Routledge, 1950) and Francis Grose's *Dictionary of the Vulgar Tongue* (1811; Bibliophile Books, 1984). Some items from letter G of the former: *G* (1000 dollars), *gab* (mouth, loquacity), *gad the hoof* (go without shoes), *gaff* (public place of amusement). Novels about gangsters and pirates often have some good examples, as will television series about the police or shady characters (such as Arthur Daly in *Minder*).

• I'm not joking when I say that there will be lots of local examples. The problem is how to extract them from the intuitions of the more street-wise members of the class.

CEL 11

article (KS 3)

• The word **article** comes from Latin *articulus*, with meanings to do with 'joint' (as in *articulated lorry*). No one knows exactly how the term came to be used in grammar, but it's easy to see how the idea of 'separate elements' (as in *articles of clothing*) could extend to language (*articles of government*) and thus to specific parts of the language.

• Because the articles don't seem, on the surface, to have much meaning, it's important to stress the ways in which the choice of an article does affect the meaning of a sentence in an important way. For example, the way we use the articles (or not) allows us to distinguish between a specific meaning (*A/The car is outside*) and a general meaning (see **generic reference**), such as *Cars are expensive these days*. More advanced students might examine the different uses of *the*. In addition to its function of referring backwards (illustrated in the entry), it can be used to refer forwards (*the president of*

Germany – which president? the one I'm just about to name), to refer to our general knowledge (*the Prime Minister, the moon* – which moon? the one we all know), and to refer to human institutions that we get involved with from time to time (*I went to the cinema, I watched the news*).

• In relation to the very last point in the entry, it may be worth mentioning the term that some linguists use for the contrast in meaning when the articles are *not* present: the **zero article**. Note how the zero article is normal when talking about human institutions and routines, means of transport, periods of time, meals, and illnesses: *go to bed, by bus, at dawn, in school, in winter, got flu, had dinner*. There's an excellent collection of examples in the big Quirk grammar (CGEL).

• Another way of getting a sense of what the articles do in English is to compare them with all the other specifying words (see **determiner**): when compared with *my car, this car, each car*, and the others, *the car* and *a car* show up nicely as the determiners which say least of all about the noun. *My* adds the idea of possession; *this* adds the idea of nearness; *each* adds the idea of number. *The* and *a* add no extra nuances to a noun, over and above the notion of particularity. The articles are the 'basic' determiners.

RG 36; SGE 5.11–24; CGEL 5.26–59

articulation (KS 4)

• When talking about articulation, it's important to get across the idea that the various vocal organs are all working *at once*. The phenomenon is technically known as **coarticulation**. So, for example, in pronouncing the word *soon*, my lips are already getting ready for the rounded vowel *oo* while I articulate the *s*. This effect is illustrated in the entry on **assimilation**.

• Counting sounds isn't as easy as it might seem. To begin with, students will want to count the letters rather than the sounds. They may 'read in' sounds which aren't usually there – for example, pronouncing *couple* as ['kʌpəl] instead of ['kʌpl]. If they say the sentence carefully, the *f* of *of* will be pronounced; if they say it quickly, it won't. And diphthongs such as the [eɪ] of *takes*, although acting as a single unit in the language, actually consist of two distinct sound elements (see the entry on **diphthong**). So, there's no one correct answer to the question: how many sounds are there in the sentence?

IPE 2.3; EPP 2

aspect (KS 4)

• It's important to read the entry on **perfect** soon after this one. I would have dealt with them both together, except that the entries were getting very long. I've mentioned the existence of the perfect in this entry, but only to show that there's more to aspect than the simple vs continuous distinction.

• Anyone brought up on a diet of traditional grammar will probably think of all these forms as 'tenses', and talk about 'simple tense', 'continuous tense', 'perfect tense', and so on. But if 'tense' is the term to use when you're talking about the time at which an action takes place, then you need a different term for what's going on here. There's much more to aspect then a simple contrast of time. Aspect is essentially a way of *looking at* time – a 'particular angle', I say in the entry, on the action. Some languages (such as Russian) have a highly developed aspectual system, in which such distinctions as whether the action is completed or not are expressed by the verb endings. The *-ing* ending is the only inflection used for aspectual purposes in English, and it can't be used on its own, but only with an auxiliary verb – a form of the verb *to be* to express the simple/continuous distinction, and a form of the verb *to have* for the present perfect / past perfect distinction.

• Students may not be sure what 'a form of the verb *to be*' means. The entry contains only *is . . . -ing* examples. Point out the existence of *am*, *are*, *was*, and *were*, as well as the compound forms *will be*, *could be*, *may be*, etc (see the entry on **auxiliary verb**).

• You'll find that it's rather more difficult to persuade students of the importance of the aspect distinction than in the case of tense. This is because the idea of a tense contrast is fairly straightforward. Aspectual contrasts are less easy to 'feel'. It's important, therefore, to develop a sense of the range of meanings or uses involved in the expression of aspect in English. The Quirk reference grammars provide a good classification – permanent vs temporary meaning, habitual action, and so on. Collect pairs of examples where there's a clear meaning contrast – for example, *John lives in London* (permanently) vs *John is living in London* (just for the moment). Play about with adverbs: we can say *Mary sometimes plays the cello* but not usually *Mary is sometimes playing the cello*. Note also that there are some verbs (they're often called **stative verbs**) that don't normally occur in the progressive: *I am liking this banana*, *She is knowing the answer* (though you'll hear these in Indian English). As a matter of fact, it's relatively unusual to use the progressive aspect. You hear it a good deal in conversation, but in other contexts only about five per cent of verbs use this form.

RG 24; SGE 4.7–12; CGEL 4.17–40

aspiration (KS 4)

• All voiceless plosives show this aspiration, [p], [t], [k] – see further, **plosive**, **voice** (in phonetics). However, because [k] is articulated so far back in the mouth, the effect is not so noticeable on that sound. Note that the aspiration is only normal when these sounds go at the beginning of words (or in the middle, if they are strongly stressed, as in *impossible*). At the ends of words, the aspiration is missing: try *cup* vs *cub*. To 'spit out' *cup* is possible – [kʌp^h], but this pronunciation would convey some special meaning, such as vexation.

• If [s] occurs before the [p] sound, it stops the aspiration: get the students to try *spin*. In fact, the sound is exactly like [b]. Phonologists say that the contrast has been 'neutralised'.

• Some regional accents aspirate very strongly – Irish English does, for instance. Some don't – South African English, for example.

IPE 8.2; EPP 4.3–4

assimilation (KS 4)

• It's important to appreciate that assimilations are a perfectly normal feature of informal conversational speech. It is actually very difficult to speak without them – as anyone knows who has had to try (such as BBC presenters, train-service announcers, or – in a broader context – people taking a part on stage). On the other hand, many people don't like to hear assimilations in formal speech situations – and they especially object when they spot them being used by employees of the BBC. Speech which assimilates a great deal is often called 'sloppy' or 'careless', but in fact it is better to call it 'normal' or 'casual', and refer to the other style as 'careful'. Everyone assimilates, in everyday conversation – even those who are most strongly critical of the speech of others.

• You'll need a tape recorder to study assimilations. If you try to do it 'face to face', there will be all kinds of arguments about whether someone did or didn't assimilate. It's essential to be able to play a piece of speech back, if necessary several times (see the entry on **phonetics** for a suggestion about how to do this). Get someone to tell a story about an event, and listen out for the assimilations. Make sure that the microphone is close to the person's mouth, to pick up the relevant features (they can be easily masked by surrounding noise). Alternatively, tape something from the radio, and see how much assimilation exists (there'll be far more on Radio 1 than on Radio 4, for instance).

• It would be useful for students to refer to the entry on **elision**, in relation to this one. The omission of sounds is another natural consequence of the speed and informality of speech.

IPE 11.3.5; EPP 14.2

assonance (KS 4)

• The quotation is from Coleridge's 'Kubla Khan' – a poem which makes considerable use of assonance. For another example, here are two lines from Hopkins's 'Thou art indeed just, Lord':

> The fine delight that fathers thought; the strong
> Spur, live and lancing like the blowpipe flame . . .

• Note that not all sounds are equal, when it comes to assonance. Long vowels and diphthongs are more noticeable than short vowels. Stressed vowels are more noticeable than unstressed vowels. Also, the vowels do not have to be identical for you to hear a phonetic relationship between them: for example, the vowels of *far* and *fan* are very similar, as are those of *seat* and *sit*.

• Students' attention should be drawn to the related entries on **alliteration** and **rhyme**.

LG 6

audience (KS 3)

• The concept of **audience** has been especially invoked in recent years as part of studies of the way children learn to write. Children need to keep clearly in mind who exactly they are writing for, as they develop their written language skills (and so, of course, do adults). Stressing this point is less necessary in the case of speech, where usually the audience is face to face with the speaker; but it can't be ignored, for it is perfectly possible to judge your audience wrongly (and 'talk down to them', 'go over their heads', and so on). And in such cases as radio broadcasting, the problem of 'knowing your audience' arises in an acute form. An interesting topic for discussion is the way our sense of audience varies between speech and writing. Does the existence of body language and the availability of immediate feedback have much effect?

• A sense of audience variation can be obtained by comparing material plainly aimed for different target audiences, such as 'tabloid' vs 'quality' press, specialised vs general magazines, publications with different political biases, and the varying levels of the main radio channels. Students might try writing a text (or rewriting one) aimed at a younger age group, writing to friends vs strangers (always a good test of what information can be presupposed), writing formally vs informally, or writing from different points of view (wishing to persuade, inform, defend, antagonise, etc).

CEL 10, 34

auxiliary verb and main verb (KS 3)

• Main verbs are also called **full verbs** or **lexical verbs**. The basic idea is that these are the verbs which carry the major meaning in a verb phrase. A main verb may be the only verb in a verb phrase (*I walked home*); if there are several verbs, the main verb is always the last one (*I have walked home*) – everything preceding it is an auxiliary. There are several other differences between auxiliary verbs and main verbs not mentioned in the entry. In particular, notice that auxiliary verbs are followed by the word *not* (or *-n't*); main verbs aren't. Compare *I may not go* vs **I go not*. Incidentally, the link between **mood** and **modal** may not be obvious, and may need pointing out. The notion of modality is discussed in the entry on **mood** in the KS 4 book.

- The very first auxiliary in a verb phrase is also a special one – for example, it is the form which goes before the subject when you're turning a statement into a question: *They are leaving – Are they leaving?*; *They have been running – Have they been running?* (notice you can't say **Have been they running?*). The Quirk grammars give this special use of the auxiliary a special name: the **operator**. They talk about the auxiliary being used 'as an operator' – that is, it's the word which carries out an operation on the basic structure of a sentence, such as turning a statement into a question.

- The three verbs *be*, *have* and *do* are special: they can act both as main verbs and as auxiliary verbs. Moreover, when they are auxiliary verbs, their role is different from all the other auxiliaries. For example, they have a 3rd person singular form in the present tense, whereas modal verbs don't: compare *she is/has/does* and **she mays/wills/cans*. They have an infinitive form and participle forms, whereas modal verbs don't: compare *to be/have/do, being/having/doing, been/had/done* and **to may/can*, **maying/shalling*, **mighted/shalled*. And they can be used in commands, whereas modals can't: compare *be quiet / do come in / have a seat* and **may sit!*, **can go!* For these reasons, these three verbs are sometimes called the 'primary' auxiliaries.

- Remember that neat classifications rarely work in language analysis. There are some verbs which fall midway between the apparently clear-cut distinction between main and auxiliary verb. Forms such as *have to*, *be able to*, and *be going to* are a nuisance, because they seem to combine some of the properties of main verbs and some of auxiliary verbs. They are often called **semi-auxiliaries**. There are also differences between the modal auxiliaries: *used to*, *ought to*, *dare*, and *need* are different from all the others. But I'd leave this kind of thing to a later stage of enquiry.

- It can be really interesting drawing up a table of all the auxiliary verbs and discovering the similarities and differences between them. Students are usually amazed that such a small area of grammar can be so intricate, and that these 'small words' are so important. A good angle is to collect examples of the way children get the grammar wrong when they're learning these verbs, between the ages of about 2½ and 7. Here are some from my own collection: *He willed go, I did fell, I'm want some dinner, What did you did, Please may you jump me high, I used to did*.

RG 15, 18; SGE 3.11–18; CGEL 3.21–51

baby talk (KS 3)

- A third context in which people use baby talk is during very intimate conversations – teasing between parent and older child, the members of a gang, or husband and wife, for example.

- Try getting some real data to illustrate the range and complexity of baby talk. One of the most amusing tape recordings, in fact, comes from recording someone talking to their pet – especially if they don't know the tape recorder is on! In particular, it will show up the exaggerated intonation patterns and tones of voice which people use (and which are impossible to illustrate in a written entry).

• A good discussion point is: should parents use baby talk to a child? Some people think they shouldn't, because it is presenting the child with a wrong model. In fact, there's no evidence that children are hindered in their learning by hearing this kind of thing, so we have to ask the question why it is that baby talk is used at all. Most people produce it without any conscious awareness of what it is they are doing. It can be argued that forms like *choo-choo* actually help the process of learning, because they present the child with a repeated chance to hear the nature of particular sounds and syllables. You'll find some discussion of this in my *Listen to your Child* (Penguin, 1986), pages 61, 86–8.

back (KS 4) see **front**

back slang (KS 3)

• In fact, there are two ways of playing this game: pronouncing the letters of the words backwards, one at a time (which is what is shown in the entry); and pronouncing the sounds of the words backwards, one at a time. So, *police* comes out as 'ekilop', using the first method, and as 'seeluhp', using the second. Also, the game doesn't have to be word by word. It could be sentence by sentence – but that's extremely difficult.

• There are all kinds of word games which play about with the sounds or letters. For example, you can put an extra syllable (such as 'guh') inside each word, add an extra sound at the end of each word, or put the last sound at the front of a word. Inventing the most intricate game is quite good fun. The class works out a set of rules. You then tape record the game being played, and listen to the tape afterwards, to see if the rules are being accurately followed, and how people adapt the rules to meet awkward situations. You can even have a class (or school) back-slang competition!

EL 7

bilabial (KS 4)

• This term is used only when talking about consonants. Phoneticians don't talk about a lip-rounded vowel as a 'bilabial vowel', because the two lips are actively involved in the production of *all* vowels.

• Actually, there's another bilabial consonant – [w], as in *wall* – which I didn't mention in the entry because it's very vowel-like in the way it's made (see the entry on **approximant**). In some accents, there's a voiceless equivalent to [w] – the *wh* of *why*, which is written [ʍ] in phonetic transcription. Do the students pronounce *Wales* and *whales* differently? These days, it isn't usual to find the contrast in RP speakers (see **Received Pronunciation**) – but you may well hear it in older speakers, especially men, and in people who have had some speech training. It's also common in Scots and Welsh English.

IPE 8.9.2; EPP 7.4

bilingual (KS 3)

• A bilingualism survey in the school, or in the area, can produce some interesting results. The trick is to develop a good questionnaire – which isn't as easy as it sounds. Bilingualism turns out to be something rather more complex than it might appear to be at first sight. Just how bilingual is the person? Do they read and write as well as speak and listen, in each language? Do they use each language at home, or just one of them? What language do they use at school, in the playground, at church, at work . . . ? If you can get hold of a copy of the national census form, look to see how the government asks these questions. Get the students to criticise the census form (it won't be difficult). If you want to see a survey done professionally, look at the Linguistic Minorities Project, *The Other Languages of England* (Routledge & Kegan Paul, 1985), especially its Appendix 3, which lists 156 questions to ask!

• Don't be too 'purist' in your approach to bilingualism. Often, bilinguals aren't sure which language they use on which occasion. Sometimes, they switch languages within a single conversation, or even within a sentence (the phenomenon is called **code switching**). It's very normal to mix languages when talking (**code mixing**), and there are some famous cases of this happening around the world – Tex-Mex, for example, which mixes English and Spanish in southern Texas. *Donde esta el thin-sliced bread*? asks a customer in a supermarket ('Where's the . . .'). *Esta en aisle three, sobre el second shelf, en el wrapper rojo* replies the sales assistant ('It's in . . . on the . . . in the red . . .'). For a good introduction to the realities of bilingualism, see François Grosjean, *Life with Two Languages* (Harvard University Press, 1982).

ET 5

blend (KS 3)

• For the record, the others are: *helicopter* + *airport*, *breath* + *analyse*, *electricity* + *execute*. Some other examples are *Eurovision*, *paratrooper*, *travelogue*, *smog*, *moped*, *Ms* (*Miss* + *Mrs*).

• Some of the elements are used so often that they begin to resemble affixes, eg *Euro-* in *Eurodollar*, *Euroenergy*, *Eurocrat*. On this basis, get the students to make up some blends of their own, and work out possible

meanings for them, eg *alphanesia* (inability to remember the alphabet?), *pizzangle* (the shape of a slice of pizza?).

CGEL App I.76

block language (KS 3)

● Block language is everywhere, so it shouldn't be difficult to compile a collection. A couple of other places to look are in shops (the labels and price tags on the products) and in libraries (the titles of books). Any language which is highly abbreviated, especially when resulting from pressures of space or time, can display the characteristics of block language – examples include messages on postcards (*Having wonderful time*), addresses, telegrams, and the language of diaries.

● Notice there are several different types in the list I've given in the entry. In some, the item contrasts with only a small number of other possibilities – for instance, the road sign *30* contrasts with *40*, and a few other possibilities; *No smoking* with *Smoking*; *For sale* (hopefully) with *Sold*. Notice that the main structural feature is the lack of normal sentence structure – in particular, the lack of a verb. On the other hand, *Dog bites postman* is one of thousands of possible headlines, identified only by the typography and elliptical grammar. The language of newspaper headlines makes an interesting study in its own right.

RG 2; SGE 11.22; CGEL 11.45–7

body language (KS 3) see **communication**

borrowing or loan word (KS 3)

• This entry is good motivation for digging in dictionaries. If you have an etymological dictionary available, this provides even fuller information. Notice that, in a complete account, the dictionary will give the whole of the word's history, stage by stage. For example, a word may have originated in Latin, and come down to Modern English via French and Middle English. You'll also find that there are several words marked simply 'etymology unknown'. An interesting angle is to look at a restricted area of language, to see where its words come from. First names, for example, are given excellent etymological treatment in Leslie Dunkling and William Gosling, *Dictionary of First Names* (Dent, 1983).

• Borrowings can lead to an interesting sociolinguistic discussion. Many people object to using a borrowed word when there is an equivalent already available in the language. The French Academy, for example, has been very critical of English borrowings in French official writing. Where are borrowings most apparent in present-day English (eg French words in perfume names)? Note that it will take a while before a borrowed word settles down. For a time it may preserve its foreign pronunciation, retain any accents on its letters (see **accents**), and be written in italics in print. There's a good collection of words still felt to be alien in John Ayto, *Making Sense of Foreign Words in English* (Chambers, 1991).

CEL 54

braces see **brackets**

brackets (KS 3)

• I say 'in British English' because in American English the term **brackets** is usually reserved for square brackets only. Incidentally, the warning about overusing brackets should be taken very seriously. Some students develop a bracket obsession. Examples such as the two at the bottom of the entry shouldn't be copied, unless the writer is very sure of the effect to be conveyed. Bracket sequences are effective only in very restricted contexts – as here, where they give the entry a jocular 'lift' at the end.

• I haven't given any examples of different kinds of brackets inside each other. Students may be familiar with these conventions from mathematics. More advanced students should note the conventional use of square brackets to indicate an ironic comment, as in 'There were three interested [sic] children waiting for the teacher'; an explanation of special typography, as in 'This was *not*, he said, the solution [my emphasis]'; an omitted piece of text in a quotation, as in '[They claimed] it was a disaster';

and an authorial gloss: 'I said that she [the defendant] would be able to read the notes'.

CGEL App III.20

cant (KS 4) see **argot**

capital letter (KS 3) see **upper case**

cardinal numeral and ordinal numeral (KS 4)

• Try where possible to follow up the usage aspect of numerals. There's more to them than merely the mathematical side. An example is how we say '0' – *nought, zero, oh* (in telephone numbers and a few other places, such as James Bond's number), *nil* (football), *love* (tennis). Another is how we say 'roughly': *eightish, about eight, 30-odd, a good 30, 30 or so, some 30, approximately 30* (and *approx 30*), *circa 30* (and *c 30*). Note, we can't say **33-odd*. And how are numerals said or written in dates, times, fractions, mathematical formulae, money (eg how many ways are there of saying £8.50?)? Also, punctuation, especially the use of hyphenation, is an important aspect, when numerals are written out in full. For large numbers, the comma is increasingly avoided. It is ambiguous on the Continent, where the comma is used for a decimal point. The International Organization for Standardization recommends the use of a thin space, and this is increasingly to be seen in print.

• Budding linguists can try working out the rules governing the way we form larger numbers from smaller ones. Superficially it seems that, for cardinals, after 10 we add *-teen* and *-ty*, and for ordinals we add *-th*. However, there are several exceptions (*eleven* not *oneteen*, *twelve* not *twoteen*, *thirteen* not *threeteen*, *fifteen* not *fiveteen*, *eighteen* not *eightteen*, *twenty* not *twoty*, *thirty* not *threety*, *fifty* not *fivety*). There are seven irregularities among the ordinals (relating to 1, 2, 3, 5, 8, 9, 12).

RG 38; SGE 6.28; CGEL 6.63–9

cardinal vowels

• A set of standard reference points for describing the position of the tongue in the mouth when it is articulating a vowel. It was devised by the British phonetician Daniel Jones (1881–1967). The diagram takes the form of a quadrilateral representing the area of the mouth in which vowels are articulated. The horizontal dimension shows whether a vowel is articulated towards the front, centre, or back of the vowel area, and the vertical dimension shows whether it is articulated high up, mid, or low down in the vowel area. The position of the lips is also noted. (See entries on **close vowel**, **front** and **rounding**.) The diagram is a very helpful teaching tool, but I think it would be asking too much of students to go into it at KS 3 or 4. Given the fineness of the phonetic distinctions involved, and the diagram's general applicability (to all languages), it is more a tool for specialists than for introductory-level students.

EPP 2.2; IPE 4.4

case (KS 3)

• The idea of **case** isn't always easy to get across in relation to English, simply because English isn't a language which makes use of cases very much. In the tradition which comes down from Latin, cases are word *endings*, and there are very few such endings in the language (see further, **inflection** and **morphology**). If you were taught English using the techniques of Latin grammar, once upon a time, you may have gained a different impression, of course. In nineteenth-century approaches to English grammar, there was a widespread tendency to refer to all the uses of nouns as 'cases', whether they had an ending or not. So, for example, *fish* in *The fish was hungry* would be 'nominative', *O fish* would be 'vocative', *fish* (in *I saw the fish*) would be 'accusative', *the fish's fin* would be 'genitive', *I gave it to the fish* would be 'dative', and *I took it from the fish* would be 'ablative'. Grammarians no longer try to force the categories of Latin grammar on to English. Because there is only one ending (the 'apostrophe *s*'), there is only one case to be recognised. If you need to talk about all the other uses of the noun, you could call them, collectively, the 'unmarked' case. These other uses are signalled either by word order, the particle *O*, or prepositions.

• More advanced students might investigate the genitive in further detail. For example, what other meanings does it express, apart from possession (consider examples such as *a week's leave* and *a summer's day*)? The relationship between the case ending and the *of*-genitive (as in *the cover of the book*) might be explored: we sometimes prefer one form rather than the other – such as *the front of the house* rather than *the house's front*, and the *women's college* rather than *college of the women*. Budding linguists can compare the cases (or lack of them) in English with those present in other languages. Some languages have no cases in the noun at all (Chinese, French), some have many more (German, Latin). Finnish has 16.

RG 34; SGE 5.48–55, 6.6–7; CGEL 5.112–26, 6.2–5

cataphora (kuh-**ta**-fuh-ruh) see **anaphora**

catenative (kuh-**tee**-nuh-tiv)

• This is a useful term for describing a lexical verb which governs (the nonfinite form of) another lexical verb. Take *She likes to ski* or *I hate waiting*;

the most important verbs are *ski* and *waiting*, respectively. So what are the other verbs? They aren't auxiliaries, such as *can*, *may*, and *is* – they seem to have much more content (see the entry on **auxiliary verb**). They are called **catenatives** because they can act in a 'chain' (*catena* is Latin for 'chain'): *I didn't seem to want to keep on trying to practise*.

RG 19; CGEL 3.49

central vowel see **front**

circumlocution (KS 3)

• It's worth pointing out that not all circumlocution is bad. It may provide comic effect in literature (especially as a feature of character). In some literary periods (such as the eighteenth century), periphrasis was considered a desirable trait. In everyday settings, when people are being very formal or polite (especially if they're unused to talking in a formal style), they often resort to circumlocution. To say something in a roundabout way may, at times, be an aid to communication, especially if the subject-matter is awkward or sensitive. It's not always right to go straight to the point. Can students think of contexts where this could happen?

• An interesting exercise is to make a collection of periphrases and evaluate them. It isn't enough simply to identify the examples; their function needs to be discussed. Any kind of 'officialese' will contain some good instances. People may criticise it, but why do officials use it in the first place?

clause (KS 3)

• The first example is deliberately a very simple one, in which each clause is linked by *and*. Some students might think from this that the crucial indicator is the word *and*, and proceed to analyse *mummy and daddy* as two clauses. Rather, the important feature is the structure itself, which in almost all cases must contain a verb (the exceptions include the so-called 'verbless' clauses, such as *Although tired, Maria watched TV*, where the first clause has the subject and verb missed out). There should be one main verb in each clause.

• There are many sentences which don't have a clause structure. They include: *Yes*, *Exit*, *Mhm*, and many examples of formulaic language (see **block language**, **formula**). They tend to be very short. But the size of the sentence isn't the crucial point. You can have a one-word sentence which is a clause, such as a command: *Stop!*

RG 2; SGE 2.2; CGEL 2.11

clause analysis (KS 3)

• This entry gives only the briefest of overviews. It needs to be followed up, but gently, and over a period of time. It's at this point that any approach to language study has to be very careful, to avoid ending up as a series of boring and apparently purposeless exercises which simply 'name parts' (as in the old days of parsing). The crucial thing (which becomes clearer in the entries on the individual clause elements) is that each element actually expresses a meaning. Clauses are patterns of meaning, such as 'who did what to whom – and when or where?' Incomplete and ambiguous sentences can help sharpen a student's sense of this: *Michael put the car* (adverbial omitted). Playing about with element order is useful: *Cat savages mouse* (not news), *Mouse savages cat* (news!). Note clauses such as *Mary kicked*, where, if the object is omitted, the verb must have a figurative meaning, such as 'objected'. Get students used to abbreviations, such as S, V, O, C, and A. Get them used to talking about an 'SVA structure' or an 'SVOA' structure.

• Another angle is to show how children learn clause structure, gradually building up these patterns from their elements: *Daddy*, *Daddy eating*, *Daddy eating cake*, *My Daddy is eating the cake* . . . Indeed, any domain where people are having problems with language will show the need to know about clause structure. The clauses of a language-handicapped child, or of an adult who has developed aphasia following a stroke, or of a foreigner in the early stages of learning English will all display unusual patterns of development. Keep an eye open for alien-speak: Yoda, in the *Star Wars* films, says things like *Strong with the Force you are* and *Your father he is* – where the complement element is placed before the subject and verb.

• The entry says 'just a few exceptions'. The chief one is the command type of sentence, which may consist only of a verb (*Go!*), and where a subject is optional (*You children sit on your chairs!*). Another is the elliptical kind of sentence (see **ellipsis**), where the context allows you to leave out one or more elements (as in a reply to *Where are you going? To town*). There are also some exceptional types of sentence which aren't easily analysed into a neat sequence of clauses: see the entries on **existential sentence** and **cleft sentence**.

• When students are beginning to practise looking for clause elements, keep them off subordinate clauses (see **subordination**). These are tricky, because a subordinate clause is a 'clause within a clause'. There are *two* levels of structure going on at the same time. For instance, *I saw that he fell*, at one level consists of a subject-verb-object structure (*I saw 'something'* – like *John saw Jim*). But the 'something' itself consists of a clause, basically *he fell*, which is a subject-verb structure. Students have to be able to see these two levels, and this kind of analysis is best left to a much later stage of grammatical study.

RG 3–4; SGE 2.3–5; CGEL 2.13–19

cleft sentence (KS 4)

• It's the flexibility of the cleft sentence construction which makes it such an important feature of speech. Almost any clause element can be brought to the front of the sentence and emphasised. It's also a very useful device in writing, as it gives the reader a clear-cut indication of where the emphasis in the sentence should lie, and (as the Shakespeare quotation shows) it gives writers several options in their efforts to match syntax, rhythm, and meaning. You'll also find certain types of cleft sentence used in certain styles. In radio reporting, for example, sentences often begin with a time phrase: *It was in the early hours of this morning that an attack took place . . .*

• Notice that clefts can apply to questions (*Who was it who left early?*) and exclamations (*What a lovely cake it was you made!*). These sentences often pass unnoticed in speech, but in writing they can become inelegant without care: *It was because it was Sunday that the shop was shut*. They will quite often turn up in essays where the writer is being influenced by the patterns of conversational speech.

RG 71; SGE 18.18–20; CGEL 18.25–30

cliche (KS 3)

• Stress the point that cliches aren't always bad, even though few people have a good word for them. But cliches can play an important social role, such as keeping a conversation going, and forging rapport. However you evaluate them, cliches always have a function – even if that function is simply to demonstrate that someone hasn't got anything to say. But don't stop the discussion there. If someone hasn't got anything to say, what is it in society or in that person which accounts for the need to communicate at all? Notice also how pervasive cliches are – they turn up in proverbs, slogans, propaganda, jargon. Social stereotypes (eg of race, sex) rely on them. If you start collecting cliches, you will end up collecting more of the language than you bargained for.

• Cliches are old uses of language which refuse to die. They are the opposite of neologisms – the latest linguistic inventions (see **neologism**). It's very worth while to relate these two processes. An excellent source discussion is Walter Redfern, *Clichés and Coinages* (Blackwell, 1989). Note especially how cliches can be recycled, used with subtle changes in word-play and other forms of ingenuity. It's as plain as the nostril on your face.

click (KS 4)

• You'll find that everyone can do clicks – including some that are somewhat ruder than the ones I've illustrated in the entry. From a general language point of view, it's important to stress that these sounds really are consonants, just like [p] and [b] in English. Some of the South African languages have a very wide range of clicks – made in various parts of the mouth, some nasalised, some with lip rounding, and so on. If you can get hold of Miriam Makeba's 'The Click Song', it will be a fine illustration of the resonance that can be given to these sounds.

• I haven't given precise descriptions of the click sounds, because of their marginal status, but of course this could be done. For example, the kissing sound is a *bilabial click*, and its phonetic symbol is a small circle with a dot in the centre. The 'tut tut' sound is a *dental click*, and its symbol is a thin vertical line (formerly, an upside-down *t*). The IPA chart gives the complete set of standard symbols (see **International Phonetic Alphabet**).

CEL 22; IPE 4.3.9

clipping (KS 3)

• The others are: *public house, gentleman, photograph, demonstration, because, telephone, fried potatoes, advertisements, television*. Some other examples are: *brill, gents, mike* (microphone), *stereo, plane* (aeroplane), *fridge*. Notice how clippings usually drop the end part of a word. *Fridge* and *flu* are interesting because they drop an element both at the beginning and at the end. A fertile source of clippings is proper names: *Liz, Rich, Stu* . . .

• It's important to emphasise that clipping is one *type* of abbreviation, along with acronyms and blends. A student of mine once wrote 'Current trends include the use of abbreviations and clippings', which illustrates the kind of uncertainty that can arise.

CGEL App I.74; ET 15

close vowel and open vowel (KS 4)

• The 'more subtle distinctions' referred to are **mid-close** (or **half-close**), for vowels which are made nearer to close than open, and **mid-open** (or **half-open**), for those nearer to open than close. In RP (see **Received Pronunciation**), the first vowel quality of *bay* is mid-close, often transcribed with an [e] symbol, whereas the first quality of *bear* is mid-open, often transcribed with an [ɛ] symbol.

• The distinction between close and open is largely of theoretical significance. Very few vowels are made at the extremes of closeness and openness. Almost all are 'somewhere in the middle'. Their exact positions will be shown in a phonetics textbook, using a special diagram of the vowel area in the mouth (see **cardinal vowels**). As vowel qualities are not always easy to hear, I wouldn't introduce this diagram at KS 3 or 4, nor investigate differences in vowel quality too closely. Consonants are a much easier way into phonetics. On the other hand, you may find yourself without a choice. Differences between regional accents are primarily located in the use of different vowels. If you've a class where the students have different accents (so that, for example, they say the word *bear* in various ways), and they show interest in these differences, you may have to do some vowel quality analysis sooner than you expect.

IPE 4.4.5; EPP 2.2

cluster (KS 4)

• This term is used only with reference to consonants, and not to vowels. Sequences of vowel qualities are described as **diphthongs** and **triphthongs**. In the study of the written language, clusters are sometimes called **blends** – especially in the context of teaching young children to read.

• The Sound Warning is a serious one. Students do have trouble keeping the spoken and the written apart in their minds. They will very easily think 'There are three sounds in *box*', just because they see three letters. It can take a lot of effort to dissuade them. And the other risk is that, when they see a letter, they imagine that it should be pronounced. Use words with silent letters to make the point: *debt, write, knife*.

IPE 9.8–9; EPP 8.2

coarticulation see **articulation**

code mixing/switching see **bilingual**

coherence (KS 4) see **cohesion**

cohesion (KS 4)

• This entry and **coherence** need to be taken together. The crucial point is to get students to appreciate that there are two distinct notions involved, as indicated in the Word Warning. I don't think there's much more to say about coherence and incoherence, which are intuitively rather obvious notions, and the subject-matter of much traditional language study (in comprehension exercises, for example). It's worth stressing that a text can be incoherent in a number of ways – leaving out crucial information, adding irrelevant information, sequencing the information wrongly, and so on. Incoherence can also result from ambiguity or from failing to spell out one's assumptions properly. Also, cases of incoherence aren't usually as obvious as in my example. It may even be quite difficult to pin down the incoherence of a text, especially when subtle points of argumentation are involved. And it's always easier to see the incoherence in others' language than the incoherence in oneself. Exercises which present texts into which particular difficulties are introduced, in a carefully controlled manner, can be useful in focusing students' attention on the need for careful listening or reading.

• Cohesion is much easier to pin down. Once the range of relevant items is recognised, it can be quite interesting to go through a written text and mark the items which are cohesive. An exercise which presents cohesion 'errors', of the type I illustrate in my opening passage, usually makes the point clearly enough – and several real examples of such errors will be found in many a school essay (eg pronouns which don't have a clear cross-reference). Examples of texts analysed in this way are given in RG page 207 and CGEL 19.69–84. The focus on these topics came especially from Michael Halliday and Ruqaiya Hasan, *Cohesion in English* (Longman, 1976). My entry concentrates on the grammatical feature of cohesion. Other ways of making a text hang together include the *graphic* (layout, sub-headings, etc) and the *prosodic* (intonation and stress, in particular). *Lexical* cohesion is especially important. Take the sequence, *The car lurched around the corner. Typical old Ford, said Julian. Vehicles aren't allowed in that street, said Marge.* Because we know that Fords are cars, which are vehicles, everything hangs together. Notice what would happen if words lacking lexical links were introduced: *The car lurched around the corner. Typical old shop, said Julian. Animals aren't allowed in that street, said Marge.* You could of course construct a scenario which made sense of such a sequence, but it would require a lot more work!

RG 73; SGE 19; CGEL 19

coinage (KS 3) see **neologism**

collective noun (KS 4)

• Emphasise that the alternative numbers after a collective noun are not a matter of 'right' vs 'wrong'. It is a difference in point of view – seeing the impersonal collectivity of a group vs the personal individuality within the group. Some other collective nouns are: *army, association, audience, club, crew, crowd, department, enemy, family, gang, government, group, herd, jury, majority, Parliament, population, staff, team, the United Nations.*

• There's a difference between British and American English: the latter tends to have a singular verb after collectives. It would be unusual to find *The government are . . .* in American English.

RG 33; SGE 5.46; CGEL 5.108

collocation (KS 4)

• Although the term may be unfamiliar, the basic idea underlying **collocation** is not. It is simply our intuitive expectation that certain words keep company with each other. We get to know the meaning and use of words by the company they keep. When a collocation becomes so predictable that it is, in effect, a fixed phrase, we talk about idioms (*spick and span*), cliches (*every Tom, Dick and Harry*), proverbs (*too many cooks spoil the broth*), and the like. Notice that *spick* is somewhat unusual, in that it has no other use in the language. Only a few words are like this (*amok* is another, only precedable by *run*). By contrast, many words occur in such a wide range of contexts that we don't have any clear intuitions about their collocations – *have, want, be . . .*

• An interesting way in to the study of collocations is to look at their level of mutual predictability. Try putting together a *Blankety-Blank* game in class – it isn't quite as easy as it seems, incidentally. Another angle is to deliberately break expectations – such as *He popped the letter into the porridge* or *She was dressed to die*. Another is to look at the way authors do this professionally, such as Dylan Thomas's phrases *all the moon long* and *a grief ago*. Figurative language always introduces fresh collocations – such as Wordsworth's city which doth 'wear the beauty of the morning' ('Upon Westminster Bridge') or Hopkins's 'Elected Silence' ('Habit of Perfection').

CEL 17

colloquial speech (KS 3)

• No difficulty getting samples of this kind of speech? Actually, it's the most difficult variety of all to capture on tape. The problem is that, when people see a microphone, they become self-conscious, and the naturalness of their spontaneous speech is the first victim. If a good conversation develops, the participants may well forget the tape is on, of course. Alternatively, you could hide the tape recorder somewhere, but be prepared for trouble if you do. (Remember President Nixon! You could start a Schoolgate scandal.) Apart from anything else, though, surreptitious recording tends to be of very poor acoustic quality. (It's also possible to use samples of authentic conversation, produced by publishers specialising in teaching English to foreigners: *Advanced Conversational English*, by myself and Derek Davy (Longman, 1975) is an example.)

• You can get a good conversation going by choosing the right topic – such as a particularly alarming experience – where the participants get carried away with their story. Don't use too academic a topic (such as a discussion of a novel), as the subject-matter will prompt the use of language of a more formal kind. If you're going to use the tape to make certain points in class, later on, you'll need to spend some time pre-listening. *Don't* think that the features of colloquial speech will somehow manifest themselves by magic as soon as you press play on the tape recorder. A great deal of a spontaneous conversation is unusable, for pedagogical purposes, because several people are speaking at once, background noise obscures a point, or you can't distinguish between the different speakers (it's remarkable how similar people sound on tape). Half an hour spent out of class, listening out for the best passages, and noting where they are, using the tape numeral indicator (make sure your machine has got one), is time very well spent.

CEL 31

colon (KS 3)

• There are several other uses of the colon, which students might like to track down. It is often used to introduce an example, or a list of examples. It may be used to separate the elements of a time (3:20). Some people (especially in American English) follow the 'Dear X' invocation in a letter by a colon. Note that, in general, the colon is not a very commonly used punctuation mark.

• The reference to British English distinguishes this convention from American English, which regularly uses a capital letter for an independent clause after a colon. Another typographic variation is that some printing styles have a dash following the colon (:–), but this goes against the modern trend for printed matter to present as uncluttered an appearance as possible.

CGEL App III.10–11

comma (KS 3)

• I did win. But I wouldn't want that to be taken as a recommendation for students to put commas everywhere. There's a real danger of comma scattering, especially when students think that a comma marks a pause. The main message about a comma is that its role is primarily to show the structure of a sentence. But the comma is the most flexible of all the punctuation marks, so it's not possible to sum up its uses in a simple sentence or two. It certainly isn't possible to have a short lesson dealing with the comma. A particular complication is that comma usage is a matter of tendencies rather than rules. For example, it isn't possible to say definitively whether there should or should not be a comma before the conjunction in the following sentence: *The dog was furious and the cat was pleased*. Because the clauses are fairly short, many people wouldn't bother to put one in. In fact, about 50 per cent of clauses linked by *and* don't have a comma before the *and*. On the other 'and, if the conjunction were *but*, then about 75 per cent of clauses *would* have a comma. Or, to take another area: in a series of adjectives before a noun, a 'serial comma' is sometimes put in before the conjunction (*a tall, dark, and handsome prince*) and sometimes not. Usage is completely split in Britain; American English generally puts it in (though not always in newspapers).

• It's difficult to be definite about where a comma should be present, but it's fairly easy to say where it shouldn't be. In particular, the main elements of clause structure (subject, verb, object, complement) cannot be interrupted by punctuation – so it isn't possible to have **I said, that he was in* (where the comma is separating the verb and the object clause) or **The lady standing by the bar, is my auntie* (where the comma is separating the subject and the verb). Nor can a simple phrase be interrupted in this way: we cannot have **the big, cat* or **has, been running*.

• There are some nice examples where the comma is contrastive, especially between an adverbial and the rest of the sentence. Compare *They walked in naturally* ('in a natural way') and *They walked in, naturally* ('Of course they walked in'); *You know he was angry* ('You are aware that he was angry') and *You know, he was angry* ('I'm telling you: he was angry'). In these cases, the comma is following the prosody of the speech.

CGEL App III. 6–9, 17–19

command (KS 3)

• I've used the familiar term here, rather than **directive**, but in fact the latter term is a better label for what goes on when verbs are used in this way. Only one of the uses of the imperative form of the verb is to give commands. Others include inviting (*Have a drink*), warning (*Mind your head*), pleading (*Help me*), advising (*Take an aspirin*), requesting (*Open the window, please*) and expressing good wishes (*Have a nice day*). Get the students to look up what a command is in a dictionary, and then see how far these other examples can legitimately be called 'commands'. See if they can work out the other meanings for themselves. What's *Go to hell*, for instance? An imprecation. Or *Take three eggs* (in a cooking commentary)? An instruction. It's difficult to think up a satisfactory term for such a wide range of functions. If students don't like the term **directive**, let them have a go at thinking up something better. (Students oughtn't to develop a fear of terminology. They won't, if they're given responsibility for it. Can they do better than the grammarians?)

• Investigate other kinds of command, apart from those with a single verb: *Get lost*; *Be doing your homework when I get in, or else*; *Do come in*; *Don't do that*. Note also that some verbs can't be used as a command (**Need a bike*). Nor can commands be used with a past time reference: **Sit down yesterday*. Sometimes a subject can be expressed: *You sit down*; *Nobody move*; *All you children stand up*.

RG 6; SGE 11.15–19; CGEL 11.24–30

comment clause (KS 4)

• There is a widespread antipathy to comment clauses, because there is a widespread tendency to overuse them, and they then become a sign of

unclear, lazy, or devious thinking. A politician who answers a question by smothering the sense in comment clauses fails to impress. And there are some people who put a 'you know' between every few words – a mannerism which can intensely irritate. But if speakers use these clauses in a varied and limited way, they can add a great deal of smoothness, interest, and conviction to what is being said. Certainly, *everyone* uses them. Even those who object to *you know* will be heard on occasion to use such clauses as *frankly speaking, I venture to say, I assume, it appears, you must admit, it transpires,* and so on. Use the brackets criterion to identify the comment clauses in a sample of recorded conversation.

- Then discuss why people put them in. Some of them are there for stylistic effect, softening the force of a sentence, as in the sympathetic teacher example. Some express the speaker's tentativeness (*I believe, they allege*), some express certainty (*I'm certain, there's no doubt*), some express an emotional attitude (*I regret, I'm pleased to say, to put it bluntly, speaking candidly*), some ask for the listener's attention (*you know, mark you*). Some are very common in speech (*mind you, you see*); others are very common in writing (*it would appear, as was pointed out above*).

RG 67; SGE 15.32; CGEL 15.53–6

common noun (KS 3) see **noun**

communication (KS 3)

- There are two main points to be appreciated here, and both arise from the observation that **language** and **communication** aren't the same thing.

There are other ways of communicating, apart from using language, as the entry illustrates. And there are other functions of language apart from that of communication (in the sense of transmitting information from person A to person B). This last point isn't illustrated in the entry – but consider, for example, the way in which language is used to express social solidarity (in chants at football matches) or in play (children's games, as when someone is bouncing a ball against a wall and calling out a rhyme at the same time).

• Beware the several metaphorical uses of the term **language**, in such phrases as 'body language'. Spoken and written language have a highly sophisticated structure (as the terms in this book illustrate). In particular, spoken and written language demonstrate a high level of creativity (an unlimited number of new words can be created, and there is no limit to the ways you can add to the length of a sentence) and two levels of structure (meaningless sounds/letters are combined to make meaningful words/ sentences). By contrast, the gestures and facial expressions of body language lack this creative range and this complexity of structure. I prefer to talk about **nonverbal communication**, therefore, rather than to use the potentially misleading phrase 'body language'. A good review of the research in this field is to be found in Michael Argyle, *Bodily Communication* (Methuen, 1975). A popular account is Desmond Morris, *Manwatching* (Triad/Granada, 1978).

CEL 65

comparative (KS 3) see **degree**

competence

• This term is widely used in language study these days, but I felt that, like several other terms in linguistics, its status as part of a general linguistic theory placed it beyond the level of the student books. Nonetheless, from time to time you might find it useful to introduce the notion, which refers to our unconscious knowledge of our language. It is the system of rules that we have mastered, which enables us to produce and understand an infinite number of sentences, and to recognise grammatical mistakes and ambiguities. The term, introduced by Noam Chomsky in the 1970s, was distinguished from **performance**, which refers to the actual utterances of native speakers, such as would be found in a corpus of linguistic data. A later development introduced the idea of **communicative** or **pragmatic competence**, referring to our ability to use sentences that are appropriate to the situational context in which they occur (eg our awareness of rules of politeness and formality).

CEL 65

complement (KS 3)

• Students find this notion somewhat trickier than the idea of **object** – perhaps because the relationships involved are somewhat more abstract. The verb to concentrate on at the outset is the verb *to be*, which is by far the commonest complement-taking verb (students should relate this entry to the one on **copula** in due course). Other verbs which take complements include the following (I list them with some typical adjective complements): *appear (interested), look (nice), seem (calm), keep (interested), become (older), go (sour), turn (cold)*. To check whether the word after the verb is a complement or not, see if the verb can be replaced by a form of *be*, without fundamentally altering the meaning of the sentence. So, *The weather's turning cold* → *The weather is cold; You look nice* → *You are nice.*

• Notice that not everything following the verb *to be* is called a complement, in this approach. In *Horatio is in the garden*, the phrase *in the garden* (answering the question 'where?') is an adverbial (of place). So, there are *three* types of three-element structure in English (see the entry on **clause analysis**): SVO (*Erika saw the doctor*), SVC (*Erika is a doctor*) and SVA (*Erika is in the garden*). Having said this, it must be stressed that the adverbial here does have a similar complementing function, and some grammarians really stress this point.

• There's a (poor) joke which points up the role of the complement to the object. *Rude hotel guest: Call me a taxi. Doorman: Sir, you are a taxi.* The guest intends the sentence to be a double object construction ('call a taxi for me'). The doorman takes it as a complement-to-the-object construction ('the taxi is me').

• Beware: there's a general use of the word **complementation** which can confuse. You could argue that *anything* after the verb 'completes the meaning of the clause'. So, all three of the Erika sentences are incomplete when they get to their respective verbs, and need 'finishing off': *Erika saw, Erika is*). If you argue like this (and the Quirk grammars, for example, do), then you will end up saying that the object is one form of complementation, the complement is another, and the adverbial is another. There are many kinds of complementation, in this sense – but only one complement.

RG 11; SGE 16.12–13; CGEL 16.21–4

complementary terms see **antonyms**

complex sentence (KS 4)

• I lied. It *is* quite complex, at times. An essential point is not to confuse complex sentences and long sentences. You can have a complex sentence that's quite short (*Stay where you are*) and a long sentence that isn't complex (*The red book and the green pen and the yellow screwdriver and the orange egg-cup were lying on the table in the garden*). For the definition of complex sentence given here, the crucial point is that one clause must be *part of* another clause. Stringing a host of phrases together, on this account, doesn't make a sentence complex – just long! (If you're into linguistic theory, you'll find that approaches differ, on this point.) Also, stringing clauses together using conjunctions such as *and* doesn't make a sentence complex, in this approach. They are given a separate label: **compound sentences**.

• My entry doesn't go into a further point, which can cause confusion when it's encountered for the first time. The entry talks about a clause which takes up the *whole* of a clause element. It doesn't actually mention clauses which take up only a *part* of a clause element – such as relative clauses (see **relative**). Consider this: *The book which is lying on the table is Mary's*. The subject is: *The book which is lying on the table*. The relative clause is: *which is lying on the table*. It isn't the whole of the subject, just part of it. Should this be called a complex sentence? Linguists' opinions vary. Some say that such sentences are indeed complex, in the same sense as before. Having a clause within a clause like this, they argue, is enough to make anything complex! Others, though, think that such sentences – despite the relative clause – are basically simple in structure. Their reasoning is that you can leave out the relative clause and still have a complete sentence: *The book is Mary's*. It's essentially a very simple sentence. They point out that you can't do this with sentences such as *What I said was the truth*. Here, the subject is *What I said*. If you omit that clause, you're left with an ungrammatical fragment: **was the truth*. At this point, you are either totally fascinated or totally lost (or possibly both). Either way, I would keep off such ramifications until a much later stage of study.

RG 63; SGE 14; CGEL 14

compound sentence (KS 4)

• I say the three 'main' linking words. Actually, there are only three coordinating conjunctions: *and*, *or*, and *but*. However, you can say *and/or*, and there are some other words which resemble these in certain respects – such as *yet*, *so*, *nor*, and *for*. (See the entry on **conjunction**.)

• Notice that it is possible to use punctuation to join clauses together, without the use of any conjunctions. For example, if you wrote *I came, I saw, I conquered*, you would have a compound sentence. In theory, the same thing happens in speech, through the use of intonation and rhythm; but intonation isn't as clear-cut a signal of structure as is punctuation. If you said *I came . . .* out loud, for instance, it can easily sound like three separate sentences, though you can get round this to a degree by giving each clause a 'continuative' lilt (using a rising tone).

RG 63; SGE 13.2–3; CGEL 13.5–18

compound word (KS 3)

• The point about criteria really needs working on. Students will think that, to be a compound, the two elements need to be joined together. Note that the writing convention changes over time: as the compound becomes more established, so the spelling moves from 'open' through 'hyphenated' to 'solid' (joined together). Hyphenation is less common in American English than in British English. The crucial point is the semantic one: the two meanings must merge in some way. Usually the first element modifies the second (almost like a prefix) – it indicates a special feature or characteristic. You can state this relationship in a full sentence: *chewing gum* is *a gum for chewing*. A *dance hall* is *a hall for dancing*. The big Quirk grammar classifies compounds into the types of clause structure which underlie the compound. For example, a subject + verb structure underlies *heartbeat* ('The heart beats') and *toothache* ('The tooth aches'). A verb + object structure underlies *book review* ('Review the book') and *computer-designer* ('Design a computer'). A verb + adverbial structure underlies *waiting room* ('wait in a room') and *sewing machine* ('sew with a machine').

• A good game is to contrast compounds and separate word sequences. A *hot dog* might need stroking or eating. Not all *black birds* are *blackbirds*. Not all *dark rooms* are *darkrooms*. In speech, the stress pattern differs: *'black 'bird* vs *'blackbird*. Almost all compounds have a single-stress pattern. Keep an eye open for unusual compounds – in particular, **reduplicative** forms, which contain elements that are either identical or very similar (*walkie-talkie, bow-wow, shilly-shally*). See also the entry on **blend**.

RG 74; CGEL App I.57–70, 72

concord (KS 3)

• In some grammars, concord is called **agreement**. In the entry, I've picked on a rather unusual kind of concord in English (the agreement between reflexives and their antecedents). The most important kind I've illustrated only in passing, so this needs to be followed up straight away. This is the concord of number between subject and verb in the 3rd person singular of the present tense: *He/she/it moves* vs *I/you/we/they move*. A singular subject requires a singular verb (marked by *-s*), and a plural subject a plural verb. The past tense isn't affected – except for the unusual number concord in the verb *be* (*was* vs *were*). *Be* is also unusual in that, in the present tense, there is 1st person concord as well: *I am*. Other kinds of concord include that between subject and complement (*The boy is an idiot / The boys are idiots*) and between object and complement (*I consider that boy an idiot / I consider those boys idiots*). There is also gender concord between pronouns (*Fred broke his leg, Mary broke her leg, The chair's broken its leg*). Note that *Fred broke her leg* is possible, but it must mean 'someone else's leg'.

• There are many problems of usage affecting concord. Sometimes, the choice of concord depends on what the meaning of the noun is (see the entry on **collective noun**). Noun phrases expressing a quantity or measure are often plural in form, but they take a singular verb (*Ten pounds is all I have*). There are special problems with coordination, especially when the subject contains both a singular and a plural noun phrase (*Either your clutch or your brakes is/are the cause of the problem*). And there are problems when referring to indefinite pronouns (such as *everyone*), where the traditional *he* is now often avoided, and the gender-neutral *they* used instead (though not without vociferous objection from usage critics who resent the loss of grammatical concord): *Everyone thinks he knows what to do / Everyone thinks they know what to do.*

• If you get on to this kind of discussion (hardly avoidable, because 'errors' of this kind are common in students' written work), draw attention to the three different (and partly conflicting) principles involved. Between subject and verb, for example, you will find strict **grammatical concord** operating: a singular subject must go with a singular verb, at all costs. That's the principle given in all the grammar books, which everyone is supposed to follow. But in addition there is **notional concord**, followed instinctively by native speakers: here, a singular *meaning* for the subject is followed by a singular verb (regardless of whether the subject is singular or plural in form), and a plural meaning is followed by a plural verb (again, whatever the form of the subject): *None of the people are going* (where traditional grammar would insist on *is*). Lastly, there is **proximity concord**, which people find themselves drawn to in speech, but which they would often correct (if they noticed it) in writing: the verb agrees with the number of the noun nearest to it (regardless of whether it's the real subject or not): *The king together with his eighty wives are going on holiday*.

RG 14; SGE 10.19–30, CGEL 10.34–50

concordance (KS 4)

• The best way to understand what a concordance does is to use one. It only takes a few minutes, and the power of the book becomes clear. In particular, by showing all the uses of a word together, it becomes easier to see which are an author's favourite words, whether the author is using a word in a range of different meanings, whether it has any figurative senses, and so on.

• The Bible is another work which has been well treated in concordances.

concrete noun (KS 4) see **abstract noun**

conditional clause (KS 4)

• In some languages, a special form of the verb appears in a conditional clause, and the grammars, quite properly, talk about a 'conditional tense'.

However, no special form of the verb appears in English, so this term would be something of a misnomer. A few people still continue to use it, though, because of the influence of the Latinate tradition of grammatical study.

• Apart from the use of *assuming, provided,* and *supposing* (all of which could have been followed by *that*), referred to in the last paragraph of the entry, other subordinating conjunctions include *as long as, given (that), in case, in the event that, on condition (that).*

• At some stage, you should go into the different meanings of the conditional clause. An **open conditional** sentence doesn't say whether the proposition expressed in the main clause is true or not: *If Mary is in school, she'll be in the gym*. Is Mary in the gym? Maybe, maybe not. It's left open. By contrast, in a **hypothetical conditional** sentence, the speaker believes that the proposition expressed in the main clause is false: *If Mary were in school, she would be in the gym*. Is Mary in the gym? Almost certainly not – because she probably isn't in school, anyway! Notice how the verb forms shift backwards in time, in the hypothetical type. There are also some special kinds of conditional clauses: they may have a rhetorical function (*If you did that homework by yourself, I'm the King of Siam*); they may express politeness (*if I may say so, if I may interrupt*); and they may make a comment on the language being used (*if you know what I mean, if that's the right word*).

RG 66; SGE 15.17–20; CGEL 15.32–8

conjunct see **adjunct**

conjunction (KS 3)

• There are only three coordinating conjunctions (*and, but, or*), along with a few special cases, such as *and/or* (*Anna and/or Susie will be there*), and the **correlative** conjunctions, where one form introduces the first clause and another form introduces the second: *either . . . or, neither . . . nor, both . . . and, not only . . . but also*. It's important to note that coordinating conjunctions connect words and phrases as well as clauses: *a new bicycle and a box of Lego, Fred or Pamela*.

• Here's a list of the main subordinating conjunctions. Several consist of a single word: *after, although, as, because, before, if, once, since, that, though, till, unless, until, when(ever), where(ver), whereas, whereupon, while*. Several consist of more than one word, often ending with an obligatory *that* (*in order that, such that*), an optional *that* (*assuming, considering, except, excepting, given, granted, provided, so, supposing*), or *as* (*as far as, as soon as, insofar as*). There are also several correlative subordinators: *No sooner did they leave than the roof fell in; So many people arrived that they had to find extra chairs*.

• Don't forget to talk about the meanings of the various conjunctions. *And*, for example, can express simple addition (*I read magazines and Jane read comics*), time sequence (*John got up and (then) went out*) or result (*I worked hard and (therefore) got promotion*). Several subordinating conjunctions express time: *after, as, before, since, till, until, when, while*. Just two express place: *where* and *wherever*. Four express reason: *because, since, for, as*. The reference grammars give a complete list. There are some further examples in the entry on **conditional clause**.

RG 64–6; SGE 13.3–16, 14.7–9; CGEL 13.5–42, 14.11–19

connectivity (KS 3)

• It's important to appreciate that this notion is much wider than that of **conjunction**, in that it includes the whole range of connecting adverbials, as well as the kind of examples discussed under the headings of **coherence** and **cohesion**. This cluster of entries should be interrelated, at some point, therefore.

• Connectivity has attracted particular attention in the recent flurry of reports on the English language, probably as a reaction against the previous tradition of language study, which was almost entirely restricted to the sentence. In linguistics, major branches of the subject now have as their focus the investigation of stretches of language larger than the sentence (see the entries on **discourse** and **text**). Note that, in the context of child language studies, although the acquisition of the first connectivity features is fairly early (*and* and other conjunctions emerging at around age 3), the various patterns of adverbial connectivity do not emerge until much later – largely after age 7, and with very little development until around age 10. Some of the relevant research is reviewed in a paper by Cheryl Scott in the *Journal of Child Language* 11(2), 1984: 'Adverbial connectivity in conversations of children 6 to 12'. Some teaching implications are discussed in a follow-up paper with Dathan Rush: 'Teaching adverbial connectivity: implications from current research' in *Child Language Teaching and Therapy* 1(3), 1985. It seems that the earliest connectives include *then, so, now, though*, and *anyway/anyhow*. Such items as *however, therefore, in other words, nevertheless* are rarely encountered until after age 12. Also, there are major differences between spoken and written language. Among the teaching suggestions these authors make are:
- identifying connectives with similar functions (*I am hungry, so/therefore I'm going to eat*);
- paraphrasing (*X happened, therefore Y happened. Because X happened, Y happened*);
- filling the gap (clozing) (*We have a long wait before our turn comes up, — let's go get something to drink*. Choose between *otherwise, in the meantime* . . .);
- finishing off (*Barry hated his job, yet* . . .);
- judging acceptability (a judge saying *anyhow*, a yob saying *notwithstanding*);
- discourse formulation (write a paragraph containing the words *therefore* and *in conclusion*);

– across-speaker cueing (Speaker 1 says a sentence. Speaker 2 has to reply using a particular connective. *A: I don't want to eat at Smith's.* (CUE: *then.*) *B: Where do you want to eat, then?*).

RG 73; SGE 19; CGEL 19

connotation (KS 4) see **denotation**

consonant and vowel (KS 4)

• This is a difficult entry to work with, because of the way sounds vary around the country. One of the first things to do is work out whether the class mainly uses RP (see **Received Pronunciation**), or whether there are major regional differences. If there are, what are they? There won't be much of a problem with consonants (typical examples will include the replacement of [t] by a glottal stop (eg in *bottle*), the dropping of [h] (eg in *happen*), and the replacement of [ŋ] by [n] in such words as *running*). The major problem comes with the vowels, which can vary dramatically from one accent to the next. It takes a while to work out the vowel patterns used in your area, but once you've done it, you won't have to do it again. If you're unhappy about your own ear, try to find a tame phonetician in a university linguistics department to check what they are. A local speech therapist might be able to help, too. Gimson's book is a handy reference for all the main regional vowel variants.

• Students will never sort out the sounds/spellings point until they've made some progress in using phonetic spelling. They must appreciate that *come*, for example, has only three phonemes in it. They don't have to master the 'official' transcription to do this, of course. Indeed, many of them may still be using a phonetic spelling in their everyday written work without realising it!

• Students should ask themselves why the consonants in *king* and *fusion* have to be mentioned separately. The reason is that their distribution is different: all other consonants can occur at the beginning of a word; [ŋ] can't and [ʒ] is very unusual in word-initial position – only in such French loan words as *genre* and *gigolo* (and *Jacques*).

• The 'information value' of consonants and vowels is very different – as anyone knows who does crossword puzzles. If you have the clue – E – A – E, you don't stand much chance of working it out; whereas if the clue is – P – N – T, you feel you can get somewhere. Relate this point to the frequency of occurrence of the various vowels and consonants (see the entry on **alphabet** for the written frequency list). A frequency list for RP phonemes is given in Gimson's book: sections 7.14 and 8.10.

• I've deliberately chosen easy examples for the syllable structure illustration. With more complex words, the syllable structure won't be so straightforward, and there are lots of syllables which aren't neatly consonant-vowel-consonant (or CVC, to use the usual abbreviation). For example, *elephant* breaks down into *e-le-phant* ['e-lə-fənt], which is V-CV-CVCC; Anthony into *An-tho-ny* ['an-tə-ni], which is VC-CV-CV. In a more precise formulation, you would say that the typical (or **canonical**) position for a consonant is at the beginning or end of a syllable. A vowel is the syllable **nucleus**. The only occasion when a consonant can be a syllable nucleus is in the case of **syllabic consonants**, in the case of nasals and [l] (in such words as *bottle*, *button*, *prism*) where the final consonant carries the whole weight of the syllable. Apart from these, it's very very rare to have a syllable consisting only of a consonant (as in [ʃ], 'shhh').

EPP 2.2; IPE 4, 5.5

constituent

• This is a useful term to refer to any linguistic unit which is a component of a larger construction. The most obvious constituents of the present sentence are the words. Less obviously, they are the elements of the clause, such as subject and verb. The word *elements* has, in turn, two constituents: *element* and *-s*.

CGEL 2.4

content word see **grammatical word**

context (KS 4)

• It's important to appreciate that this notion applies at several levels of generality: in its linguistic sense, words have to be seen in the context of sentences; sentences in the context of paragraphs; paragraphs in the context of chapters, and so on. The most general notion is of course a very familiar one, in literary studies, where students are routinely advised to see a piece of text 'in its context' – which would include a whole range of non-linguistic considerations, notably the biographical, social, and historical background. Some writers, worried about the potential ambiguity here, use the term **co-text** for the linguistic context and **context** for the non-linguistic. Others talk about the 'linguistic context', the 'historical context', and so on.

• Examples of the importance of context can be found everywhere. The phenomenon of irony is a good example of the need for context to arrive at a correct interpretation (see the entry on **irony**). Another is the way context resolves the different meanings of a pun. Jokes may be funny in one context and not in others. Satire often takes a topic, and places it in an unexpected or incongruous context. Get students to look out for linguistic features which alter their value depending on the context in which they appear: for example, *good*, in general conversation, is the opposite of *bad*, but in some contexts (eg a tourist classification of hotels) it may be at the *bottom* end of a scale which goes from 'good' through 'excellent' to 'superb', and thus has a somewhat negative value.

LG 11

continuous (KS 3) see **progressive**

contour (KS 4)

• This can be a difficult entry to follow, from the text, though students who are used to reading musical scales shouldn't have a problem. (They must beware of taking the musical analogy too literally, though – people do not speak 'out of tune'.) Textbooks vary somewhat in the way they represent contours. Some use a dot for each syllable, varying the size of the dot (the louder the syllable, the bigger the dot). Some use a continuous line.

• It's important to give as wide a range of intonation contours as possible, when following up this entry. Another example is the level contour, in which the words come out in a monotone, which expresses boredom or sarcasm. There is also a contour which rises and then falls, and which usually conveys an emotional response, such as being very shocked or very impressed. Get the students to relate certain contours to familiar contexts, to help fix the 'tunes' in their auditory memory. For example, the difference between a home win, an away win, and a draw in the reading of football results each week on the radio can be identified in terms of contours: rising contour followed by high falling contour = draw; rising contour followed by higher falling-rising contour = away win; rising contour followed by flattened falling contour = home win.

IPE 10.5; EPP 15–17

contraction (KS 3)

• Note that a contraction isn't the same as an **elision**. An elision simply omits a sound (see that entry for examples). In a contraction, one word loses a sound (or sounds) and so gets joined onto another word. In some languages, the sounds of the two words can be completely fused, as in French *du* from *de le*. A complete list of the contracted auxiliary verbs is: *'m* (*am*), *'s* (*is, has*), *'re* (*are*), *'ve* (*have*), *'d* (*had, would*), *'ll* (*will*), and the various negative forms: *aren't, isn't, wasn't, weren't, haven't, hasn't, hadn't, don't, doesn't, didn't, can't, couldn't, mayn't, mightn't, shan't, shouldn't, won't, wouldn't, mustn't*. Note that two of these are ambiguous: *'s* and *'d*.

• When is the contracted form used? It is partly a matter of style, as the entry says, but the use is also conditioned by the context. You're much more likely to get *'s* when the preceding word is a pronoun, *there*, or *here*; you're more likely to get *is* when the preceding word is a noun. There are also usage variations to take into account. *She is not going* can contract in two ways: *She isn't going* and *She's not going* (note you can't do both at once: **She's isn't going*). The former is more common in most dialects (though not in Scotland and some parts of the North of England). *Mayn't* and *shan't* are very rare in British English, and would hardly ever be used in American English.

• Contractions also appear as a marker of non-standard writing, especially when an author is trying to represent dialect or very informal speech. *The* is often contracted in this way, for example (to *t'*). Examples include *y'all, see'd, t'other, we's hae* ('we shall have' – used by Joseph in *Wuthering Heights*), *th'wast* (an example from *The Return of the Native*), and *Tha'd better* (an example from *Sons and Lovers*).

RG 18; SGE 3.13–16; CGEL 3.23, 31–6

conversation (KS 3)

• Emphasise that the naturalness of conversation is deceptive. We have all learned hundreds of rules and strategies which we unconsciously put to use, each time we engage in a conversation. Can students work out the rules governing the way we say *Good morning/afternoon/evening/night*? (To take just one example, when we meet someone we know in the morning, we say *Good morning* to them; if we see them again a few minutes later, we don't repeat the greeting. To do so would sound very odd! *Good morning* is said only once. On the other hand, if we say *Good night* to someone, and then see them again a few minutes later, we can repeat the greeting without it being thought odd.) Another area where the rules are fairly easy to work out is the opening exchanges in a telephone conversation (who speaks first, and what is said). Restrictions on the choice of topic can be interesting: for example, in English it is the done thing to comment on the excellence of the meal when eating in someone else's house, but not the done thing to enquire about how much the meat cost. All these conventions differ between languages. Ronald Wardaugh's *How Conversation Works* (Blackwell, 1985) is a good introduction to the subject.

• Students might look at specific issues within a conversation, such as how people show they want to speak (*but –, erm,* or just a sharp intake of breath), show they're paying attention (*mhm . . . mhm*), or ask their listener for agreement (*you see, you know*). How do you check that a listener is following you? (*Are you with me? Do I make myself clear? Do you see? Let me put it another way.*) How do you tell a listener you're ready to conclude a topic? (*So it goes. Well that's life. Makes you think, doesn't it?*) How regular are the turns in a conversation? How do people interrupt (politely and impolitely)? Don't forget eye contact: by looking at someone, a speaker can signal it's that person's turn to speak next. Get students working in groups of three (one speaker, one listener, and one observer), swapping roles from time to time.

• Another angle is to get hold of a textbook teaching English to foreigners, and see whether its sample conversations sound natural. Conversations sound artificial at times.

CEL 20–1, 31

converse terms see **antonyms**

conversion (KS 3)

• *To tree* doesn't exist – but there's no harm in students imagining what it *could* mean, and trying to find a context for it, such as a dog who persistently chases cats up trees (*Our cat's been treed again*). It's important to show students that they can experiment with parts of speech. They shouldn't have the belief that a given word 'is' a part of speech. As the *round* case shows, everything depends on how you use it.

• Here are some classified examples of conversion: verb to noun (*a desire, a smell, a laugh, a throw*); adjective to noun (*a daily, a comic, regulars, a wet*); noun to verb (*to carpet, to mask, to peel, to glue*); adjective to verb (*to dirty, to empty, to narrow*); noun to adjective (*brick wall, reproduction chairs*). Note the somewhat unusual examples of nouns from grammatical words (*ifs and buts, the how and why*), affixes (*ologies and isms*), and phrases (*also-rans, has-beens, down-and-outs*).

RG 74; CGEL App I.43–56

coordination (KS 3)

• Coordination is an enormous topic, so all I can do is point to some of the interesting features which you might use as a focus. For instance:

– When noun phrases are coordinated, there may be two different meanings: the two nouns may combine to express a single meaning, or they may retain their separate identities. Compare *John and Maria go to church* and *John and Maria make a nice couple*. In the first case, we can 'expand' the sentence, and say: *John goes to church and Maria goes to church*. In the second case, we can't do this: it doesn't make sense to say *John makes a nice couple and Maria makes a nice couple*. Notice that *John and Maria own a house* is ambiguous, therefore: do they each own a house?

– There's also ambiguity in constructions such as *I collect Greek stamps and models*. Do I collect Greek models? or any models? *There are some old men and women in the bus*. Are the women old?

– Don't forget the meanings of the conjunctions. *But*, for example, has to have a context where relevant contrast applies. We can't easily say *It's raining in London but my egg's hard*. I can imagine Edward McLachlan making sense of it, though!

– Point out the need to be careful linking figurative and literal phrases: *Ella made up her mind and the bed*. The incongruity might be deliberate, of course. Comedians revel in such possibilities, and it can be found in literature, where the effect is traditionally referred to as **zeugma** (from the Greek for 'yoking'). An example is Pope's '. . . *or lose her Heart, or Necklace, at a Ball* (*The Rape of the Lock*).

– *Respectively* is an interesting construction: *Jules and Jim are French and English respectively*. *Anna and Susie visited their respective aunts*. In this second example, the word resolves the ambiguity apparent in *Anna and Susie visited their aunts*, which could mean 'Anna visited her aunt(s) and Susie visited hers' or 'They both visited each other's aunts' or even 'They both visited just the aunts they have in common'. The use of *respective(ly)* is restricted to formal contexts.

– Note the special intensifying meaning of *We talked and talked and talked*, and the ironic nuance of *There are prime ministers and prime ministers, you know!*

• My entry concentrates on cases where the marker of coordination is present (technically, the coordination is **syndetic**). There are also many cases where no explicit marker is present (the coordination is **asyndetic**): *I bought apples, oranges, bananas – all kinds of things*. Note how the 'open-endedness' of this list contrasts with the 'closed' implication of *I bought apples and oranges and bananas*.

• Coordination raises questions of **ellipsis**, as is illustrated towards the end of the entry. Students can experiment with which clause elements can be left out. Some can be quite complex: *I finished the exam in two hours and Mike in three* (where 'finished it' and 'hours' have been omitted.

RG 64; SGE 13; CGEL 13

copula (KS 4)

• I haven't put *copulation* into the entry, pointing out that this is the only commonly used word in English which shares the same root – but I was tempted! Incidentally, notice that the adjective from **copula** is **copular**: the copula is a copular verb. Other copular verbs aren't illustrated in this entry. They include *become*, *seem*, and *appear*. (See **complement** for other examples.)

• The *Rediscover Grammar* reference is to the cartoon on the front cover of that book, where Tarzan is shown being corrected by Jane, who is holding a copy of *Rediscover Grammar*!

• It's important to link this entry to the one on **complement**. A copula is followed by a complement and not an object. (It may also be followed by an adverbial, of course.)

• As the Word Warning says, the distinction between copula and auxiliary often confuses because forms of the verb *to be* can be used in both functions. Emphasise that the copula is a main verb – it's the only verb in the clause, after all. It can be helpful to think of the verb *to be* as really *two* verbs, not one: *be*-auxiliary and *be*-copula.

RG 11; SGE 16.12–13; CGEL 16.21–4

co-reference see **reference**

corpus (KS 4)

• If the school compiles a corpus of material, be careful about where you get it from, and what you do with it, to avoid getting into trouble with the copyright laws. If you include a recording or written sample made locally, the author(s) should give permission. Respect confidentiality, by giving everyone pseudonyms or abbreviating their names. You can also make use of the published extracts from corpora, such as Jan Svartvik and Randolph Quirk, *A Corpus of English Conversation* (Lund University Press, 1980). At a more advanced level, of course, it is possible to gain direct computer access to some of the major collections, such as the London-Lund Corpus or the Lancaster-Oslo-Bergen Corpus. The Survey of English Usage at University College London has a very large collection of English spoken and written material.

• Useful corpora can be compiled of postcards, advertisements, cartoon captions, newspaper abbreviations, headlines – of anything, really. Written samples are easier to use than spoken, but both need a good cataloguing system. It's especially difficult to find material on a tape without a good tape numbering system. Note that you can also compile a corpus of specific linguistic features, as well as a corpus of texts. For example, you might make one from the uses of a particular sentence type (say **block language**) or a particular figure of speech (as is done in Elyse and Mike Sommer, *Similes Dictionary* (Gale Research Company, Detroit, 1988)).

CEL 65

correctness (KS 3)

• Putting the notion of correctness in perspective is one of the most difficult tasks in present-day language teaching. The attitude expressed by this entry is by no means new, but it does conflict with some 200 years of prescriptive thinking, which insists that variation is basically undesirable and ultimately damaging to the language. If you wish to develop the philosophy of this entry, you will need to emphasise and illustrate the inevitability of language change, and the fundamental role of variation in society (social, regional, occupational . . .), pointing to the way that language reflects this variety and does not (cannot) control it. It is important to stress that this view in no way dispenses with standards (as is sometimes claimed by its critics). The standard form of a language is recognised as such, within the total range of varieties which exist. The view does not reduce to an 'anything goes' position – as should be clear from my examples, which are *all* in use by educated people, and are part of standard English. On the other hand, it does commit the student to the view that all varieties (including those which are called 'non-standard') are to be taken seriously, as having a social role to play, and that linguistic change is to be understood rather than condemned. The entry should be read in conjunction with the entry on **appropriate**.

• It is important for the student to appreciate that only a small part of the language is affected by usage problems. The prescriptive grammars would pick on a few features and issues (such as whether we should say *I will* or *I shall*, whether we should split an infinitive (see the entry on **grammar**), and whether we should end a sentence with a preposition), and use these as the markers of educated awareness. The vast majority of sentence constructions, however, raise no problems of this kind. To see this, a useful exercise is to collect the letters that are published in newspapers or *Radio Times*, or are read out on listener feedback programmes, complaining about incorrectness in usage, and develop a sense of the narrow range of the complaints.

CEL 1; SGE 1.2–5; CGEL 1.15–17

co-text see **context**

count noun and non-count noun (KS 4)

• The countability distinction was usually ignored in traditional grammars, but it is of fundamental importance in the classification of common nouns. One way of showing which nouns are which is to draw a matrix of cells, in which the various criteria (such as the four listed in the entry) are placed across the top, and the nouns listed on the left. Students can then put a tick (or a plus sign) in a cell, if the criterion applies to a noun, and put a cross (or a minus sign) if it does not. For example:

	a before?	plural?	no article?	*some* before?
vacuum-cleaner	+	+	–	–
music	–	–	+	+

The different patterns emerge clearly.

• As the Word Warning says, there are several cases where the noun can be seen from both countable and uncountable points of view. Other examples are seen in these sentence pairs (the countable example first): *it's a beauty / she displays great beauty; There are many difficulties / There wasn't much difficulty; The lights and sounds were bright / Light travels faster than sound; Look at those lovely lambs / Eat your lamb.* There are also several pairs of related words (again, countable first): *laugh/laughter; poem/poetry; machine/ machinery; job/work.* Note the special cases: in *That's a happiness I'll never have,* the normally uncountable *happiness* is given a countable interpretation (meaning 'kind of'). Note too the jokey cases: *I love vacuum cleaner,* a hungry termite might say. The language also allows the use of special nouns (they're called **partitives** – see the entry on **quantifier**) to give a countable sense: *a grain of truth, a blade of grass, a loaf of bread, a stick of chalk,* etc.

RG 30; SGE 5.1–2; CGEL 5.2–9

creole (KS 4)

• The distinction between a pidgin and a creole is not as clear-cut as the definitions might suggest: it is a very gradual process, referred to technically as **creolisation**. Also, creoles (as other languages) have several varieties: some display the influence of the standard language spoken in an area (such as English in Jamaica); others display little such influence, and are very close to a pidgin.

• Students could try to work out how the rules of a creole (stress that these *are* rules) relate to the standard language. A large number of examples is given in Loreto Todd, *Modern Englishes: Pidgins and Creoles* (Blackwell, 1984), including passages from the Bible and Shakespeare, outline grammars and vocabulary lists. The rest of 'This little piggy' is: *Dis smol swain i bin stei fo haus. Dis smol swain i bin chop sup witi fufu. Dis smol swain i no bin chop no noting. An dis smol swain i bin go wi, wi sotei fo haus.* Here are the opening lines of Antony's speech from *Julius Caesar* III. 2 in Sierra

Leonian Krio:

Padi dem, kohntri, una ohl wey dey
na Rom. Meyk una ohl kak una yeys.
A kam ber Siza, a noh kam preyz am.
Dem kin memba bad wey pohsin kin du
Lohng tem afta di pohsin kin dohn dai.
Boht plenti tem di gud wey pohsin du
kin ber wit im bon dem. Meyk i bi so
wit Siza.

CEL 55

dactyl (KS 4) see **foot**

dash (KS 3)

- The dash is most commonly encountered in informal writing – in letters between friends and in note-taking, for example. It is sometimes used almost everywhere – replacing commas, full stops, colons, and other marks – a trend which works well enough in a loosely structured kind of prose – but which conveys a lack of care and organisation when used in more formal contexts – such as here. Students will need to be cautioned about overuse.

- Students should look out for other uses of the dash, such as in dates (7–3–90, 1977–87) and page numbers (pp 15–23). I also haven't illustrated the correlative (or parenthetical) dash in the entry – such as here – where the marks are an alternative to the use of brackets. In handwriting, no regular distinction is drawn between different functions of dash, and in size the dash may be the same as a hyphen. In print, a typographical distinction is drawn between the hyphen and **en** dash (as in *3–4-year-old*), and between both of these and the **em** dash (as in *This is Mr T —*). The terms *en* and *em* are typographer's terms, referring to the width of the letters *n* and *m* in traditional type. En rules usually mean 'and' (as in *Liberal–Democratic alliance*) and 'to' (as in *London–Holyhead railway*), and they are used when marking a correlation, as shown above. Note the spaces on either side of the correlative dash; these are usually absent in other cases (though there are some types of exception). Em rules often introduce lines of dialogue in a text (especially in foreign books), or mark the omission of a word or part of a word. They are also found in indexes and bibliographies, showing repeated information.

CGEL App III.20, 26

declarative (KS 4)

- The four exceptions are the three interrogative structures, *Can you . . .*, *Is there . . .*, and *Why . . .*, and the imperative structure, *Search . . .*

• The idea that we can use a declarative structure to ask a question can be confusing, until the student appreciates that the term **declarative** is a formal grammatical term, not a functional one – in other words, it describes a particular structure and not the way a type of sentence is used. Declarative sentences (or clauses) are here distinguished from interrogative and imperative ones. The functional terms would be statement, question, and command. Usually, a statement has a declarative structure, a question has an interrogative structure, and a command has an imperative structure – but there are certain important kinds of exception, such as the type illustrated by *Simon declared?*

RG 5; SGE 11.1; CGEL 11.1

definite article (KS 3) see **article**

degree (KS 3)

• **Degree** is usually discussed with reference to the comparative construction only, and this is the main emphasis in my entry too. But it's important to see that the basic meaning of 'degree' is much greater than this particular construction. Many adverbial words and phrases in English express degree notions, and some are listed in the entry. Students will find it easy to grasp the idea of degree as an *increase* in intensity, because of the way comparative and superlative usually work (*bigger, biggest*). It's important to get them to appreciate that the idea of degree also involves a *lessening* of intensity. The sub-classification provided by the Quirk

grammars may be helpful, in this respect. These grammars distinguish between **amplifiers**, which scale upwards, and **downtoners**, which scale downwards. Among the former are words which express the upper extreme of a scale (such as *absolutely, entirely, fully, totally*) and those which express a high point, not necessarily the extreme (*deeply, greatly, highly, much, strongly, a good deal, a lot*). Among the downtoners are those which express approximation (*almost, nearly, virtually*), those which express just a slight lowering effect (*sort of, more or less, rather*), those which express 'to a small extent' (*partly, somewhat, slightly, a bit, merely, just*), and those which express 'to very little or no extent' (*hardly, scarcely, in the least, at all*). A few words are ambiguous: *quite*, in particular, can scale upwards *or* downwards (*That's quite nice* could mean 'That's really nice' or 'That's not so nice').

• A term for the 'same' degree is **equative**. Note that you can also have *so . . . as* expressing an equative degree. See also the entry on **superlative** for a discussion of the choice between the inflectional (*bigger/biggest*) and periphrastic (*more/most interesting*) alternatives, in the expression of degree.

RG 51, 54; SGE 7.39, 8.37; CGEL 7.74–86, 8.104–15

deixis (**diek**-sis)

• This term is becoming quite widely used, so I thought I would bring it into this book, though I feel it has rather too abstract a sense to be of much direct use to students at KS 3 and 4. **Deictic** features of language refer directly to the personal, temporal or locational characteristics of the situation within which an utterance takes place. The meaning of a deictic element depends on the situation. Examples include *here* and *there*, *I* and *you*, *today* and *tomorrow*, and *this* and *that*. What *here* means depends on where the speaker is. What *this* means depends on how near something is to the speaker. What *yesterday* means depends on when the speaker is talking.

CEL 17

demonstrative (KS 4)

• My entry deals with pronouns only; but determiners can be demonstrative too, as in *this car* and *those apples*. Keep an eye open for unusual demonstratives, such as the mock-regional *There's gold in them there hills*.

• The 'near/far' distinction in the entry is interpreted with reference to physical distance only. Note also some related uses: *This is what you do* (said before a demonstration) vs *That's what you do* (said after); *Have you seen this new computer yet?* (which I've just been reading about) vs *Have you seen that new computer yet?* (which we were talking about last week). Note the use of *that* to express dislike (emotional distance): *There's that friend of Mike's*.

RG 44; SGE 6.19–20; CGEL 6.40–4

denotation and connotation (KS 4)

• Connotations can be shared by several people (as in the *Wimbledon* example) or they can be very personal and private – such as someone who says 'I always think of eggs when I hear the word *dictionary*' (perhaps because the speaker remembers an occasion when a dictionary was dropped on some eggs). The latter are not particularly interesting, from a linguistic point of view (though a psychiatrist might have a field day). Another example of shared connotations would be *dog* – friend, companion, etc.

• You may encounter these terms with different senses in philosophy.

CEL 17

dental (KS 4)

• The phonetic symbol which shows a dental consonant is a tooth-shaped mark placed below a consonant symbol: [t̪], [d̪], [n̪].

• Dental sounds are heard in several foreign languages, such as French and Spanish. Note also the way [t], [d], [n] become dental in English when they are used before the [θ] sound, as in *eighth*, *width* and *tenth*.

EPP 6.2; IPE 8.4.3

dependent clause (KS 3) see **subordination**

derivation (KS 3)

• **Derivation**, as the entry shows, has two distinct meanings. The processes involved in modern word-formation can be studied without reference to a historical dictionary. For example, students might plot the way affixes are used in the derivation of much contemporary vocabulary: *mega-*, *Euro-*, *-friendly*, *tele-* and *-aid*. A good source of data is John Ayto, *The Longman Register of New Words* (Longman, 1989) which gives historical notes.

• The entry on **etymology** should be read at the same time as this one; it contains another example of a derivation. Also, see **affix** for the notion of derivational prefixes and suffixes.

RG 74; CGEL App I

description see **prescription**

determiner (KS 4)

● It will be important to point out to students that, although the term is unfamiliar, determiners nonetheless constitute a distinct word class (or part of speech). They must see why this is so, and not try to learn all the determiners off by heart. The best way is to appreciate the central role of the articles, *the* and *a*. They are the chief determiners because this is the only role these two words have in English. The other determiners have other roles (notably, they can occur alone as pronouns). The crucial feature of a determiner is that there is only *one* before any noun. So, a determiner is most easily viewed as a word which can replace *the* or *a*, but which can't be used at the same time as *the/a* in the same noun phrase. If students try this out, they'll find that the determiners include the demonstratives (*this, that, these, those*), the possessives (*my, your, his, her, its, our, their*), certain words beginning with *wh-* (*what, which, whose, whichever, whatever, whoever*), *no* (as in *no car*), *every, each, either, neither, some, any*, and *enough*. Some approaches allow in a few other words as determiners (such as *much* and *many*), but as the grammar of these words is slightly different from the above set, they are often classified separately. *Many*, for example, can be used with certain determiners (as in *the many problems*).

● The determiner/pronoun distinction may be hard to grasp, so give lots of examples, such as *Look at this picture / Look at this; I haven't got any biscuits / I haven't got any*. Note the change in form with *my* (determiner) to *mine* (pronoun), *your* to *yours*, etc. Again, get students into the habit of working out for themselves whether a word is determiner or pronoun, by working with criteria – in this case, is there a noun following or not?

RG 35; SGE 5.3–6; CGEL 5.11–14

deviance (KS 4)

● This use of the asterisk shouldn't be confused with its use in philology, where it shows a hypothetical form in the pre-history of a language. Sounds and words in Indo-European, for example, will be preceded by an asterisk to show that they are not attested in historical records.

● The three deviant examples are: the wrong verb form – either the auxiliary needs to be changed (*should* becoming *have*) or the main verb needs to be changed (*had* becoming *have*); the adjective order should be reversed; and the adverb *closely* is in the wrong place (either before the verb or at the end of the sentence).

● An important extension of this entry is to show the way deviant sentences are found in literature. There are many examples in Hopkins (*The achieve of, the mastery of the thing*), Dylan Thomas (*a grief ago; all the moon long*), Cummings (*He danced his did*), and Joyce (*theirhisnothis*). See the entry on **foregrounding** for further examples. Deviance is also found in the written and spoken output of many language-disordered people, such as aphasics. A piece of written work from a profoundly deaf teenager illustrates the kind of unintelligibility which can come from a severe language problem: *The Star Wars was the two spaceship a fighting opened door was coming the Men and Storm trooper guns carry on to Artoo Detoo and threepio at go the space.*

EL 8; LG 3.2

devoiced see **voice** (in phonetics)

diachronic see **synchronic**

diacritic (KS 4)

- This notion is much broader than that of **accents**. An accent is a type of diacritic, not the other way round.
- Some languages use diacritics a great deal – Slavic languages, for example. English tends to avoid them. The phonetic alphabet is a good source of diacritics. An interesting use is the marking of stressed and unstressed syllables in traditional metrical study.

IPE 12

dialect (KS 3)

- The concept of an 'intranational' dialect is familiar, and this is what the entry largely deals with. The 'international' dialects will be less familiar, and the notion of treating British English as a 'dialect' some will find disturbing. It should be stressed that the term 'dialect' doesn't reduce the value of a language variety in any way (though it is indeed sometimes popularly used in a demeaning sense – 'It's just a dialect, not a real language'). You can counter such an attitude if you start referring to standard English, for example, as being the dialect of English with the greatest prestige, the dialect most widely used by educated people, and so on. Seen in the context of world English language use, British English is a dialect spoken by about 56 million people (out of a world total of over 350 million speakers whose mother-tongue is English).
- Link this entry with the entries on **accent** and **variety**. Make sure the distinction with accent is clear – dialect is a matter of grammar and vocabulary. The accent in which a dialect is spoken is a separate question. Incidentally, the study of dialect is known as **dialectology**.
- Regional dialects attract widespread interest. There may well be a local dialect society near you. Dialect humour is a good source of illustration

(such as *Lern Yerself Scouse*, The Scouse Press, Liverpool): there are examples in my *English Language*, page 111. It would be good to build up a collection of local dialect words and phrases, starting with those used in school. Dialect forms in literature are well illustrated in Norman Blake's *Non-standard Language in English Literature* (Blackwell, 1981) – many examples can be found in Dickens, Emily Brontë, Eliot, Scott, Hardy. A famous example of the representation of regional dialect is in the speech of the soldiers in *Henry V*.

EL 6–7

dialogue and monologue (KS 3)

• This distinction seems straightforward enough, but in fact it isn't as clear-cut as it seems. One person talking to another is a dialogue, but talking to two people, or three, or four . . . ? Talking to 20 is likely to be a monologue. Also, if one side doesn't want to be involved, the situation hovers uncertainly between dialogue and monologue (not an uncommon experience in a classroom, I imagine).

• Find other examples of written dialogue. There are some unusual examples around, such as an exchange of letters, a form to be filled in, and examination questions. And there are some intriguing cases for the analyst of spoken language, too. For example, is leaving a message on an answerphone a monologue or a dialogue?

CEL 11

diction (KS 3)

• The metaphor that some words purr at you and some growl or snarl has been used by several authors of rhetoric (such as S I Hayakawa). A good example is the following pair of sentences: *There were some youngsters on the street corner* and *There were some youths on the street corner*. The first sentence uses the purr-word *youngster* (they are pleasant individuals); the second uses the snarl-word *youths* (best avoid them).

• Avoid giving the impression that diction is something that only literary authors have (and especially poets – the idea of 'poetic diction'). It is a very general notion, applicable to any variety of the language. Swearing in the street is just as much a matter of choice of appropriate diction as is writing an essay or a poem. On the other hand, the distinctive brilliance of much literary diction needs also to be appreciated.

• Word substitution exercises, as illustrated by the dialogue, can be useful in sharpening a student's sense of appropriate diction, but they have to be made rather more appealing. One way in is to present the student with a set of words to choose from, containing words of varying degrees of range and appropriateness – for example, with reference to pictures: *colourful, atmospheric, trendy, original, cheap, rubbish, torn, smelly*? A thesaurus provides a fine source of vocabulary. Alternatively, start with comedy sketches. *Monty Python* material, for example, often obtains its effect by the deliberate use of unexpected, incongruous, or inappropriate diction (such as the words for death used in the famous 'parrot' sketch).

LG 1.2.3

dictionary (KS 3)

- *Yomp* came to public attention in the Falklands War. It is British army slang, of unknown origin, which means marching with heavy equipment over difficult countryside.

- The point about the spelling of *pneumonia* is valid enough, but there are pronouncing dictionaries where it would be possible to look the word up under *n* and be led to it.

- Look carefully at the claims made by publishers about their dictionaries. Two dictionaries might claim to contain 80,000 words, for example, but one might include all the derivative and irregular forms in this total (*nation, national, nationalise*, etc; *go, went, gone*, etc), and the other might exclude them. The best way of getting a sense of what dictionaries are about is to take two dictionaries of comparable size and compare a few entries, point by point. Develop a set of test questions to ask of any dictionary (such as the sample in my *Cambridge Encyclopedia of Language*, Chapter 18). Students might choose an entry (*cat, sausage*) and get to know it really well, so that it can be a rule of thumb for evaluating the approach of a new dictionary.

diglossia

- This term is widely used in sociolinguistics to refer to a situation where two very different varieties of a language co-occur throughout a speech community, each with a distinct range of social function. A 'high' variety is the more formal variety, which tends to be learned in school and used in literature, on the radio, etc. A 'low' variety is used in family conversations and other informal settings. Greek, Arabic, and Swiss German are all examples of diglossic language situations. It's a fascinating phenomenon, half way between monolingualism and bilingualism, so it might be worth bearing in mind when dealing with those topics.

CEL 10

digraph (KS 4) see **grapheme**

diphthong (KS 4)

• There are eight diphthongs in RP (see **Received Pronunciation**), usually classified by their direction of tongue movement. In three cases, the movement is towards a front [ɪ] vowel quality, as in *they*, *cry* and *boy*. In another three cases, the movement is towards a central [ə] vowel quality, as in *here*, *care* and *sure*. And in two cases, the movement is towards a back [ʊ] vowel quality, as in *toe* and *how*. See the entry on **triphthong** for further examples.

• It can be difficult to hear the vowel movement in a diphthong, especially if someone is speaking very fast. This is an especial problem when there is only one letter in the spelling. Some people refuse to believe that there is a diphthong in *my*, for example. To get round this, find a word where this problem doesn't arise (such as *pie*), and then point out that the two words rhyme.

EPP 3.2; IPE 7.10–12

directive see **command**

direct object and indirect object (KS 3)

• Verbs which take two objects are technically called **ditransitive** (this is *not* the name of a Welsh grammarian) (sorry). The indirect object is usually animate, and usually precedes the direct object.

• The transformation works mainly with verbs where the preposition is *to* or *for*: 'give X Y' / 'give Y to X' and 'order X Y' / 'order Y for X'. It's interesting to try it out on a range of ditransitive constructions, to see what happens: *I offered Jane some help, I envied my friend his job, I wished her good luck, She blamed me for the problem, They warned me of the danger*.

RG 10; SGE 16.31–6; CGEL 16.55–63

direct speech and indirect speech (KS 3)

• *Say* is the commonest reporting verb, but there are hundreds of others: *admit, answer, ask, claim, cry, declare, insist, object, promise, repeat, reply, warn, write*. Also note the verbs which add some information about manner of speaking, such as *mumble, snap, sob*. Varying the reporting verb effectively is one of the most difficult tasks when writing a novel. Get the students to write a dialogue and see.

• There are five types of change in wording required as we move from direct to indirect speech and back again: verb tenses, other time references (such as *now, yesterday, next week*), place references (such as *here, there*), personal pronouns, and the demonstratives *this* and *these*. The change of tense is called **backshift**, because we 'shift' the time-scale backwards in indirect speech. The relationship between the verb forms in each style is called the **sequence of tenses**.

● Note the relationship between this entry and **free direct/indirect speech**. In literature, 'mixed' styles of narrative are commonly used. An excellent example is the trial of Charles Darnay in *A Tale of Two Cities* (Book 2, Chapter 3), where the speech shifts from direct to indirect, correlating to a considerable extent with the attitude of the witnesses towards the prisoner (sympathetic to the prisoner – direct speech; hostile to the prisoner – indirect speech). It is even possible to change point of view in the middle of a sentence. A good example is from Chapter 12 of Alexander Solzhenitsyn's *Cancer Ward*:

> She pulled on her overcoat in the doorway, and her grandmother only just had time to slip some lunch into her pocket before she left. It was a dampish chilly morning, but not wintry. People would be wearing raincoats on a day like that back in Central Russia, but here in the south people have different ideas of hot and cold. They wear woollen suits in the heat . . .

RG 69; SGE 14.17–22; CGEL 14.28–35

discourse (KS 4)

● The auditory 'paragraphs' in news bulletins tend to be based on intonation: the paragraph starts relatively high at the beginning and falls to a relatively low point at the end. Another good example of spoken discourse organisation is sports commentary, where there is a typical cyclical progression of introduction + event + reaction. Some further examples are given in the entries on **conversation** and **foregrounding**. Don't forget to link the notion to traditional concepts, such as plot and sub-plot in drama and the novel, and other aspects of narrative structure. There is value, also, in studying particular features of discourse, such as the use of *well, OK, you know, hello, good morning, please*, and *yes*. There are obvious contexts where we say these words, and there are also many less obvious contexts. An example of the latter: see if students can work out when there could be an exchange like the following. A: *Hello*. B: *Goodbye*. (A is arriving at work and finds B rushing to catch a train).

● Some linguists restrict the term **discourse** to spoken language only, reserving **text** for written language. I prefer a more general application, and talk about 'spoken and written discourse'. Michael Stubbs, *Discourse Analysis* (Blackwell, 1983) is a useful introduction to the subject, which deals with several of the above points.

disjunct see **adjunct**

ditransitive see **transitive verb**

double negative (KS 3) see **negative**

downtoner see **degree**

drafting (KS 3)

- A lot can be learned from a study of the manuscripts of well-known authors. A good collection is in P J Croft, *Autograph Poetry in the English Language* (Cassell, 1973, 2 vols). Many of the samples show considerable emendation (the extracts from Whitman and Hopkins, for example, are full of deletions and changes of mind). I should perhaps explain how I know that I made over 400 drafts of a piece of mine: the piece was written on a word processor, and I memorised the text each time I made a change in the wording.

- The importance of drafting has been repeatedly emphasised in recent studies of writing, though for some reason it remains difficult to persuade students that it is a legitimate activity. Note that a similar process of drafting takes place in speech, too, as when one speaks 'off the top of the head' – an activity which may well need some subsequent redrafting ('Let me make myself clear . . .').

CEL 34

echo utterance (KS 4)

- Echoes are so different from other kinds of sentence that some grammars (such as the Quirk grammars) classify them as a separate sentence type. They can take the form of any utterance, or part of an utterance. Their function is to act as a question or an exclamation. The questions either recapitulate something, in order to confirm it (A: *I didn't go out*. B: *You didn't go out?*) or ask for clarification (A: *Look at that!* B: *Look at what?*). Note that there are other ways of expressing these meanings, such as adding *did you say?* to the recapitulation echo (*The car, did you say?*).

- The interpretation of these sentences depends very much on the tone of voice in which they are uttered. Students could role-play various possibilities, to see the effects it is possible to obtain. Say *Look at what?* in tones of voice expressing surprise, resignation, anger, etc. This is a

standard technique in drama training.

RG7; SGE 11.14; CGEL 11.33–7

-ed form (KS 4) see **participle**

elision (KS 4)

● Muddling the terms **elision** and **ellipsis** is common. Try a mnemonic: *eli**s**io**n** for **s**ou**n**d*, with the *s* and *n* in both words; or *ellip**s**i**s** for **s**entence**s***, with the two *s*'s in both. Not brilliant. It might take just as long to remember the mnemonic!

● Elisions can be grouped into those which take place within single words and those which take place as a result of their location in connected speech. In the former category are such words as *temp**e**rature*, *lavat**o**ry*, *fact**o**ry*, *cam**e**ra*, *ordin**a**ry*, *prob**a**bly*, *p**o**lice*, *g**e**ometry*, where a vowel is often elided, and *han**d**some*, *han**d**bag*, *coas**t**guard*, *perfec**t**ly*, *fi**f**ths*, where a consonant has been elided. Sometimes whole syllables may be elided, such as in *Feb**rua**ry*, *lit**era**ry*. (Many of these elisions don't apply to American English.) In the latter category are the shortening of *and* to *n*, the loss of *h* in unstressed pronouns (*he*, *his*, etc), and the elision of a final consonant in such sequences as *nex**t** day*, *jus**t** now*, and *kep**t** quiet*. These variations are typical of informal speech, but some of these forms will be heard in formal speech too (such as *camera* and *handsome*, which sound un-English if articulated with full vowel values).

EPP 9.1, 14.3; IPE 9.6, 11.3.6

ellipsis (KS 4)

• Sometimes a full sentence response is used, but always for special effect. Music hall comedians used to reply in this way (A: *I say, I say, I say. Why do people in the desert never go hungry?* B: *I don't know. Why do people in the desert never go hungry?*). People also respond with a full sentence when they're being angry or sarcastic, or needing to repeat something (see further, **echo utterance**). And, pedagogically, there is often a point in extracting a full sentence from a reluctant respondent, in order to check that there has been comprehension (or, at least, audition). *What did I just say, Midgely?*

• The crucial criterion, in ellipsis, is that the omitted material is retrievable. So, in the sentence *I drove to London and then to York*, the words *I drove* are predictable. Sometimes the deleted material is recoverable by looking at the surrounding language, as in that sentence. Sometimes it can be recovered only by looking at the situation in which the sentence occurred, such as *See you later*, where the *I'll* is omitted. Sentences such as *Thanks* and *Hello* can't be called ellipses, therefore, because we don't know what has been left out. (*I give you my thanks? My thanks are due to you?* . . .) See the entry on **coordination** for some further examples.

• Incidentally, people often talk about the deleted material having been **elided**, but as this introduces an ambiguity with the entry on **elision** (where it's routine to talk of 'eliding' sounds), some grammarians have invented a new verb, to *ellipt*: the material, they say, has been *ellipted*.

• All right. Because of the sandwiches there. (What did you expect? A *new* joke?)

RG 62; SGE 12.14–23; CGEL 12.1–7, 31–70

embedding

• This term is sometimes used (especially in transformational grammar) to refer to the phenomenon of subordination – when one construction is used within (ie 'embedded within') another. For example, in the sentence *The lady who has a car is outside* the clause *who has a car* is embedded within the clause *The lady is outside*. I've used the more widely recognised term, **subordination**, in these books.

emotive meaning (KS 4)

• This is a familiar notion, which has long been the focus of attention in English classes – for example, examining a text to find instances of words which show the attitude of the author. It is important, though, to ensure that the concept is applied to spoken as well as written language – and to all styles of speech and writing. The analysis of broadcast material (in contexts where neutrality is expected) makes an interesting exercise, to see whether the author has managed to maintain objectivity. Equally, the analysis of a broadcast from the House of Commons, or an extract from Hansard, will show the opposite.

● Literary extracts provide excellent material, but students will need to develop their vocabulary for describing the emotions involved. *Could you on this fair mountain leave to feed,/ And batten on this moor?* (*Hamlet*, III.4). Personality trait studies in psychology can provide some help, as can the section on 'emotion' in *Roget's Thesaurus*.

CEL 17

epigram (KS 4)

● The quotations are from Pope's *An Essay on Criticism* and Oscar Wilde's *Lady Windermere's Fan*. Chapter 17 of *The Picture of Dorian Gray* provides a conversationful of examples.

● There are many activities which can focus on epigrams. They can be collected from Christmas crackers, book and chapter openings, statues, and tombstones (an excellent day's outing, which under LMS can be combined with a visit to the graves of former governors). For graffiti, there are the several collections of Nigel Rees (Unwin paperbacks), but doubtless the students can provide their own samples.

epithet (KS 4)

● The nickname survey generally produces some interesting results. Advertising is another area where an epithet survey is easy to do, because the copywriters are continually searching for the 'right' word for their product.

● A comparison of newspaper reporting styles generally brings to light some interesting differences in the use of epithets: *Tall red-haired 33-year-old Belinda said . . .* The 'summarising' effect of an epithet commends itself especially to the headline writers.

equative see **degree**

etymology (KS 3)

● Some other examples: a *publican* was a public servant, a *bonnet* was a man's hat, *vulgar* meant ordinary. *Glamour* and *grammar* were once the 'same' word, as were *lobster* and *locust*. Geoffrey Hughes's *Words in Time* (Blackwell, 1988) provides a fascinating study, in which groups of words belonging to political, religious, advertising, and other areas are interrelated.

• The study of place names is a topic that usually attracts great interest. Does the student live in a town or village ending in *-chester*, *-caster* or *-cester*? It was a Roman town or fort. A place containing the element *wick-*, *wig-*, *-wick* or *-wich* was originally a farm or dwelling. There are several books on place names which will provide plenty of material, such as John Field's *Place Names of Great Britain and Ireland* (David & Charles, 1980). Laurence Urdang's *Names and Nicknames of Places and Things* (Grafton Books, 1987) is also a helpful collection. And Leslie Dunkling and William Gosling, *Dictionary of First Names* (Everyman, 1983) will do nicely for first names.

• There is plenty that can be done by way of primary research. A house name survey? (Why did you call your house such-and-such? Householders love to be asked.) A survey of the names of locomotives, horses, magazines, pop groups, ships, cats, pubs, streets . . . How do local authorities devise new names for new streets? How do you set about tracing the origin of a family name? (There's an excellent illustration in Leslie Dunkling's *Guiness Book of Names* (1974, page 70), which also contains information on pretty well everything to do with names.)

euphemism (KS 3)

• By 'sex', I mean notions to do with sexual identity – euphemisms for menstruation, for example (*time of the month*, *curse*). In Victorian times, many words were proscribed in polite company (such as *legs* – even tables were affected, as the use of the phrase *table limbs* illustrates).

• I've given very few examples in this entry, which leaves plenty of scope for activities. What other areas are prone to euphemism? Religion, certainly (for example, names for the devil – *Old Nick, Old Harry, the Old Gentleman*). Illness (*under the weather*, *off colour*, *below par*). Different jobs may have their individual euphemisms: unemployed actors sometimes say they are 'resting'. What euphemisms do people use if they wish to avoid saying that someone is unemployed, drunk, in prison . . . ?

CEL 11

euphony (KS 4)

• This is a very unclear notion, and it's difficult to be precise about it. It isn't difficult to find examples of texts which people agree to be euphonious (such as Coleridge's 'Kubla Khan' or Gray's 'Elegy'), but it is quite a different matter getting people to agree on what exactly it is in the sound which promotes the feeling of euphony. It's illuminating to experiment with different sequences of vowels and consonants to see how people react. Long vowels, diphthongs, and continuants usually prompt judgments of euphony; short vowels and plosives don't. 'Doctor Foster went to Gloucester' will not, I opine, be considered euphonious.

• The opposite term is not so widely used in language description or criticism, but it has quite a common popular use: **cacophony**.

LG 6

exclamation (KS 3)

• This term needs to be related to the verb *exclaim*. Note that any kind of sentence can be said in an exclamatory way, using tone of voice; but from a grammatical point of view certain ones are distinctive. Some are minor sentences (see the entry on **major sentence**), such as interjections (*Gosh!*, *Phew!*), and alarm calls (*Help!*, *Fire!*), and some have an idiosyncratic clause structure (*How nice it is!*, *What a good boy you are!*, where the word order following the question word is subject + verb).

• As with all emotional punctuation marks, there is a real danger of overuse in students' writing. Scattering exclamation marks throughout an essay reduces their force. Keep an eye open for particularly apt uses of exclamation marks, either singly or (more rarely) in combination. For example, there's a lovely sequence in A A Milne's *Winnie the Pooh* in which exclamation marks are used alone to represent enlightenment:

> 'We might go in your umbrella', said Pooh.
> !!!!!!
> For suddenly Christopher Robin saw that they might.

Note also the ironic (!) use of the exclamation mark.

CGEL App III.23

existential sentence (KS 4)

• This is quite an advanced concept, and I was in two minds about including it at KS 4. On the other hand, it is a very common type of sentence, which turns up in several forms. In addition to the examples in the entry, the construction can be used in questions (*Is there any other business?*), and in other tenses (*There was a silence*). Other verbs than *be* are often found, especially in literary styles: *There sprang up a gale*, *There arose in his mind . . .*, *There may come a time . . .* Note that some kinds of verbless sentence (see the entry on **block language**) can be regarded as being existential, with an 'omitted' *there is/are*: *Men at work*, *No exit*. Slogans could also be analysed as an omitted *there must be*: *No discrimination*, *No more war*.

• The essential difference between the two uses of *there* in the Word

Warning is that the adverbial use has a strong stress and the existential use is unstressed.

RG 72; SGE 18.30–6; CGEL 18.44–54

expansion (KS 4)

- The view that parents use expansion as a teaching technique seems plausible enough. But the point that they do this especially when other people are present suggests that other factors are involved too. In such a case, parents seem to be expanding the sentences not so much for the benefit of their child as for the benefit of the other adults!

- The use of expansion in classrooms is well worth studying, as it can simultaneously develop knowledge of language and knowledge of subject-matter, as well as promoting student/teacher rapport. Any tape recording of a classroom dialogue will bring to light several examples. There is a well-established educational interest in the study of teacher/student dialogue, as demonstrated by Douglas Barnes, James Britton, and Mike Torbe, *Language, the Learner and the School* (Penguin, 1986, 3rd edn).

- The term **expansion** is also sometimes used in grammar for the way a phrase can be made bigger by the addition of optional elements: *the cat*, *the fat cat*, *the big fat cat*, etc.

expletive (KS 4)

- Obviously, this is a sensitive topic. A fruitful way in is to adopt a historical perspective, looking at the way swearing practice has changed over the centuries and between languages. What expletives are to be found in Chaucer, Shakespeare, and so on? Make a collection of such items as *'swounds* and *by my troth*, and examine their meaning. Another angle is to study the way in which swear words are 'softened' in force – *Gosh*, *Golly*, *Jeepers*, etc. Geoffrey Hughes's *Swearing* (Blackwell, 1991) is an excellent source-book, as is Ashley Montagu's *The Anatomy of Swearing* (Rapp & Whiting, 1968).

- Stylistic issues need to be addressed. Expletives are 'deleted' in certain contexts – which? (Remember Watergate?) What is the BBC policy on the use of expletives? Why do some people use so many expletives (the answer is more to do with social solidarity than anything else – it's the 'done thing' to swear in certain social groups). With advanced students, it is possible to develop in them a dispassionate interest in taboo linguistic phenomena ('like doctors'). This may not be possible lower down the school.

eye rhyme (KS 4)

- The quotation is from 'The Passionate Shepherd to his Love'. It's important to distinguish between words which are eye rhymes now, but which weren't when the poet wrote them (because the pronunciation has since changed); these are sometimes called **historical rhymes**. In other cases, historical change is irrelevant to the rhyme's visual status.

LG 6.2

feedback (KS 3)

- This entry should be related to **conversation**, where other examples of feedback are given. Feedback by smell? Well, sweating to show anxiety, for example.

- Distinguish external feedback (where the speaker senses the listener's response) and internal (or kinaesthetic) feedback, where the speaker senses internal body movement (such as tongue movement) or the sound of his/her own voice. It's because we hear our own voices through the bones of the skull that they sound strange when we hear them through the air for the first time, from a tape recorder.

CEL 20, 46, 64

feminine (KS 3) see **gender**

figure of speech (KS 3)

- The literary examples are from Shakespeare's *A Midsummer Night's Dream*; Tennyson's *The Princess*; and Coleridge's *The Rime of the Ancient Mariner*.

• This entry is little more than a general perspective for the more detailed studies of the different types. It would be as well to get on with those entries as soon as possible. The 'finishing off' exercise has in fact been used in studies of the emergence of figurative language in young children. There are several stages through which children pass. Pre-school children use short and conventional endings, not always sensible (*tall as tall, tall as you, tall as a giant, warm as snow*), but sometimes quite poetic (*soft as a rainbow, quiet as a magic marker*). Seven-year-olds are a very literal-minded group, preferring concrete comparisons (*soft as a pillow*). Eleven-year-olds also use concrete comparisons, and often personal names (*hard as stale bread, tall as Wilt Chamberlain*). Older children are more of a mixture, sometimes producing elaborated endings (*warm as a summer's night in Montana*), sometimes making inappropriate comparisons (*hard as rubber*), and sometimes being quite poetic (*colours as light as an old folk tune*).

CEL 12; LG 9

finite and nonfinite (KS 4)

• This entry is a long one, but it is essential that students understand what these terms *mean*. They have been around for centuries, and millions of people have learned to use them – yet very few understand where the terms come from, and why grammarians use them. Note that these labels are used to refer to clauses as well as verbs: a **finite clause** is one containing a finite verb; a **nonfinite clause** contains a nonfinite verb. The subject is usually expressed in a finite clause. It isn't helpful to talk about finite and nonfinite *sentences*, because a sentence often consists of a combination of finite and nonfinite clauses.

• Beware the case where the same form of a verb can be used in both finite and nonfinite constructions. There is one in the entry – *looked*. This can be a finite form, as the past tense of the verb *look* (*I looked*) and it can be a nonfinite form, as the past participle of *look* (as in *I have looked*). You have to look at the whole clause to see which one it is. When *I have looked* changes to *He has looked*, you can see immediately that *have* is the finite form, as that's the one which changes in relation to the subject. *Looked* stays the same. Examples of other verbs where there is identity (homophony) between past tense and past participle are *bend* (*bent*), *leave* (*left*), *hit* (*hit*) and *shut* (*shut*).

RG 17; SGE 3.3, 19–20; CGEL 3.2, 52–3

first language and second language (KS 3)

• Some language scholars don't talk about 'second' languages at all, but call everything other than the mother-tongue a 'foreign language'. However, I think it's useful to distinguish those non-native languages which have been given a special standing in a community, and those which haven't.

• English is given special status in over 40 countries; French in about 30. Countries where English has some kind of official status include Botswana, Cameroon, Fiji, Gambia, Ghana, Guyana, India, Kenya, Malta, Nigeria, Pakistan, Tanzania, Uganda, Zambia and Zimbabwe.

EL 1; CEL 59

fluency (KS 3)

• It's important for students to appreciate that fluency isn't just a matter of speaking rapidly. Several factors are involved, including the ability to comprehend as well as to speak. 'You may not be perfect . . .'? True. And if someone *is* perfect, we would normally have to use such a phrase as 'native-like fluency'.

• Draw attention to the main types of fluency disorder – **stuttering** and **cluttering**. Cluttering is less common: it is the inability to control the speed and rhythm of speech, so that syllables get left out, words run together, and speech becomes extremely erratic and disjointed. Stuttering is the more familiar notion (it's also called **stammering**, incidentally – there is no difference in meaning, so the phrase 'stammering and stuttering' is a tautology). Note the wide range of symptoms which will be heard, including the repetition of sounds, the prolongation of sounds, the avoidance of difficult words, and the insertion of abnormally long pauses into a sentence as the stutterer fails to release a sound (the difficulty is called 'blocking'). A certain amount of everyday non-fluency is normal – such as when we are excited or nervous. Non-fluency becomes a handicap when the speaker's speech problems become severe, interfere with communication, and generate high levels of anxiety.

CEL 46 (p 278)

focus (KS 4)

• Normally (in some 90 per cent of cases) the last semantically important word in a sentence is the focus, and carries the main emphasis, signalled by a melodic peak (see the entry on **intonation**). If you bring the focus forward, it is always to express some kind of contrast, as in the case of *ham* in the entry. Note what 'semantically important' means. In the sentence, *I've got clothes to wear*, it wouldn't be usual to emphasise the word *wear*, because it is obvious – that's what one normally does with clothes. On the other hand, if the sentence were *I've got clothes to burn*, the last word would be likely to receive a stress, because it is unusual, and worth focusing upon.

• Students won't be used to listening to spoken sentences in this way, so it will be important to provide clear examples of focus contrast. Choose sentences where the semantic contrast is clear:

Jean bought a blue car and Mary bought a red one.
A: Who's got a pen? B: John's got a pen.
A: You did lose the book. B: No, I didn't lose it.

RG 70; SGE 18.5–12; CGEL 18.9–18

foot (KS 4)

• The quotation sources are: Gray's 'Elegy'; William Cowper's 'The Poplar Field'; and T S Eliot's 'Dry Salvages' (from *Four Quartets*). The next few lines of the Eliot poem are also worth referring to, as the word *time* recurs, and there is a fine rhythmical conclusion in the final two lines of the section: *And the ground swell, that is and was from the beginning/ Clangs/ The bell.*

• There is a well-established tradition of metrical analysis, which can be so illuminating and yet can go horribly wrong if used in a mechanical and unthinking way. To classify feet, and to count their number in a line, so that a student triumphantly recognises an 'iambic pentameter', say, has limited value. Learning the foot terms off by heart, along with the associated line-length terms (dimeter, trimeter, quadrameter, pentameter, sexameter, etc) can kill metrical appreciation. The crucial point is to be able to recognise that a metrical change has taken place: as the entry implies, we need to assume that there's a reason for everything. Focus the student's attention on the semantic effect that the poet conveys by the change. (We may not know what poets intend, but we can certainly evaluate what they convey.)

• The notion of 'weight' is very important, especially in the context of free verse. This is more than simply a matter of stress, or loudness. It includes the use of pause, intonation, speed, vowel and consonant length, and other such factors. Play about with the lines of a poem to see what happens when line weight is altered. For example, take *Clangs/ The bell*, where the single-word line places enormous phonetic and semantic weight on *Clangs*. Note what happens when these lines are conflated as *Clangs the bell*. The word is said more rapidly, with much less prominence, and much of the climactic force of the language at this point is lost.

LG 7

foregrounding (KS 4)

• It isn't difficult to find examples of foregrounding. It is present, for example, in cases of alliteration, assonance, rhyme, unusual word order variations, archaism, abnormal spelling or punctuation, and unexpected juxtaposition of style. Colloquial speech is foregrounded in the middle of T S Eliot's *The Waste Land* (*I said to her myself . . . Hurry up please it's time*); spelling is foregrounded in the middle of 'East Coker' (*daunsinge, signifying matrimonie*); typography is foregrounded in e e cumming's 'Four III' (*jerks Here &, here, gr(oo)ving the room's Silence . . . gonE*).

• This entry should be read in conjunction with the one on **deviance**, which is a much wider notion, including all cases of ungrammaticality.

LG 4

formal and informal (KS 3)

• The informal features include: contractions, such as *you're*; idiomatic phrases, such as *come to think of it* and *in a way*; elliptical sentences (*Correct*); and conversational features, such as direct address questions and commands. Several other informal features will be found, if students go through other entries.

• The second B sentence is over the top, I admit, but I hope it makes the point. The style-switching exercise is a good one, even though it's rather artificial. Students might try turning a BBC news broadcast into an informal style; or reporting a story in two versions (such as telling it to a mate and telling it to the head). They shouldn't ignore the 'obvious' features, such as the use of formal titles (*Sir, Mr Jones*), and nicknames, slang and colloquial vocabulary (*chap, mum*). Find some examples of extremely formal speech, such as the Queen's speech from the throne, or a judge summing up. Contrast two newspaper styles (the *Sun* vs *The Times*) or two radio channels (Radio 1 and Radio 3).

CEL 10–11

formula (KS 3)

• Formulaic language is often referred to as 'stereotyped'. The entry on **block language** contains other examples. All such sentences fall under the general heading of **minor sentences**, in that they cannot be analysed in terms of regular grammatical patterns (see the entry on **major sentence**). All you can do to formulae is classify them in a general way into functional types, such as greetings, farewells, apologies, expletives, and toasts. Further examples include: *Hello*; *All the best*; *How do you do?*; *Cheers*; *Here's to the future*; *I beg your pardon*; *Get lost*; *Hear hear*.

• In a few cases, slight changes can be made to formulaic sentences. We can drop the *very* from *Your very good health*, for example, and maybe pluralise *health* when toasting several people. But there's not much that can be done to *God save the Queen*, as the entry shows. Even lexical changes are unlikely. Although God can in theory save everyone, there are very few people who can be saved in linguistic practice: *God save the butcher* is not possible in serious speech or writing.

RG 2; SGE 11.22; CGEL 11.45, 54

free direct/indirect speech (KS 4) see **direct speech**

fricative (KS 4)

- The quote is from *Saul*, xiii. The fricatives in the final task are in bold face: *And* ***h****ere'****s*** *a* ***sh****ort* ***s****enten****ce*** ***f****ull o****f*** ***f****ricati****v****e****s****, wi****th*** *lo****v****e and ki****ss****e****s*** ***f****rom me, to end* ***th****i****s*** *entry*. Note that *sh*, *ss*, and *th* are single sounds, despite their spelling.

- The /r/ is a fricative in Received Pronunciation in such words as *drive*, *bedroom*, *price* and *fry*. It's devoiced in the latter two cases (see the entry on **voice** (in phonetics)).

- The [ʒ] is different because it isn't easy to illustrate it at the beginning and end of a word. See the entry on **consonant** for some examples.

EPP 6.2; IPE 8.4

front and back (KS 4)

- I haven't illustrated diphthongs and triphthongs in the entry; these, of course, may contain both a front and a back sound, as in *boy* (see the entry on **diphthong** for examples). I also haven't illustrated **central** sounds, such as the vowels in *cup*, *bird*, and at the end of *sofa*.

- The other front vowel is the one in *sit*; the other back vowels are those of *dog* and *put*. A detailed description of the English vowels, with their positions marked on diagrams, is given in the introductions to phonetics. Gimson's book also gives details of the main regional variations in pronunciation. Only the gross distinctions need be appreciated at this stage. I doubt whether it would be worth while trying to get students to sense more detailed vowel locations until a more advanced stage of language work.

EPP 2–3; IPE 7

fronting

- This term can be quite useful in syntax, referring to the way a constituent of a construction is put at the front of a sentence – such as for extra emphasis. In *Ramsbottom my name is*, the complement element has been fronted. You might find it helpful in describing word order variations, especially in poetry, where fronting is very common (see the **word order** entry).

RG 71; SGE 18.14–15; CGEL 18.20–1

full stop (KS 3)

- The triple dots are often called 'suspension dots' or 'ellipsis dots'. They are used in other contexts, too, such as to signal the omission of part of a quotation. If the omission comes at the end of a sentence, a fourth dot is sometimes added.

- When an abbreviation occurs at the end of a sentence, only a single full stop is used. However, abbreviations increasingly omit the full stop, these days, as part of the modern trend towards typographical simplification. Forms such as *ie*, *eg*, *Mr D Smith*, *BC*, *PhD*, and so on, are usual, especially in British English. Acronyms rarely have full stops (*BBC*, *NATO*).

- Look for interesting uses of the full stop, such as to separate money units (£5.50), units of time (5.30), acts, scenes and lines in a play (III.1.12), section numbers in a book (3.1), and decimal numerals (3.5 – though often a raised dot is used here).

CGEL App III.14

function word (KS 3) see **grammatical word**

future tense (KS 3)

- For people brought up on traditional grammar, it will sound like heresy to say that there is 'no future tense' in English. But, if by 'tense' you mean a type of verb ending, then you cannot avoid this conclusion. (If you don't, but define 'tense' to mean any form of time expression, then you can salvage the notion, but at the cost of allowing in all kinds of other 'tenses', such as might be expressed by auxiliary verbs and time adverbials.)

- To show the wide range of meaning expressed by *will* and *would*, consider such sentences as the following: *I was told I would be released tomorrow* (prediction in the past), *That'll be John now* (prediction in the present), *Mary WILL keep ringing at lunchtime* (habitual prediction), *Oil will float on water* (timeless prediction), *John will talk for hours, if you let him* (personal description), *We won't stay more than an hour* (intention), *Will you help me?* (willingness), *If you WILL go out at night, what do you expect* (insistence), *Would you kindly ask her to come in* (tentativeness), *John WOULD do that, wouldn't he!* (exasperation).

RG 23; SGE 4.27–8; CGEL 4.57–8

gender (KS 3)

- The distinction between natural and grammatical gender in the Word Warning is an important one, when it comes to the comparison of languages. It may take some explaining, though. Students can be confused by the traditional use of the terms *masculine*, *feminine*, and *neuter*, thinking that they inevitably mean 'male', 'female', and 'no sex'. Point out that these are just labels of convenience, which are used to show the different ways in which nouns work. In French, for example, there are nouns which go with *le* and nouns which go with *la*. We could call the first set 'Class A nouns' and the second set 'Class B nouns', if we wanted. But the traditional labels, deriving from the study of the classical languages, are now totally established. The terms **animate** and **inanimate**, for the same reason, will not be familiar, and may need careful introduction.

• There are two contrasts in natural gender in English: **nonpersonal** (*it, which*, etc) vs **personal** (*who, he, she*, etc), and **masculine** (*he, himself*, etc) vs **feminine** (*she, herself*, etc). Several types of gender-marked nouns can be distinguished, including:

- noun pairs which correlate with *he* and *she* (*brother/sister, Mr/Mrs, boy/girl*);
- noun pairs where one item adds a gender ending (*prince/princess, hero/heroine, widower/widow* – in this last case, and also in *bridegroom*, it is the male item which has the ending);
- nouns with dual gender – they can be *he* or *she* (*artist, professor, student, guest, parent, singer* – and those in the entry);
- nouns with common gender – they can be *he, she* or *it* (*baby, cat, rabbit*);
- collective nouns – these have a separate KS 4 entry (*army, club, team*).

• The sexism issue is a good talking point with older students. Distinguish the development of new sex-neutral noun uses (*chair* for *chairman, spokesperson* for *spokesman, flight attendant* for *airline hostess*) from the problems of pronouns (using *he* in a generic sense, as in *A student should give his work in . . .*). Discuss the merits of the various solutions which have been offered, such as the use of *s/he* (written form only), *he or she*, and inventing a new pronoun (among the suggestions have been *co, thon, hesh, mon, hir, per* and *tey*). How do I get round this problem in this book? (By using plural forms – I would write *Students should give their work in . . .*). Look out for cases where the issue comes to the fore, often in an incongruous way: *Man overboard!, Mind that child – he may be deaf!* Also consider cases where it is difficult to find alternatives, such as *Stone Age Man*.

RG 33, 47; SGE 5.45–7; CGEL 5.104–11; CEL 10

generic reference (KS 4)

• The cancelling-out effect doesn't always happen when the nouns are used in this way in other parts of the sentence: compare *I like Lilliputians* (which is definitely generic) and *I like a Lilliputian* (which might be generic, but which could also mean that I like a particular Lilliputian).

• Here are some other sentences containing noun phrases with generic reference (or 'generic meaning'): *Learning a language is important, Cigarettes are bad for you, When was the wheel invented?, I play the violin, The English are good at cricket, It's in support of the blind, I gave her a good education.*

RG 36; SGE 5.22–4; CGEL 5.52–9

genitive case (KS 3) see **case**

genre (KS 3)

- Students should look for examples of other genres – in religion, for instance, the distinction between prayers, invocations, blessings, rosaries, litanies, chants, hymns, psalms, sermons, exorcisms, scriptural readings, creeds, sutras, catechisms, prophecies, testimonies, and so on.
- The notion of genre is often interpreted with reference to the written language only, but there are many examples of spoken genres: sports commentaries, news broadcasts, weather forecasts, soap operas, sit-coms, chat shows, game shows . . . In each case the student should ask: has the event got definable, predictable linguistic features which enable us to identify it as a genre? In some cases, these features are easy to define (such as radio weather reports from coastal stations). In others, the features are much more difficult to pin down (such as the essay). See the entries on **haiku** and **limerick** for examples of other genres.

CEL 12

gerund, gerundive see **participle**

given and new (KS 4)

- The terms are easy, as the entry says, and usually the application to sentences is straightforward enough. But applying them to samples of spoken and written language can be quite tricky, because a great deal depends on what the speaker assumes the listener to already know. If, out of the blue, I say *Michael goes fishing on Thursdays*, and stress the word *Thursdays*, I show by my emphasis that I think this bit of information is what my listener will find interesting. If, however, my listener replies by saying 'I didn't know he fished', then I have made the wrong assumption about what I am taking for granted. Even more so, of course, if the listener were to say, 'Who's Michael?'

RG 70; SGE 18.4; CGEL 18.8

glottis (KS 4)

- Other sounds can be made at the glottis, such as whisper and various kinds of breathy and husky voice qualities. These effects can change the meaning of what is said (whisper can convey a conspiratorial meaning, for example), but they do not act as consonant sounds in English.

• Glottal stops can also occur in other parts of a word. In RP, for example (see **Received Pronunciation**), a [p, t, **k**] occurring at the end of a word or syllable is often replaced in this way. Listen out for this happening in such words as *Scotland* and *football*, or in such phrases as *not much* and *at least*. A glottal stop is often heard before a vowel at the beginning of a word, when the word is spoken forcefully: you can hear it if you say *eight*, for example, as loudly as you can. There's a slight catch in the throat which is not present when this word is said in a quiet, relaxed way.

IPE 8.2.7; EPP 6.4

grammar (KS 3)

• The sense of **grammar** in the entry is rather more abstract than the senses often found in everyday speech. 'Grammar' often means simply a grammar book or a grammar lesson. 'We've got grammar now. Bring your grammars.' In the linguistics literature, even more abstract senses can be found. For example, in the approach to grammar associated with the American linguist, Noam Chomsky (**generative grammar**), the term is used in a very broad sense, to include the sound system and the lexical system as well.

• The distinction between descriptive grammar and prescriptive grammar is implicit in this entry, and it is important to bring out the difference in attitude between the two approaches. The attitudes relate to those described under **appropriate** and **correctness**. In a descriptive grammar, the grammarian is attempting to state what happens in the language, without making any value judgments about the social standing of the usages being described. It is thus very different from a grammar which **prescribes** (gives rules about how you should speak or write) and **proscribes** (gives rules about how you should *not* speak or write). The state of mind which present-day language courses try to inculcate is very much a descriptive one, in which students are taught to be accurate in their observations, to search for explanations of how language works, and to be tolerant in their judgments of varieties of language which they do not themselves use. This need not conflict with the demands of a pedagogical approach, as practised in a school, which has to be prescriptive to some extent when teaching children how to use the educated (or standard) variety of their language fluently and effectively. We can view all language varieties as having their individual role to play in society, and try to become linguistically informed about each of them, while recognising that the standard variety has a special place, for historical and social reasons.

RG; LG 2

grammatical word and lexical word (KS 3)

• You'll also hear grammatical words called **form words**, **functors**, **structure words**, and **closed-class words**. Sorry. All the terms refer essentially to the fact that these are a small ('closed') set of items which have a primarily grammatical ('structural') function. The reference to 'little' words is somewhat tongue-in-cheek. Some grammatical words are quite big – *because*, *several*, and *without*, for instance. There are also some multi-word items with a grammatical function, such as *out of*, *according to*, and *for the sake of*.

• The distinction between the two types of word seems clear enough, but there are some unclear cases which I haven't referred to in the entry. Some grammatical words *do* have a great deal of meaning, such as *if*, *into*, *what*, and *you*. The important point to stress is not the semantic one, but the structural role of these words in building up a sentence. All pronouns, conjunctions, prepositions, and determiners are grammatical words. Frequency is a good guide: they are the commonest and most repeated words in the language.

SGE 2.6; CGEL 2.39–40

grapheme (KS 4) see **graphology**

graphology (KS 4)

• A possible point of confusion is that 'writing system' here means not just handwriting, but printed and typewritten material as well. I've made no distinction between **graphology** (the study of the written language system) and **graphetics** (the study of the properties of the graphic

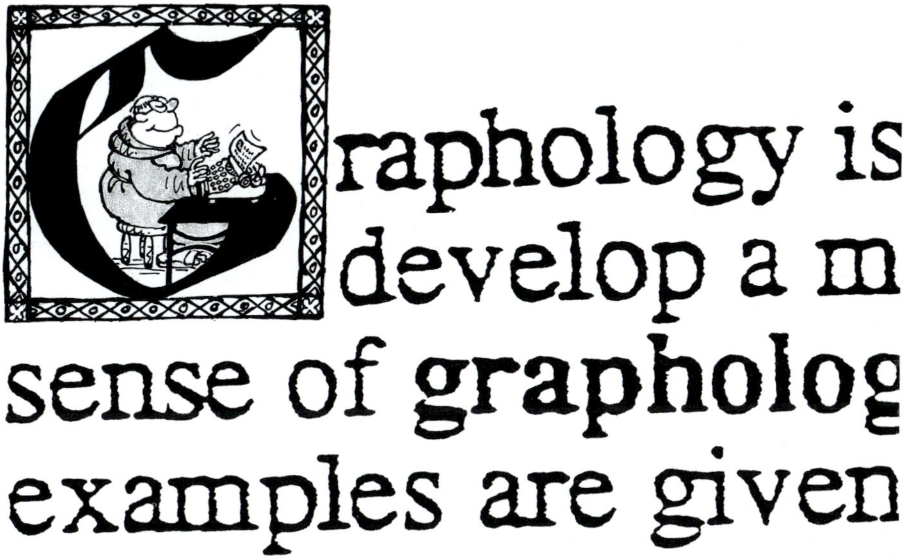

medium). I do draw an analogous distinction in the study of speech (see entries on **phonology** and **phonetics**), but that distinction is a well-established one. The linguistic study of the written language is not so well advanced, and the terminology is not standard, so I have not introduced students to the distinction at this point.

• I haven't gone into typographical questions much in these books. There are *thousands* of typefaces. I do have an entry on upper- and lower-case letters (see **upper case**), but that's about all. Some of the basic typographic terms could therefore be introduced at this point, such as **italic**, **bold**, and **roman**. Older students might appreciate knowing about some of the classic typefaces (such as Gothic, Times Roman), especially now that word processing and other home computer packages make reference to some of them.

• Letters are graphemes, and that is how I introduced the notion. More generally, any contrastive visual element is a grapheme, such as a full stop, comma, and colon, and the symbols @ and & (see the entry on **logogram**). Note that graphemes may vary from language to language, such as the inverted question mark in Spanish or accents in French.

• One way of getting a sense of typographic values is to play about with different typefaces, to see whether they suit a particular context or meaning. *Ye Olde Tea Shoppe* would be fine in Gothic print. On the other hand, you would be unlikely to find a go-ahead firm marketing their slogan, *The firm for the future*, in Gothic. Gothic type harks back to the past. Students might build up a collection of interesting graphological examples, using newspapers, magazines, ads, TV guides, and so on. The collection might include lists, tables, figures, tree diagrams, and other ways of laying out information, as well as distinctive lettering, colour, and use of space.

• Graphology isn't just a matter of print, but includes handwritten material as well. Students might develop a metalanguage for describing handwriting styles. There's no harm in investigating the other sense of **graphology**, where handwriting is interpreted in terms of character and personality. Some examples are given in the *Cambridge Encyclopedia of Language*, page 189. Compare also typewritten documents, which differ from print in several respects: what are the differences, in fact? Look at the use of underlining, for example. What difference has the advent of the electronic typewriter made? And how is printed information to be conveyed on the computer screen (the problem of 'graphic translatability')? How should emphasis be conveyed, for instance – through underlining, colour, capitals, spacing, flashing lights . . .?

CEL 32–3

group genitive (KS 4)

• To avoid the ambiguity, you have to rephrase – for instance, *Look at the bald-headed teacher with a cat*.

• This structure is also sometimes called the **embedded genitive**. Technically, the genitive ending is being attached to a postmodifier. It is especially common following names which contain several elements, such as *the Bank of England's policy*, *the Wife of Bath's Tale*, and *the Professor of History's moustache*.

RG 34; CGEL 5.123, 17.119

haiku (KS 4)

• The purpose of the haiku is to evoke a feeling through the use of a natural image. The lines do not rhyme. The verse form arose in Japan in the sixteenth century. Poets who used it include Basho (Matsuo Munefusa, 1644–94) and Kobayashi Issa (Kobayashi Nobuyuki, 1763–1828). Western poets who have used haikus include the Imagists (Ezra Pound, T E Hulme, and others) and James Kirkup. The point of including this entry is to raise the question of poetic discipline and its purpose. Any self-discipline can be imposed – a poem of four lines of three, four, five, six syllables, or whatever. Students could experiment with new forms – or alter old ones (eg modifying a sonnet or a limerick, to see what happens).

head (KS 4)

• It really is important for students to recall the entry on **phrase**, at this point. Notice that the prepositional phrase is different from all the others, in that it seems to have two heads – the preposition and the noun phrase which follows (sometimes called the 'prepositional complement'). It would be difficult to say, really, which was the 'chief word' – which is why I changed the phrasing at that point in the entry, and said that the preposition 'controls the construction'.

• You might explore in greater detail what 'chief word' means. The head is the most important word semantically, of course – it is what the phrase is about. But it is also the most important word grammatically. In particular, it is the word with which the verb agrees. In the sentence *The girl with the books is sleeping in the garden*, you know that *girl*, and not *books*, is the head of the subject noun phrase because it agrees with the singular verb *is*. You also have a semantic clue – *girls* sleep; *books* don't. A good diagrammatic classification of phrases is given in CGEL 2.28.

RG 27; SGE 2.4; CGEL 2.28

high vowel (KS 4) see **close vowel**

historic present (KS 4)

• The 'feel' of the historic present is that of an eye-witness account. You'll see it used in photographic captions (*Prime Minister arrives at Downing*

Street) and in historical summaries or tables of dates (*1914: First World War begins*).

• Note that there is an important difference between historic present sentences and such sentences as the following: *Smith tells me that John's going away*. Like the historic present, the telling took place in the past, but in this case the information is still relevant and operative. John is still going away, whereas the drunk is not still striking matches or the Prime Minister still arriving in Downing Street. These sentences all contain verbs of communication (*We read in the Bible . . ., I hear on the grapevine . . .*). The idea that artists are still able to 'speak' to us also explains the use of the present tense in *Shakespeare gives us an insight into . . .* Note the contrast, incidentally, between *Smith writes of poverty in the early nineteenth century* and *Smith wrote in the early nineteenth century* (not **Smith writes in the early nineteenth century*).

RG 23; SGE 4.4; CGEL 4.8

holophrase (KS 4)

• The idea of a 'single-word sentence' upsets people who think that an utterance has to have all its elements (especially a verb) before it can count as a sentence. But when you examine the way in which holophrases are used, it's plain from the intonation and other prosodic features that the utterance is being made to function as a sentence. One child I know said *dada*, with a high rising, querying tone, when he heard footsteps on the gravel outside his house, at the time when he expected his daddy to come home from work. When the father entered the room, the child said *dada* again, but with a falling, 'there he is' tone. This was plainly the difference between question and statement, though the utterances lacked all the usual grammatical signs of that distinction. Similarly, utterances such as *dindin* and *allgone* aren't difficult to interpret. However, often the function of a holophrase isn't so easily identified. Students should expect many of them to be ambiguous, when they start listening to a tape.

• To reduce the ambiguity, it is essential to keep careful observational notes while recording the child (eg describing what the child is doing; saying who is being looked at). Video recordings are of course invaluable, in this respect. With the growth of home videos, this suggestion is no longer as impracticable as it once was.

CEL 41

homographs (KS 4) see **homonyms**

homonyms (KS 4)

• There is also a literary dimension to the use of homonyms, as they form the basis of many puns – usually the more obvious ones. Homonymic puns are very common in Elizabethan drama, and especially in Shakespeare, whose word-play has been the subject of several studies. For example, Surrey in *Richard II*: *That lie shall lie so heavy on my sword . . .* (IV.1). The activity is even appreciated by the characters: *I moralise two meanings in one word*, says Richard III. *Can sick men play so nicely with their names?* asks Richard II. A fine discussion of these matters is in Walter Redfern's *Puns* (Blackwell, 1984), especially Chapter 3.

LG 12.2

homophones (KS 4) see **homonyms**

hyperbole (KS 4)

• The term **hyperbole** tends to be used only in the context of literature, where the effect is widely employed. Bombastic speeches, very common in Elizabethan drama, contain a great deal of hyperbole: see the speeches of Tamburlaine, for example (*We'll chase the stars from heaven . . . an easy leap/ To pluck bright honour from the pale-faced moon*). Many instances are to be found in the heroic drama of the Restoration period (Dryden, Davenant, and others). Burlesque loves hyperbole – for example, Bottom's speeches as he prepares for the drama of Pyramus and Thisbe: *I will move storms . . .* (*A Midsummer Night's Dream*, I.2). Bottom knows exactly what he is doing: *This is Ercles' vein*.

• Although the term has a literary application, the effect certainly isn't restricted to that domain, as the other examples in the entry illustrate. Exaggeration is absolutely everywhere.

LG 10

hypernyms (KS 4) see **hyponyms**

hyphen (KS 3)

• 'You won't find any hyphens there'? I lied, I'm afraid. Even with ragged-edge typography, it's sometimes necessary to have a hyphen – but only, in this book, where a compound word approaches the right-hand edge of the page, and where to transfer the whole item to the next line would leave an ugly space. In such cases, the compound is split, and a hyphen is left. There's an instance in the entry on **thesaurus** (KS 3), where the compound form *nineteenth-century* is divided in this way. Let the students find the exceptions for themselves. It may motivate them to read the book!

• Studying where you put line-break hyphens is interesting. They should occur at a natural point within the structure of a word. Students take a while to appreciate this, and will divide, for example, *strongly* after the *r*, in immature writing. But not everyone will agree on what a natural dividing point is. Should it be *frac-ture* or *fract-ure*? (American English prefers the former; British English the latter.) Dictionaries sometimes give guidance on this, by marking hyphenation points (usually, syllable-division points).

• There are many differences of practice in hyphenating compounds (see **compound word**). American English has fewer hyphens than British English, preferring to write the words **open** (a space) or **solid** (no space). Publishing houses devise their own set of recommendations, and these differ widely. Students could carry out their own survey, comparing the styles of different publishers. Try to work out the rules guiding usage practice – for example, the difference between using a compound after a verb and before a noun: *They stood face to face* but *a face-to-face meeting*. There are some nice contrasts of meaning involving the hyphen: *re-form* vs *reform*, *re-cover* vs *recover*.

CGEL App III.4

hyponyms (KS 4)

• The **hypernym** is often called the 'superordinate term'. Vast numbers of words don't have very specific hypernyms. Dip into *Roget's Thesaurus*, for example, and you'll discover them straight away. Of course, all words have an abstract hypernym: we can always say that something is a type of 'quality' or 'process' or 'action'. Dictionaries use this strategy when they define words. In fact, dictionaries are a good source for hyponymy examples (though they may not actually say 'a type of'): I've just looked up *coquina*, for instance, and the definition given is 'a small marine clam . . .' – so, *clam* is the hypernym of *coquina*. Nouns are the easiest words to deal with, in terms of hyponymy.

• Notice that there are sets of terms which belong together within a particular hypernym. These can then be called **co-hyponyms**. For instance, within the hypernym *instrument* there are the co-hyponyms *flute*, *oboe*, *clarinet*, *trumpet*, and so on, and these can be grouped in various ways. *Flute* is a hyponym of *woodwind*, and *woodwind* in turn is a hyponym of *instrument*. If you want to clarify this, you can say that *flute* is an 'immediate' hyponym of *woodwind*, and *woodwind* is an 'immediate' hyponym of *instrument*. It's still true, of course, that *flute* is also a hyponym of *instrument*. Any hierarchical classification will involve this kind of relationship (types of animals, plants, etc). Look out for interesting cases. For example, in English there is no true hypernym for all the colour words: the term *coloured* usually excludes *black* and *white* (as in the context of TV, race). Notice, too, how *dog* (when opposed to *bitch*) is a type of *dog* (in a more general sense). A good discussion of hyponymy is in F R Palmer's *Semantics* (CUP, 1981, 2nd edn), 5.2.

CEL 17

iambic foot (KS 4) see **foot**

ideogram (KS 4)

• A distinction is commonly made between ideograms and **pictograms** (or **pictographs**), which I haven't introduced in the entry. Ideographic writing is usually considered to be a later development of pictographic. Pictograms are much more immediately recognisable (such as a series of wavy lines suggesting a river). A typical modern ideogram is the prohibition symbol (eg a diagonal line through a cigarette, meaning 'no smoking'), often seen on road signs. The symbols in the story in my entry seem to be partly pictographic, partly ideographic. The distinction between the two types is not always clear. Very few pictographic symbols, in fact, are decodable without understanding the context first.

• This topic can be very illuminating for students interested in the history of language. Any introduction to the history of writing will provide examples – such as Florian Coulmas, *The Writing Systems of the World* (Blackwell, 1989). Building up a collection of ideographic (including pictographic) signs from the street, shops, airports, etc is a useful exercise.

CEL 33

idiolect (KS 4)

• Most of the time, in language work, we study the features of language which people have in common – the rules of grammar, pronunciation, and so on which enable people to communicate with each other. From time to time, though, it is important to study a person's idiolect – those features which *distinguish* that person from others in the community. Examples include the forensic investigation of someone's spoken or written language, as part of a police enquiry, and the analogous stylistic detective work which has to take place when critics wish to establish who was the author of a particular literary work (did Shakespeare write all those plays? did St Paul write all those letters?). The study of language-disordered people, both children and adults, can also require a detailed study of individual patterns of ability and disability. But literary stylistics is the domain most involved in the idiolectal use of language. 'Style is the man.'

• There's no reason why students shouldn't get involved in some elementary language detective work. Each of a group could write an account of something, using two separate pages. The pages are mixed up, and people have to try to work out who wrote what. The handwriting usually gives the game away. To eliminate this, get the accounts typed, and see how far everyone gets. Some students will have linguistic fingerprints which stand out a mile. Others will be difficult to separate. The same exercise could of course be done using literary samples, but that would probably be a more advanced task, as the language involved would usually be rather more complex.

CEL 8, 12

idiom (KS 3)

• There are several handy collections of idioms, such as Martin Manser's *A Dictionary of Contemporary Idioms* (Pan, 1983) or the *Longman Dictionary of English Idioms* (1979). Under *devil*, for example, the former lists *be a devil*, *be the very devil*, *go to the devil*, *talk of the devil*, *there'll be the devil to pay*, and several others. The latter includes no less than 26 entries under the headword *eyes*. There are a lot of idioms about.

• Spend some time discussing *why* a sequence of words is an idiom. In the entry, I present a semantic criterion – you can't work out the meaning of the whole by looking at the individual parts. There's also a grammatical criterion: we can't use idioms like a normal sentence. Their grammatical potential is restricted, often markedly so. We can't easily add words to an idiom, or leave words out, or change the word order, and so on. *It's raining cats and dogs* doesn't singularise to **It's raining a cat and a dog*. You can't put all your cards on the chair, or the desk – unless you want the sentence to be taken literally, of course. Which reminds me: the entry on **literal** should be read closely in association with this one.

CGEL 16.12

illiterate (KS 3) see **literate**

imagery (KS 3)

• I'm using a fairly narrow definition in this entry. There is a much broader (and somewhat vaguer) sense in which an image isn't just a vivid mental picture, but any state of mind or experience on the part of the speaker or writer. Figurative language is often present, but not always. To say *I smelled the rose* is an olfactory image, in this sense, though the sentence doesn't use any figure of speech. The images may appeal to any of the senses, not just the visual: tactile, auditory, olfactory, gustatory, and kinaesthetic (based on our internal sensation of body movement). Plainly, the further discussion of this issue is going to involve considerations of a psychological and critical nature, which would move me away from the central concern of these books. I've therefore kept the entry quite short, and apologise now to the topic which is, in its literary application, quite vast.

LG 5

imperative (KS 4) see **command**

impersonal style (KS 4)

- The point about teacher difference of opinion isn't new, of course. It was one of the points made early on when people debated the proposals for 'language across the curriculum' in the seventies. Each subject area has to be examined in its own terms, in this respect. The balance of personal to impersonal allowed into a history essay will not be the same as that allowed into a geography essay – and the same point applies to different branches of a subject (eg physical vs human geography).
- A useful exercise is to get students to go through my two books and look for features of personal style. I think the KS 4 book is somewhat less personal than the KS 3. Many entries, though, adopt a mix of styles. Indeed, it is wise not to think of personal and impersonal as a dichotomy, but as at either end of a continuum. They could look at any materials from this point of view – spoken as well as written. Where would a sports commentary go on this continuum? a sermon? the weather forecast (which is an interesting mixture, actually)?
- This entry could be related to the one on formality (see **formal**). The distinction between formal and informal is a much more general one; but impersonal styles are usually formal, and personal styles are usually informal.

CEL 63

inanimate (KS 4) see **animate**

incoherence (KS 4) see **coherence**

indefinite article (KS 3) see **article**

indefinite pronoun (KS 4)

- The term **indefinite** is here being seen in contrast to the other classes of pronoun: personal (*I*, etc), reflexive (*myself*, etc), possessive (*my*, etc), reciprocal (*each other*, etc), relative (*who*, etc), interrogative (*who*, etc) and demonstrative (*this*, etc). They are not usually referred to in a combined way as the 'definite pronouns', except by implication. The indefinite pronouns lack the element of definiteness which is found there.

- The compound pronouns divide into two types: personal (ending in *-one* or *-body*) and impersonal (ending in *-thing*). In manuals of usage, the pronouns ending in *-one* are regarded as being rather more formal and polite than those ending in *-body*. They are also used more frequently. American English uses *-body* pronouns more widely than does British English. Note the grammar of the compound pronouns. They can be followed by *else* (*Anyone else coming?*). The personal items can take a genitive ending (*It's nobody's fault*). Adjectives have to follow them, not precede them (*Nothing new*, not **New nothing*).

- The simple indefinite pronouns can be followed by *of*. Here's a list of them: *all*, *any*, *both*, *each*, *either*, *few* (*fewer*, *fewest*), *little* (*less*, *least*), *many*, *more*, *most*, *much*, *neither*, *none*, *one*, and *some*.

RG 44; SGE 6.21–8; CGEL 6.45–62

indentation or indention (KS 3)

- Indents are employed in many interesting ways, and students might go hunting for them, apart from their use in paragraph division. Look at the way they are used in letters, for example. In some styles of letter-writing, you have to indent each paragraph so that it begins beneath the comma of the opening vocative (*Dear Sir,*), and the closing formula (*Yours sincerely,* etc) is markedly indented. The address on the envelope could have each line indented compared with the previous line. In contemporary letter styles, indention is little used, with some styles avoiding it altogether – every line is placed against the left-hand margin ('ranged left'), and paragraphs are separated by a line of white space. Other areas for investigation include the use of indention in the layout of bibliographies, poetry, glossaries, indexes, stage directions, and tables.

CGEL App III.14

indicative (KS 4) see **mood**

indirect object (KS 3) see **direct object**

indirect speech (KS 3) see **direct speech**

inference (KS 4)

- Inference has always been an important part of the study of language comprehension, and is now a particular focus of early language work, especially in the junior school. Nonetheless, the distinction between **infer** and **imply**, referred to in the Word Warning, is widely misunderstood, and will need special attention. It is actually also a common source of confusion among adults, and usage manuals regularly worry about it. (The common direction of error is that people use *infer* where the standard language requires *imply*.)

infinitive (KS 3)

- The importance of the infinitive is that, following the Latin grammatical tradition, it is the form which is cited when you want to identify a verb in the first place. Not all languages use the infinitive form for this purpose (Arabic doesn't, for instance), but it makes sense to do so in English, as it is the simplest form of the verb. See the entry on **grammar** for a discussion of the split infinitive.

- There are aspects of the way the infinitive is used in the sentence which are worth following up. It's a nonfinite form of the verb, to begin with (see the entry on **finite**). Also, in places where you can have a bare infinitive, it usually isn't possible to have a *to*-infinitive, and vice versa. Compare *They wanted me to learn French*, where you can't omit the *to*, and *They let me answer the letter*, where you can't put it in. There are many verbs in the former category, and very few in the latter. *Help* (and, to a lesser extent, *know*) is the only verb which can be used with either construction: *I helped him (to) get into the car*; *I have known him (to) leave by six*.

RG 17; SGE 14.4, 16.27–8; CGEL 14.6–7, 16.50–2

inflection (KS 3)

- Here's a complete list of all the frequently used inflections in English (but without giving details of all the irregular forms): *-ing* (on verbs), plural (typically *-s*), the past tense (typically *-ed*), past participle (various types), present tense 3rd person singular (*-s*), genitive (*-'s*, *-s'*), comparative (*-er*) and superlative (*-est*). In addition there are endings attached to small classes of words: auxiliary contraction (eg *-'ll*), copula contraction (eg *-'s*), negative (*-n't*), object pronoun (eg *him*).

- It's important to distinguish inflectional endings from the other kinds of ending which can be added to a word – the various suffixes (see **affix** for a brief discussion).

RG 74; SGE 3.4–9, 5.35–55, 6.2, 7.39–44

informal see **formal**

informant (KS 4)

- These days, informants are often referred to as **consultants**, in language research projects.

• When I say 'telling someone the facts about your language' I don't mean that the informant is doing grammatical analyses for the linguist. It means, first and foremost, eliciting sentences in the language from informants, and getting them to react to sentences in terms of whether they are acceptable or not. This kind of activity is fairly straightforward when informants are bilingual. It's much more difficult, obviously, when linguists have to start from scratch and work out everything by observing how people speak. It can take many months before a reasonably complete outline grammar of a new language can be written.

• The same issues arise when researching our mother tongue. Dialect researchers buzz around the country asking questions very much like those used in investigating a foreign language. 'What do you call the thing a dog sleeps in at night?' might elicit some local words for *kennel*. When researching the standard language, the tasks to be given to an informant have to be rather more ingenious. You can't just go up to someone and say 'Is it grammatical to say *It is I*?' They won't necessarily know what you mean by 'grammatical'. But you can't simply say 'Do you say *It is I*?' either. People aren't so good at remembering what they typically say, when it comes to problems of usage, and are likely to give you back an imaginary answer. Many respond by giving you the answer which they think they 'ought' to give (usually, the alternative which is more careful or formal). Another approach is to present people with extracts on a page (or on tape) and ask them to comment when they hear something odd. That works quite well, but some people hear too many oddities! I once presented someone with sentences which they were to rephrase, if they noticed anything they didn't like. I gave: *The bus I got off of was a red one*. 'Oh, I don't like that,' said the informant. 'Great,' I thought. But then he said 'We don't have red buses round here.'

CEL 65 (p 410)

-ing-form (KS 4) see **participle**

instrument see **agent**

intensifier (KS 4)

• The two intensifier-less sentences are the ones beginning *By the way* and *And also*.

• Students shouldn't have much trouble sensing the idea of words which intensify upwards; but the concept of intensifying downwards is a bit unusual. The crucial point is to get across the concept of a *scale* of intensity, from maximum to minimum, with a 'middle' level to which these words relate. At this middle level, people just express themselves more emphatically. *Almost*, for example, scales downwards because it says that something is 'below' a particular norm – *We're almost there, I've almost finished*. *Greatly* scales upwards because it says that something is 'above' a particular norm – *I admire her greatly, I'm greatly interested*. And *definitely* neither scales upwards nor downwards – it simply adds emphasis: *I'm definitely going, definitely interested*. Other examples of adjective intensifiers which scale upwards: *utter folly, total nonsense, complete stranger, close friend*. Adjectives which scale downwards: *feeble joke, slight effect*. Adjectives which add extra emphasis: *clear failure, certain winner, plain nonsense*. Adverbial intensifiers which scale upwards: *totally, completely, a great deal, by far*. Adverbials which scale downwards: *virtually, more or less, partly, scarcely*. Adverbials which add extra emphasis: *clearly, definitely, indeed, really, of course, literally*. See the entry on **degree** for further examples.

RG 56; SGE 7.32–5; CGEL 7.33, 8.99–115

interdental (KS 4) see **dental**

interjection (KS 3)

• In older classifications, interjections were thought of as a separate part of speech. There's no real harm in that, but it needs to be appreciated that interjections aren't really part of the grammar at all. They're outside of grammar. They aren't used in a predictable and productive way as part of sentence structure. They are a type of minor sentence (see **major sentence**). Other examples are *Mm, Hey, Ooh, Ouch, Pooh, Uh-huh, Wow, Yippee*, and the archaic *Alas*. Some spellings vary: *Sh, Shh, Shhh; Tut-tut, Tsk-tsk*.

• There are a few exceptions to the final point in the entry. Some interjections have indeed taken on a lexical 'shape', such as *shush* and *boo*. They can be used as verbs, in the usual way: *I shushed him up*, *They're booing us*. The majority aren't like this, though.

RG 2; CGEL 11.55

International Phonetic Alphabet (KS 4)

• Some more information about the IPA might be useful. The International Phonetic Association was inaugurated in France in 1886 by a small group of language teachers. The idea of producing a phonetic alphabet was proposed by the Danish linguist, Otto Jespersen, and the first version was published in 1888. It has since been revised several times, most recently in 1989. The Association is based at University College London. The IPA has now been widely used in dictionaries and textbooks, and some of its symbols have been employed when new languages have come to be written down for the first time. A copy of the IPA can be found in many textbooks on phonetics, such as Gimson's.

CEL 27; IPE App

interrogative (KS 4)

• Note that, just as a declarative structure can be turned into a question by the use of a questioning tone of voice, so an interrogative structure can be turned into an exclamation by the use of an exclamatory tone of voice. *Hasn't she grown!* may be interrogative in structure, but it has the force of an emphatic statement – *She has grown!* Similarly, *Am I hungry!*, *Was he cross!* Notice, too, how sometimes the distinction between negative and positive structures all but disappears, in this kind of context: *Hasn't she grown!* and *Has she grown!* are very similar.

• This entry should be read in association with the one on **question** (and also **rhetorical question**).

RG 5; SGE 11.1; CGEL 11.1

intonation (KS 4)

• Listening out for intonation patterns can be quite difficult, so in the early stages concentrate on just the main features of pitch movement in the sentence. These are, firstly, the division of the utterance into **tone units** (or **tone groups**) – the main rhythmical contours which divide a sentence up into its components. If you read aloud the first sentence of this paragraph, for example, you'll probably introduce a major pitch/rhythmical break after the word *difficult*. The sentence would have two tone units, therefore. Many people would pause again after *stages*, adding a third tone unit to the utterance. And if it were being read in a slightly more disjointed way, you might hear rhythmical breaks after *patterns*, *features*, and *movement*. Next, within a tone unit, listen out for the word which carries the greatest emphasis (see the entry on **focus**). In the first sentence, said as two tone units, I would expect the most emphatic words to be *difficult* and *main*. A lot depends on how you feel the sentence meaning should be conveyed, though. To take a different example, consider the meaning changes which accompany the shift in emphasis in this sentence: *It WAS nice of Mary to volunteer*, *It was NICE of Mary to volunteer*, *It was nice of Mary to VOLUNTEER*, *It was nice of MARY to volunteer*. Lastly, you can try to detect whether the pitch movement is falling, rising, staying level, or doing some combination of these movements on the various words of the sentence. This last point is the most difficult to determine, unless you have a reasonable musical ear.

● Whether they have a good ear for music or not, there are ways in which you can start training students to listen out for the difference between falling and rising pitch. Find examples where the distinction is between asking and telling. *Mike's hurt his knee?* vs *Mike's hurt his knee*. In the former, I'm asking, and my voice rises; in the latter, I'm telling, and my voice falls. Or take a well-known speaking situation, and listen to the way the pitch makes differences in the meaning. One which always goes down well is the intonation of football results on the radio, where the difference between a home win, an away win and a draw is signalled by the different pitch movements on the second team. See the entry on **contour** for further details.

RG 75; IPE 10.5; EPP 15–19; CGEL App II

intransitive verb (KS 3) see **transitive verb**

intrusive *r* (KS 4) see **linking sound**

inversion (KS 4)

● The poetic extract is from 'On First Looking into Chapman's Homer'.

● The entry deals only with one kind of inversion, that between subject and verb – or, to be more precise, between the subject and the first auxiliary verb in the verb phrase (the operator – see the notes on **auxiliary verb**). Other types of inversion exist, in which the order of all the clause elements is reversed: *Loud grew the sound of the train* (an inversion of *The sound of the train grew loud*), *Down came the rain*, *Equally inexplicable was his behaviour*.

● There are also several types of subject-operator inversion, as can be seen from the following types of sentence: *He was angry and so was I* (where a second clause, introduced by *so*, has something left out); *Nor would she say what had happened* (where the inversion follows a negative word); *I asked more questions than did Fred* (in certain kinds of comparative clause); and *Had I known, I would have left* (in clauses which express a condition).

RG 71; SGE 11.3, 18.14–17; CGEL 11.5–23, 18.22–4

inverted commas (KS 3)

• In discussing where quotation marks are used, and why, don't forget the obvious use – to mark a quotation! They're also used in some styles to show a title. Be prepared for idiosyncrasy, too: some authors have developed their own style for using these marks – such as single marks for words used in a special sense and double marks for quotations. In my linguistics writing, I always use single quotes for a translation of a foreign word (Welsh *fy* 'my'), but not everyone follows this practice.

• There is a trend for printers to use single marks, these days, as part of the general preference for simplification. Incidentally, 'scare quotes' are sometimes called 'sneer quotes'.

• There is a difference between American and British usage over the question of whether punctuation marks should be inside or outside the inverted commas. American preference is to place the inverted commas after the other punctuation marks; British preference is the reverse. The closing inverted comma typically precedes all punctuation except an exclamation mark, question mark, dash or parenthesis belonging to the quotation.

CGEL App III.25

IPA (KS 4) see **International Phonetic Alphabet**

irony (KS 4)

• '. . . as when characters speak ironically in a play'. I haven't illustrated this in the entry. A good example is 'Thrift, thrift, Horatio! The funeral baked meats/ Did coldly furnish forth the marriage tables' (*Hamlet*, I.2). Authors renowned for their use of irony in English include Pope, Dryden, Swift, Fielding, and Jane Austen. Literary critical works have paid considerable attention to the notion, distinguishing various kinds of irony in addition to the dramatic irony mentioned in the entry (tragic irony, cosmic irony, romantic irony, structural irony, etc). To go into these distinctions would be to be involved in a different kind of book; but it is worth stressing the importance of making a connection at some stage between the subject-matter of this entry and the approaches of literary studies of irony.

LG 10

irregular (KS 4)

• It would be a very long list, which is why my reader wouldn't be amused. But it wouldn't be too big a job to concentrate just on nouns or on verbs. In any case, it ought not to be just a list, but a classification, in which different types of irregular form are placed together. In the nouns, for example, there are those which are irregular because they change their vowel (*feet*, *geese*, *men*), those which are irregular because they change their consonant (*knives*, *thieves*, *wives*), and those which add no ending at all (*sheep*, *cod*, *deer*). Then there are all the foreign plurals, which can also be classified in various ways (*criteria*, *theses*, *strata*, *stimuli*). There are nouns which look singular and are plural (*cattle*, *police*), and nouns which look plural and are singular (*news*, *linguistics*). And so on. The Quirk grammars give excellent classifications (in Chapters 3 and 5).

• In the entry, I've concentrated on irregularity in word structure (see **morphology**). There is also irregularity in syntax. For example, the normal word order in a statement is subject + verb, but after certain negative adverbs (*hardly*, *barely*, etc) the order is inverted (*Hardly had I left when . . .*). Most of the exceptions in a grammar of English illustrate this kind of irregularity, in fact.

RG 16, 31; SGE 3.9–10, 5.37–44; CGEL 3.11–20, 5.73–101

irrelevance (KS 3) see **relevance**

isogloss

• If you do any detailed work on dialects, using maps, then you'll need this term. It refers to a line drawn on a map which marks the boundary of an area in which a particular linguistic feature is used. For example, to the north of the line, speakers might use a short [a] vowel, in such words as *bath*; south of the line, they might use a long vowel [ɑ:]. When a whole 'bundle' of isoglosses fall together, in a particular part of the country, it shows the existence of a dialect boundary.

CEL 8

jargon (KS 3)

• I deliberately didn't say 'linguists'. It has to be admitted, though, that a mystique has grown up around the study of language, which it is partly the purpose of this book to help destroy. The mystique inevitably emerges when terms are concentrated upon to the exclusion of the realities to which they supposedly refer. It happened in the old days when students learned grammatical terminology by heart without relating it to everyday language

patterns and problems. It could happen again, if the terms in the National Curriculum literature distract critical attention away from the realities of language structures in use. Being aware of the dangers is the first step. The discussion of this point is not, incidentally, for the staff room only. It is for the classroom. Share the problem of terminology with the students.

• Jargon is fine, in its place. That's the message of this entry. Those who issue a blanket condemnation of jargon are missing a crucial point: between specialists, it is an extremely important feature, adding precision and economy to their communication. Draw students' attention to the existence of the Plain English Campaign, its aims and achievements. Get hold of their literature. The address of the campaign in the UK is Vernon House, Whaley Bridge, Stockport SX12 7HP. Get the students to do their own version of the Golden Bull awards for the least intelligible language, using textbooks, newspapers, handouts . . . And, at the same time, discuss the extent to which it is possible to have a truly 'plain English'. When language is simplified, something is inevitably lost as well as gained.

EL 12

labial, labio-dental (KS 4) see **bilabial, rounding**

language (KS 3)

• This entry obviously has to be in, but it's hardly possible to write a short item on such a large concept. All I've done, therefore, is outline the main components of a 'model' of language, such as will be found in the recent reports on English in the Curriculum, to draw together some loose ends. The important point, however you follow this up, is to aim for a balance between all the various dichotomies in this model – in particular, between structure and use, production and comprehension, speaking and writing, and listening and reading. Pay especial attention to listening, as a foundation skill, which has been somewhat downgraded in the National Curriculum. Above all, avoid the pendulum swing which has been apparent in language study in recent years, as the focus shifted from structure (parsing sentences without relating the analyses to real-life situations) to use (plenty of real-life situations, but no language terminology to talk about them). The current Curriculum has made language-teaching history, in its emphasis on a balanced approach, with structure and use being brought together into a single pedagogical model for the first time. This theoretical position motivates the present series, and a great deal else in current teaching practice. However, theory is well ahead of practice, at present. It is possible to see the direction in which we should be moving, but there are as yet few studies of the efficacy of different materials, strategies and techniques. I have no doubt that this is a temporary problem. Examples of good practice are already accumulating – in the various LINC projects, for example – and an ethos will gradually emerge. How temporary is 'temporary', however, largely depends on the openness of the political till rather than on intellectual will or pedagogical skill.

CEL, I suppose

larynx (KS 4) see **glottis**

lateral (KS 4)

• The Welsh sound is technically a lateral fricative (see **fricative**) – the friction is a really noticeable feature. Another type of *l* is the palatal *l* which you hear for example in Spanish – the front of the tongue makes contact with the front of the palate. There's also a voiceless *l* in English (see **voice** in phonetics): listen to what happens after a [p] or [k], in such words as *plan* and *clear*. Also, listen to what happens to dark *l* in Cockney: with the *l* sounds of RP (see **Received Pronunciation**), the tip of the tongue is in contact with the upper teeth ridge; but in Cockney it isn't, and the sound emerges as a back vowel. Listen to a Cockney saying *rail* and *row* (in the sense of 'argument'), and you won't hear much (or any) difference between them. You certainly won't hear a distinct *l* sound at the end of *rail*.

• The two types of *l* mentioned in the Sound Warning are not contrastive in English (they're not phonemes – see the entry on **phoneme**): they don't change the meanings of words, as would the contrast between, say, *l* and *r* (*led*/*red*) or *l* and *m* (*lop*/*mop*). If you replaced a clear *l* by a dark *l* you wouldn't get a new word, just the old word with a strange sound. However, in some languages, the difference between clear and dark *l is* contrastive – Russian is an example.

EPP 7.2; IPE 8.7

level

• This is a convenient term for a major dimension of the structural organisation of language which can be studied in its own terms. Linguists talk of the 'grammatical level', the 'semantic level', the 'phonological level', and so on. It's handy because it enables people to focus their discussion: 'At the level of grammar, such-and-such happens,' they can say. Another term with a similar application is **component**.

CEL 13

lexeme (KS 4)

• An alternative term is **lexical item**. Lexemes (or lexical items) are the basic units of meaning in a language. Dictionaries list them. There's no harm, of course, in following the long-established tradition, and continuing to say 'look the word up in a dictionary', as long as students realise that what they're really doing is looking up a lexeme. Most of the time, you can carry on talking about 'words', and there'll be no ambiguity. But **lexeme** is a handy term to have available when students need to talk about such matters as variant forms (the *go* problem) and idioms. An idiom is a lexeme, because regardless of the number of words it contains it acts as a single meaning, as in the case of *kick the bucket* (which incidentally derives from old pig-slaughtering practices, when pigs were hung from beams).

• Other examples of variant forms: plurals (*boy* and *boys* are the same lexeme), comparison (*big*, *bigger*, and *biggest* are the same lexeme), possession (*girl* and *girl's* are the same lexeme). Other examples of idioms: see the entry on **idiom**.

CEL 17

lexical word (KS 3) see **grammatical word**

lexicography (KS 4) see **lexicology**

lexicology (KS 4)

• A fascinating exercise (to my mind, anyway) is to research these famous lexicographers. A good source-book is K M Elisabeth Murray, *Caught in the*

Web of Words: James Murray and the Oxford English Dictionary (OUP, 1979).

• An interesting area for lexicological study is the way we talk about family names – *cousin, aunt, grandfather*, and so on. Notice what English does and doesn't do – for instance, it has no single words for 'male cousin' and 'female cousin' (French simply changes the gender), and we aren't able to distinguish in single words between relatives on the mother's side and relatives on the father's side (unlike many other languages) – *uncle* could mean either your mother's or your father's brother. Also, note the way in which we use these terms for non-relatives: a close friend of the family might be called *uncle*, an old lady in the street might be called *granny*. Some areas of kinship can remain permanently obscure, even for adults: how many people know what 'once removed' means, for example? (Your *second cousin* is the child of the first cousin of one of your parents. He or she is the same generation as you. A *first cousin once removed* is the child of your own first cousin. He or she is a generation later than you. *Once removed* means 'removed by one generation'.) Students will also find the distinction between *half-* and *step-* relations unclear. It will be helpful to draw a kinship diagram (a theoretical family tree) with 'YOU' in the middle.

• Other interesting areas are: the distinction between types of drinking implements (*cup, glass, mug* . . . – must cups have a handle? if so, what about a paper cup?) or types of chair (*chair, stool, sofa, armchair* . . . – must an armchair have arms? must a chair have four legs?) or types of colour (get hold of a paint chart, to see the extent of the problem, and look out for unusual usages, such as in snooker, where *red* is not a colour).

• Resources you should have available for lexicological study include general dictionaries of various sizes, some specialised dictionaries (eg of idioms, biography, science and technology), a thesaurus, a concordance, and a single-volume encyclopedia. Major dictionary firms include Chambers, Collins, Longman, Oxford. Also note the existence of various hybrid materials, such as the *Longman Lexicon of Contemporary English* (1981), which is a cross between a dictionary and a thesaurus.

CEL 17–18

lexicon (KS 3) see **vocabulary**

limerick (KS 3)

• There are several collections of limericks. The most famous practitioner was Edward Lear, the father of them all (see his *Book of Nonsense*, 1846).

• Note the ones which vary the form to make a special effect. Gyles Brandreth gives several examples in his very funny *The Joy of Lex* (Robson Books, 1987) – which is, incidentally, full of excellent material for language classes. Here's a nice example which plays on spelling: 'A girl who weighed many an oz/ Used language I dare not pronoz/ For a fellow unkind/ Pulled her chair out behind/ Just to see (so he said) if she'd boz.'

lingua franca (KS 4)

- The discussion can be an interesting one. You might touch on various points:

– English isn't the language with the largest number of mother-tongue speakers (that's Chinese), but it is the most widely dispersed language. There are only about 350 million mother-tongue speakers of English, but at least that number again use English as a second language, and an uncertain number more use it as a foreign language. It would be surprising if the total number of people who know English to a reasonably fluent level didn't well exceed a thousand million.
– Distinguish the desirability of a world language and the question of which language it should be. English is in its present position because of the world dominance of the United States. If the economic balance of power were to shift, another language might become more prestigious. This shift has already taken place twice in the history of Europe, as first Latin and then French became the language of education and culture. Might it happen again?
– A world language would be a useful instrument of international communication, at all levels – diplomacy, research, trade, and so on. English is already widely used in this capacity, but there are still many parts of the world where little English is spoken.
– There is a natural reluctance on the part of speakers of other languages to give pre-eminence to English. It will be essential for them to devote a great deal of educational time to learning the language. It places at a considerable disadvantage researchers and diplomats who do not have the language as a mother tongue, and who find it difficult to 'think' in the language.
– For some, English is the language of real or imagined imperialism (formerly British, now American). Some object to the way English is affecting minority languages – such as in the Celtic-speaking areas. There is anti-English feeling in Wales, Jamaica, India, and several other places.
– As English spreads around the world, it is taking on regionally distinct features. Might these become so great that the dialects would become mutually unintelligible (as happened to the Romance languages), or will the contacts between countries fostered by radio, TV, fax, the telephone, and the press, along with the greater mobility of people, produce a levelling and a genuine international standard?

EL 14; CEL 59

linguistics (KS 4)

- As with the entry on **language**, there's little point in trying to cover our entire field in a short entry. It's important to appreciate, though, that linguistics is a subject of *general* application – by which I mean that it deals with all languages, not just English. When linguists try to work out rules of grammar, pronunciation, and so on, their interest is in finding ways in which these rules are applicable to the properties of English, French, Chinese, Swahili, and all the other 5000 or so languages in the world. That's why linguistic theories, and the models which they generate, can look so complex and abstract – they are trying to make universal statements about language. While the underlying philosophy of this book, and many of the terms, come from the field of linguistics, therefore, the true power of the subject can't be appreciated through the study of a single language, such as English. The more difficult notions especially (such as phoneme, existential sentence, transformation, and all the phonetics terms), come into their own when we compare and contrast languages. If you find yourself in a setting where English and Modern Languages are trying to work together, the value of a shared language for talking about language (see the entry on **metalanguage**) will be apparent; and the source of this language will largely be found within linguistics.

CEL 65

linking sound (KS 4)

- The linking of sounds is often referred to as **liaison**. The use of [r] is the chief liaison feature in English; other examples include the insertion of a vowel in such words as *umb(e)rella*, and of a plosive consonant in such words as *some(p)thing*.

- Where does the intrusive *r* come from? It's the result of speakers extending a pattern already present in their accent (the 'linking' pattern). Although there are thousands of words in English which end with an *r*, only four kinds of vowel are involved: the [ɔ:] of *four*, the [ɑ:] of *car*, the [ɜ:] of *sir* and the [ə] of *brother*. Over the years the linking *r* has been extended to all words ending in these four vowels, when they're followed by another vowel, whether there's an *r* in the spelling or not. The effect is most noticeable on the more open vowels (see the entry on **close vowel**), and especially on those ending in [ɔ:], as in *law and order*, because there aren't many words ending in this sound in the language, so the usage stands out. Intrusive *r* is particularly disliked when it occurs within a word – such as when *drawing* is said *drawring*. Note that the use of linking features is much less noticeable in those accents where *r* is pronounced – that is, the majority of British English accents.

- The existence of 'Laura Norder' is often a source of complaint by listeners to the BBC. Some radio presenters are so worried by it that they mark their script to draw their attention to the need to take care. It is unclear why this particular feature of pronunciation should have attracted so much dislike by native speakers. It seems to show the awe in which people stand of the written language.

EL 4; IPE 11.3.7; EPP 14.4

lipogram (KS 4)

• This word-game is ancient: examples can be found in Greek from the sixth century BC. The Latin author Fulgentius wrote a work of 23 chapters, each chapter omitting one letter of the Latin alphabet.

• There is a game called *taboo*, in which answers to questions must not contain a particular letter. An extension is to answer questions without using a particular word (such as *yes* or *no*), as in the TV game *Take Your Pick*, which was popular in the 1950s. Further examples, including several cases of **univocalics**, much more difficult to devise, are given in Tony Augarde's *The Oxford Guide to Word Games* (OUP, 1984), Chapter 13. He cites a sentence from Lord Holland in 1824, which reads: 'Men were never perfect, yet the three brethren Veres were ever esteemed, respected, revered, even when the rest, whether the select few, whether the mere herd, were left neglected.'

CEL 11

literal (KS 3)

• The examples in the entry are chiefly of exaggeration (see **hyperbole**). They should be supplemented by a range of figurative examples, and the entry related to those on **figure of speech** and **metaphor**, in particular.

• In literary contexts, this notion is usually contrasted with such notions as *metaphorical*, *symbolic*, and *allegorical*. Note also the concept of a 'literal translation', in which the words of one language are translated as closely as possible into words of the other.

literate (KS 3)

• This is an entry which can generate a lot of useful discussion. There are now many literacy movements and institutions, such as the National Adult Literacy Documentation Service at the University of Reading, investigating the problem of illiteracy, at national and international levels, and it is possible to obtain a great deal of useful information from them.

• Students should be prepared to undertake some research into the statistics of the problem. In 1950, UNESCO estimated a world illiteracy total of 44.3 per cent. In the late 1980s, estimates suggested that around a thousand million people were illiterate. It is by no means just a third-world problem. Estimates in the UK range from 3 per cent to 5 per cent. In the USA the estimates vary between 10 per cent and 20 per cent.

• Discuss the reasons for the variation in estimates – in particular, the difficulty of defining the notion of 'illiterate' in the first place. All kinds of 'middle of the road' notions are used, such as 'semi-literate', 'functionally illiterate', and 'basically illiterate'.

- It is now much more difficult for people to achieve an acceptable standard of literacy, as more demands are being made on them in such fields as business, the media, and the law. An interesting exercise is to do a survey of the demands of literacy in the student's home area. The idea is to keep notes on the contexts where written language is to be found – road signs, bottle labels, shop signs, street signs, and so on. In relation to a job, there may be safety regulations, time-sheets, explanatory pamphlets, insurance forms, income-tax forms, and much more. Note especially the dangerous contexts, such as medicine labels, cooking/defrosting instructions, health hazard warnings, etc.

- Note that literacy is a composite notion, involving at least five factors: the difficulty of the text to be read, the range of contexts in which texts appear, the need to write (or type) with fluency, the need to write in response to a wide range of demands, and the need to spell correctly. There is a continuum of ability in each of these areas. Literacy isn't an 'all-or-nothing' skill.

ET 8

litotes (KS 4)

- An interesting area to trawl for litotes is the critical review and the obituary: the writer has to draw a fine line between overstatement and understatement.

- This figure of speech is not uncommon (that's another instance of it, incidentally) in literature, though it is not as frequently used as hyperbole. An example is *He was a man* (Hamlet, about his father, I.2). More often, it is used in disparagement, or in the expression of pessimism or cynicism. (Hyperbole, by contrast, is language used in the context of eulogy, optimism, and idealism.)

LG 10

loan word (KS 3) see **borrowing**

logogram (KS 3)

- There are several other examples in mathematical symbols (square root, infinity, and so on), the sign for 'degree', and the symbols for male and female in biology. A logographic survey would be interesting, and would gain a lot of its material from the sciences. Note that not all scientific symbols are logograms (some are ideograms): the crucial point is that the symbol must clearly be speakable as a word.

- Chinese characters comprise a logographic writing system. In origin they may have been ideographic (see the entry on **ideogram**), but the symbols have changed so much over the centuries that the pictorial identity is now no longer there.

CEL 33

lower-case letter (KS 3) see **upper case**

low vowel (KS 4) see **close vowel**

main verb see **auxiliary verb**

major sentence and minor sentence (KS 4)

• I find this distinction a very useful one, as it puts all the irregular types of sentence construction under one general heading, distinguishing them from the regular kinds of structure encountered in statements, questions, commands, exclamatory and echo sentences. Major sentences are often said to be grammatically **productive** – meaning that their structural pattern can generate an indefinite number of real sentences. Once you have learned a Subject-Verb-Object structure, for example, along with the various phrase patterns and word endings available in English, and assuming you have some vocabulary, then you have command of a virtually infinite supply of sentences (*The dog saw a cat*, *A cat chased a dog*, *A man saw a horse* . . .). This is a highly productive pattern, therefore. On the other hand, minor sentences, although quite frequent, lack this productivity. The commonest examples are the greetings and reaction signals in conversation: *good morning*, *hi*, *hello*, *cheers*, *cheerio*, *bye-bye*, *good night*, *yes*, *yeah*, *mhm*, *OK*, *sure*, *right*, *quite*, *no*, *nope*, etc. See other examples under **block language** and **formula**.

• Having said this, it has to be recognised that some minor sentences do have a degree of productivity, but this is extremely limited. For example, there are several aphoristic patterns of the type *The more the merrier*, *The sooner the better*. Also, certain greetings can be extended: *Happy X* is usually found with reference to Christmas, Birthday, and Anniversary, but it could be used for feasts (*Happy St David's Day*) and other celebrations, albeit often with jocular intent (*Happy Examination Day*).

• Not all irregular sentences are minor sentences. For example, many elliptical sentences are unusual, in that they omit an element of structure normally present (*Sorry about that*), but because these patterns are clearly relatable to 'full' major sentence structure, they are best grouped along with major sentences. The Quirk grammars give a good list of all these types.

RG 2; SGE 11.21–2; CGEL 11.38–55

malapropism (KS 4)

• The name *Malaprop* itself comes from French, *mal à propos* 'inappropriately'. Note that the phenomenon is much older than the late eighteenth century: in *Much Ado About Nothing*, Dogberry makes similar errors, as does Mrs Slipslop in Fielding's *Joseph Andrews*. Emphasise to students that a malapropism must be similar in sound to the target word. They should also look at the entry on **spoonerism**.

• Distinguish malapropisms from the more general notion of slips of the tongue. A slip of the tongue may be simply a sound change, as when *reading list* becomes *leading list* or *bacon and eggs* becomes *acon and beggs*. Students could keep a note of tongue slips, as they occur, or listen out for them in a tape recording, and then try to classify them. Is the slip on a consonant or a vowel? at the beginning or end of a word? Which sound is anticipated? Are sounds added or deleted? Are words blended (eg *dreeze* for *draft* and *breeze*)?

CEL 45

masculine (KS 3) see **gender**

mass noun (KS 4) see **count noun**

metalanguage (KS 4)

• Terms for talking about language are in fact used from very early on in the course of language development. Parents use words like *noise*, *cry*, and *shout* in talking to their babies (*What's that noise all about?*). Words like *talk*, *voice*, and *loud* (and many other words for describing qualities of sound) come well before school, as do all kinds of words to do with reading (*book*, *page*, *picture*, *line*, *big letter*, and the names of the letters of the alphabet). Many parents even use basic grammatical terms, such as *word* and *sentence*. On arriving in school, words for talking about language rapidly increase in number, as the National Curriculum documents indicate. But primary school teachers mustn't underestimate the extent to which many children have previously assimilated a great deal of informal metalanguage.

• How many technical terms are there? There are 445 in my two books. This is quite small, really, if you were to compare the corresponding treatment of some subjects, such as physics, chemistry, or biology. Unlike these subjects, though, linguistic terms have traditionally been introduced 'back-to-front', and as a result the subject has been criticised as dry, boring, and meaningless. Many people remember their school grammar days with horror. It's because children were taught the terms of grammar without it being made clear what the point of the exercise was. They had to learn

terms and definitions off by heart, sometimes in lists. I remember doing this myself – adverbs of condition, adverbs of concession . . . I don't recall ever being given the chance to find out how these terms related to the real world. By contrast, botanists don't teach the terminology of plant description without *first* getting students to observe the plants carefully. It should be the same with language. Observations about and reactions to language in use provide the motivation for using linguistic metalanguage.

CEL 1, 65

metaphor (KS 3)

• The study of metaphor is so central and familiar a notion in literary analysis that it would be otiose for me to say much more here. It is worth noting, though, that the extent to which metaphors pervade our everyday speech has been a particular focus of study by linguists in recent years. Metaphor shouldn't be thought of as a purely literary phenomenon. It is remarkable, for instance, how the metaphor of conflict underlies so much of what we say: in an argument, for instance, we talk about people winning, being defeated, attacking, counter-attacking, and so on. Many everyday idioms involve metaphors (*Rise and shine*, *It's your funeral*). Metaphors from computers are everywhere (*hardware*, *input*, *interface* . . .). Some areas rely totally on metaphor – any discussion of wine, for instance (*charming*, *warm*, *fruity*, *graceful*, *majestic* . . .). Some semantic fields are a particularly fruitful source of metaphor: the human body has been the highest source of metaphorical expressions for over 300 years.

• Note that, to be a metaphor, there must be a balance between similarity and difference. The items involved must not be too similar. We cannot say *Bread is butter*, for example, without risking the charge of unintelligibility. Nor must they be too different, sharing nothing in common. We cannot say *His ears were sunshine*, again without risking unintelligibility. Metaphors need to be somewhere in the middle, suggestive of certain common properties. Students should get into the habit of looking at metaphors critically, and not taking them as 'given' (as they often are, in a work of literature). If someone says *The bread ski-jumped out of his mouth*, is that first of all an intelligible metaphor, and then, is it an appropriate one, and then, is it effective, dramatic, 'good'?

• Incidentally, you might point out that the term is from Greek, meaning 'carrying from one place to another'. An interesting follow-up is when the speaker tries to carry two ideas at once, which turn out to be incompatible (mixed metaphors). I heard once: *This is a virgin field, pregnant with possibilities*. We all run the risk of being unintentionally incongruous in this way, both in speech and writing.

LG 9

metonymy (KS 4)

• Other examples include *the press* (= journalists), *Beethoven* (= Beethoven's music), *the bottle* (= alcohol). You can very often insert some extra words to show what is going on: *the ladies and gentlemen of the press, the works of Beethoven, the magistrates' bench*. You might even describe it as a kind of semantic ellipsis (see **ellipsis**). (Metaphor is different, in this respect.) When the part is substituted for the whole, the phenomenon is called **synecdoche** [si'nekdəki], in traditional rhetoric.

• The entry doesn't give any literary examples, and indeed, metonymy is often overlooked in literature, critics' attention being taken up by the phenomenon of **metaphor**. *Peace, ye fat-guts!* says the Prince to Falstaff (*Henry the Fourth, Part One*, II.2), and again, later, *Call in ribs, call in tallow* (II.4).

LG 9.1.3

metre (KS 3)

• The quotation sources are: W H Auden, 'Night Mail'; G K Chesterton, 'Me Heart'; Thomas Gray, 'Elegy written in a Country Churchyard'; Robert Browning, 'A Toccata of Galuppi's'; T S Eliot, 'Love Song of J Alfred Prufrock'. Much simpler examples of very regular and definite metres occur in limericks and nursery rhymes.

• The *meter* spelling is standard in American English. The study of metre is known as **metrics**.

• The entry on **foot** should be related to this one. Note that, while metrical analysis is restricted to poetry, it is possible to find sentences produced with a metrical rhythm from time to time in everyday speech too. A very irritable rendition of *I really think you ought to sell the car* could be extremely rhythmical, with sharp stresses on *really*, *think*, *ought*, *sell*, and *car*.

LG 7

mid vowel (KS 4) see **close vowel**

minimal pair (KS 4)

• There's never any difficulty finding a minimal pair for the most frequent sounds, but the less frequent ones can cause trouble. Find a contrast with the [ʒ] consonant, for example: *leisure* vs *ledger*; *beige* vs *bait*; *Confucian* vs *confusion*.

• Note that to be a phoneme a sound doesn't have to contrast with *every* other sound in the language – only with some of them. It can be interesting working out what the possibilities are, for a small area of the language. For example, choose monosyllabic words, and consonants in initial position. Now introduce a syllable ending, say *-at* or *-im*, and go through all the consonants to see which words are possible (*pat*, *bat*, *tat*, *dat*, *kat*, *gat*, *fat* . . .). Check the list out before you introduce it to a class, otherwise you may inadvertently include some risqué words which you would prefer to avoid. Point out that the words which don't exist are just as interesting, as they indicate the *possible* words in the language. There may not yet be a word *fim*, for instance, but there could be.

IPE 5.3

minor sentence (KS 4) see **major sentence**

modal verb (KS 4) see **mood**

modify (KS 4)

• The example gives premodification and postmodification of nouns. In the verb phrase, English has only premodification: *She goes*, *She is going*, *She may not have been going* . . . Some grammarians allow adverbs to be seen as a kind of postmodification (*She went quickly*), but I don't find that an attractive idea. Adverbs are too mobile to be seen as postmodifying a verb: they can be used well away from the verb, and even before the verb (*She quickly went down the steps*).

• Get the students to look at a particular area of modification in some detail, to see how intricate it can be. What do adjectives usually do, for instance? They premodify nouns (*the old house*), but they can sometimes postmodify, especially in dramatic narrative (*The house, old, ruined, stood on the hill*). There are also several postmodifications in fixed expressions, such as *president elect, court martial*, and *body politic*. Among the interesting cases of postmodification are: *the person opposite, you included, Monday to Thursday inclusive, B flat/minor*. Note also *the best possible use / the best use possible, in past years / in years past, positive proof / proof positive*, and several other cases where alternative positions are possible (often with a slight difference of style).

• What do adverbs usually do? Some appear before a noun (*inside information, outside door, away game, then chairman*); some occur afterwards (*the way ahead, the day before, the way back*). Some adverbs can appear in both positions (*the downstairs room / the room downstairs*). Note that we can say both *the above quotation* and *the quotation above*, but we can only say *the quotation below* (never **the below quotation*). Of such points of detail is English grammar made!

RG 39–40; SGE 7.7–9, 32–7; CGEL 2.31, 7.20–2, 56–69

monolingual (KS 3) see **bilingual**

monologue (KS 3) see **dialogue**

mood (KS 4)

• The term **mood** is traditionally restricted to types of clause, and specifically to types of verb. However, English isn't a language which marks changes of mood in a very explicit grammatical way (unlike Latin and Greek, where moods were shown by different sets of inflections). As a result, more attention has been paid to the meanings conveyed in this area of grammar. The terms **modal** and **modality** have a much broader range of application, including all words which affect the way the truth value of a sentence can be determined. Modal adverbials, for example, can emphasise the truth value of a sentence (*certainly, indeed*) or diminish it in some way (*probably, hardly, as he claims*). Modal verbs express two kinds of meaning: notions of permission, obligation, and volition, which involve the idea of human control over events; and notions of possibility, necessity, and prediction, which don't involve human control over events, but which do involve a judgment of what is or isn't likely to happen. Notice that the modal verbs combine these meanings – *may*, for example, can mean permission (*You may sit down*) or possibility (*I may resign*).

• There aren't many modal verbs (see the entry on **auxiliary verb**), but there are many modal adverbial words, phrases, and clauses. Use a thesaurus to collect examples of modal adverbials, or look up a classification in a reference grammar (such as in CGEL 8.99–103).

RG 21, 26, 54; SGE 4.21–34, 8.36; CGEL 4.49, 8.8, 99–103

morpheme (KS 4) see **morphology**

morphology (KS 4)

- The basic idea of the **morpheme** is very simple, but of course complications arise when you try to apply it to every single word in the language. Discussion of the problem cases is probably best left to a later stage of language study. Examples include the problem of how to analyse irregular nouns and verbs. In the case of *boys*, the division into two morphemes is clear: *boy* + *s*. But in the case of *geese*, it's no longer clear where the noun ends and the plural begins. The same problem arises when we try to disentangle the verb and its past tense element in such verbs as *took* and *swam* (no problem with *jumped* and *walked*, of course, where the past tense morpheme is signalled by the *-ed*).
- I haven't introduced the following notion in the entry either, but just for the record: the term **allomorph** (also mentioned under **allo-** in the present book) is available to talk about variant forms of a morpheme. For example, the past tense morpheme has three forms, depending on the sound with which a regular verb ends: after a base form ending in [t] or [d], the ending is [ɪd] (*patted*); after all other voiced sounds (including vowels), the ending is [d] (*called*, *towed*); and after all other voiceless sounds, the ending is [t] (*packed*).

CEL 16

motherese (KS 3)

- The term **fatherese** is used as well, and there are indeed certain differences between the way fathers and mothers talk to their children – fathers, for example, often adopt a more boisterous style. I've also come across the term **parentese** used in this kind of way; but **motherese** was the first term to become widely recognised by students of child language, and it has tended to stick.
- See the entry on **baby talk** for further discussion and references.

mother tongue (KS 3) see **first language**

multilingual (KS 3) see **bilingual**

multi-word verb (KS 4)

• Technically the commonest type of multi-word verb is a verb followed by one or more **particles**. There are hundreds of these verbs in the language. You'll even find dictionaries exclusively devoted to them. The particles include many prepositions (eg *at*, *for*, *from*, *of*, *with*) and adverbs (eg *ahead*, *apart*, *away*, *forwards*, *together*). The lexical verbs are often some of the commonest verbs in the language (eg *make*, *put*, *come*, *get*, *go*). Other types of multi-word verb are illustrated by the idioms *take pride in*, *cut short*, *catch sight of*, *pay attention to*. Notice that there are a few words which only appear as a verb in a multi-word verb, never on their own: we can say *He beavers away*, but not **He beavers* (except in fun), *I eked out the sugar*, but not **I eked it*.

• The syntax of these verbs is quite intricate, and should be left until a later stage. But note the kind of thing which can happen. What's the difference between *Turn on the light* and *Look at the pictures*? You can say *Turn the light on* but not **Look the pictures at*. *I've just flown in a plane* is ambiguous, depending on whether it's said by the pilot or by a passenger. If the former, he could say *I've just flown the plane in*. The passenger can't say that, though. On the basis of differences like these, some grammars set up classifications of types of multi-word verb.

• Don't get bogged down in these verbs. You can have fun with them, too: *Jim's not up yet* means the same as *Jim's not down yet*. Older students will need to distinguish between *sleeping in*, *out*, *off*, *with* and *around*. If you *live it up* you may not *live it down*. If you *get on with* a girl/boy you might *get off with* her/him, unless she/he tells you where to *get off* (and I'm not talking about buses).

RG 20; SGE 16.2–10; CGEL 16.2–17

nasal (KS 4)

• When you have a nasal vowel (common in French and Portuguese), you show this in a phonetic transcription by putting a symbol above the vowel: [ã], [õ], etc. You can also have voiceless nasal sounds – you'll hear one immediately after the [s] of such words as *smile* and *snooze*.

• When you have a cold, the passage to your nose becomes blocked, and the speech loses its nasal resonance. This is technically called **denasalised** or **hyponasal** speech. There is also **hypernasal** speech – excessive nasality – but this is usually heard only in certain kinds of speech handicap (such as in cleft palate speech).

IPE 8.6; EPP 7.1

negative, negation (KS 3)

• Distinguish 'true' double negatives, which are acceptable in standard English: *I was not unhappy; I didn't say I wouldn't do it; I can't not go.*

• Be prepared for regional variation in the use of *not*, as in Scots *He's nae coming*. Also, there are colloquial variants, such as *I'm no way doing that*. (This is why I say that negative sentences 'usually' have the word *not* inside them.)

• There are also some adverbs with a strongly negative meaning, such as *barely* and *hardly*, which forbid the use of *not*, and which therefore could be seen as alternative kinds of negation. For example, we say *Hardly had he arrived when . . .* and not **Hardly hadn't he arrived* when . . . (though in non-standard English, a double negative form is sometimes used: *We hadn't hardly got there when . . .*).

SGE 10.33–41; CGEL 10.54–70

neologism or coinage (KS 3)

• There are excellent source materials for the study of new words, such as John Ayto's *The Longman Register of New Words* (1989). Here are a few of the words from the beginning of the alphabet which seemed to be coming into the language in the late eighties: *acid house*, *-aholic* (as in *clothesaholic*, *creamaholic*, *milkaholic*, *chocaholic*), *airmiss*, *antenuptial*, *babynap* (like *kidnap*, but for babies), *ballpark*, *bimbo*. As the entry says, there's no way of knowing whether any of these will be successful and stay in the language.

Areas where neologisms will be found include slogans, acronyms, names of new commercial products, newspaper headlines and subheadings (especially of the jokey kind).

• Students might practise coining new words. Some suggestions are made in the entry on **affix** in this book. Or, think of something which doesn't have a name, and name it. Here are some examples from a recent radio competition, sent in by Neil McNicholas: *aquadrags* (the totally useless pockets in swimming trunks), *bagonise* (to wait anxiously for your suitcase to appear on a baggage claim carousel), *brewtal* (the condition of a used tea bag), *circumtreeviation* (the tendency of a dog on a leash to want to walk past poles and trees on the opposite side to its owner), *potspot* (that part of a toilet seat which causes the phone to ring the moment you sit on it) and *hicgap* (the time that elapses between when hiccups go away and when you suddenly realise it's happened). Some students will be very good at this. Others will be hopeless.

• Distinguish between a neologism (which becomes part of the standard language) and a **nonce** usage (which doesn't). A nonce word (from Elizabethan English, 'for the once') is a word cooked up to solve a particular communication problem. The word won't enter the language, nor is there any expectation that it should. Last week I described a table as rather *coffin-like*. A man arriving at a party said he was *wettish*. It's easy to see what these words mean, but they won't be in any dictionary.

CEL 54

neuter (KS 3) see **gender**

new (KS 4) see **given**

nominative see **accusative**

nonce word see **neologism**

non-count noun (KS 4) see **count noun**

nondefining (KS 4) see **restrictive**

nonfinite (KS 4) see **finite**

n

nonrestrictive (KS 4) see **restrictive**

non-standard English (KS 3) see **standard English**

nonverbal communication (KS 3) see **communication**

noun (KS 3)

• The entry discusses the types of noun there are, but not how you recognise a noun in the first place. In many cases, a word is clearly marked as a noun by the suffix it uses: *-age* (*mileage*), *-ation* (*exploitation*), *-dom* (*kingdom*), *-hood* (*boyhood*), etc. (Appendix III of CGEL gives a complete list of all the possibilities.) A noun is also a word which can change from singular to plural (*cat, cats*) or add a case ending (*cat, cat's*). A noun is a word which can be immediately preceded by the definite or indefinite article (*a cat, the dog*). And a noun is a word which can be the head of a noun phrase acting as subject or object of a clause (*the cat saw the dog*). There are a few other criteria, too, but these are the important ones. Many nouns satisfy all these criteria, but several satisfy only some of them. *Happiness*, for example, has a clear suffix, it can take *the* (but not *a*), and it can be subject or object, but it can't be pluralised. *Cat* satisfies all the criteria except the first (it has no suffix).

• Another major area which the entry doesn't touch upon is the many types of irregular noun plural – always a large section of any grammar, and much hated by foreign students of English. The other entries on types of noun follow up this point, to some extent (and see especially the entry on **number**).

RG 28–34; SGE 5.1, 25–55; CGEL 5.1–9, 5.60–126

noun phrase (KS 3)

• The entry doesn't deal with some interesting types of exception – words other than nouns which can also be the head of a noun phrase. Adjectives are the main category. When an adjective is a head, though, it does not inflect for number or case, and it usually requires a definite determiner (such as *the, those*). The adjectives involved usually express a generic meaning (*the poor, the young, those present*), nationality (*the English, the French*), or an abstract meaning (*the unknown, the ridiculous* – often appearing as a superlative, such as *the latest, the best*).

• The full structure of the noun phrase is quite complex, as the final example in the entry shows. There, the head was preceded by a determiner (*the*), an adjective (*green*) and several predeterminers (*not quite all of*), and there was a postmodifying clause, itself quite complex (*which was left at the bottom of the test tube*). The disentangling of noun phrases of this kind is best left for a much later stage of language study. I've found that any obnoxious tendency towards linguistic precocity can be cured in most students by dropping them into CGEL, Chapter 17. (The survivors become teachers of linguistics.)

RG 27; SGE 7.10–13; CGEL 7.23–6

number (KS 3)

• In discussing irregular nouns, make a clear distinction between those nouns which have both a singular and a plural form (where the latter is irregular) and those which have only a singular or a plural form. Under the former heading, there are several types (I give the plural only):
- the final sound is voiced, and an *-s* is added: *leaves, loaves, thieves, wolves, houses* (note there is some usage variation here, with *dwarfs/dwarves*, and a few others);
- the internal vowel alters (what is technically called **mutation**): *geese, women, teeth;*
- there is an *-en* ending: *brethren, children, oxen* (only three cases);
- there is no ending: *sheep, deer, salmon, bison, Chinese, Portuguese, gross, p* (as in *30p*);
- there is a foreign ending (usually deriving from Latin or Greek): *algae, stimuli, curricula, bacteria, indices, bases, analyses, criteria* (several usage problems here, too, especially with *data* and *criteria*).

• Nouns which appear only as singular *or* as plural are the following:
- singular nouns which don't have a plural: proper nouns, *news, classics, physics, measles, mumps;*
- plural nouns ending in *-s* which don't have a singular: *binoculars, shears, jeans, tights, trousers, trunks, amends, lodgings, outskirts;*
- plural nouns not ending in *-s* which don't have a singular (not so many): *people, police, cattle, poultry, vermin.*

RG 31–2; SGE 5.35–44; CGEL 5.73–103

object (KS 3)

• It's important that students realise that not everything which can follow a verb is an object. After a verb like *go*, for instance, there may be an adverb (*I'm going now*). It's a common mistake to call *now* an object. Students who do this haven't picked up the point about the 'thing most affected by the action of the verb'. The object has to be a noun or noun-like word.

• The other main error is to fail to see the difference between an object and a complement: see the entry on **complement** for more on this. Everything depends on the type of verb. When a noun phrase is an object, it doesn't have the same or similar meaning as the subject. When a noun phrase is a complement, it does. So, in *John saw a pig, the pig* is object. In *John is a pig, the pig* is complement. Note some tricky ones: in *I turned the page, the page* is object. In *I turned green,* the adjective *green* is complement (I *was* green).

• Wait for the basic notion of **object** to sink in before telling students that some clauses can have two objects (see **direct object**).

RG 10; SGE 10.15–18; CGEL 10.7

objective case (KS 3) see **case**

onomatopoeia (KS 4) see **sound symbolism**

open vowel (KS 4) see **close vowel**

operator see **auxiliary verb**

oracy (KS 4)

• A useful discussion can come from considering how exactly to monitor and assess oracy. Don't leave the problem to the examining boards. Get the students worrying about it too. Among the factors which have to be considered are:

- the type of activity (spontaneous speech vs reading aloud, awareness of the speech situation – formal, informal, etc);
- the activities involved in listening, such as comprehension and reaction (letting the speaker know one is listening);
- phonetic factors, such as general audibility, and clear and lively voice quality;
- phonological factors, such as the clarity of articulation, appropriate intonational range, and the use of pause and timing;
- grammatical factors, such as controlled sentence structure and cohesive sequences;
- semantic factors, such as a good range of vocabulary and clear organisation;
- pragmatic factors, such as the ability to question and interrupt appropriately;
- non-linguistic factors – in particular, the quality of the ideas, the method of presentation (eg use of visual aids), physical stance, facial expression, and the level of personal enthusiasm and sincerity.

• Don't confuse oracy issues with questions of regional accent or dialect. We can be orally fluent in *any* dialect (standard English being one). Conversely, it is possible to be indistinct and confusing in *any* dialect.

CEL 44

ordinal numeral (KS 4) see **cardinal numeral**

orthography (KS 4)

- The main arguments for spelling reform are that it would save children a lot of time and effort in learning to read; it would greatly help children with special needs; foreign learners of English would benefit; people would save time while writing, as fewer letters would be used (perhaps a saving of 15 per cent); and there would be savings in typing, printing, paper, storage, transport, etc.

- The main arguments against spelling reform are that there would be a major break in continuity between old and new spellings (at least, in the more radical schemes); people who have already learned to spell have a vested interest in it, and would not want to learn a new system; the saving in costs might be outweighed by the need to reprint important works in new spelling, along with road signs, maps, etc; any phonetic principle might lead to difficulties because of divergences between regional accents; and there is no agreement among the various groups arguing for spelling reform about which proposal is optimum.

- There are several types of spelling reform proposal. Some aim simply to regularise the present system, adding no new letters; some add a few new letters to those of the regular alphabet; in a few cases, all the letters are new (as in G B Shaw's proposal).

- Don't overestimate the irregularity of English spelling. The *-ough* situation is exceptional. It's been estimated that about 75 per cent of the words in English are spelled according to a regular pattern, and only about 3 per cent are totally deviant. On the other hand, the irregular spellings include some of the most frequent words in the language, so the overall impression of irregularity is great.

- Much of the irregularity can be explained by referring to an account of the history of English, showing how and when spelling and pronunciation diverged. A good dictionary will also contain historical information about the spelling of individual words.

EL 5; CEL 34

overextension (KS 3)

- Virtually any word can be overextended. *Daddy*, for example, could be extended to all humans (eg brother, grandma), to all interesting men (eg milkman, postman), or even to all interesting objects (eg biscuit tin, dog). Not only nouns are overextended. Colour words, for example, are often treated in this way.

• How do children sort out overextension problems? Parents help a great deal, by correcting, pointing to the difference between objects, explaining a relevant distinguishing feature, and so on. These features can relate both to what the object is like (round, noisy, furry, etc) and to what it does (goes in the cupboard, lives in a kennel, etc).

CEL 42

oxymoron (KS 4)

• There are some famous literary cases, such as *parting is such sweet sorrow* (*Romeo and Juliet*), Milton's *living death* (*Samson Agonistes*), and Tennyson's *His honour rooted in dishonour stood/ And faith unfaithful kept him falsely true* ('Lancelot and Elaine').

• Unlike hyperbole/exaggeration, there isn't an everyday term to talk about the oxymorons which can be heard in daily conversation. Incidentally, teachers are usually quite good at introducing oxymorons to describe the behaviour of their charges. *Let's have some silent noise now, shall we?* A genuine example. Honest.

LG 8.3

palate (KS 4)

• Although all sounds made against the palate are 'palatal', in practice a distinction is drawn between sounds made near or at the hard palate and those made near or at the soft palate (the latter being called **velar**). [k] and [g] in English are called velar sounds, because most of their articulations are made quite far back in the mouth. However, whenever these sounds are followed by a high front vowel (such as [i]), the articulation is pulled forward in the direction of the hard palate. You might be able to feel this difference between the words *key* and *go*.

• Examples of foreign language palatals include German *ich* and the first *n* in Spanish *mañana*. There's a palatal *l* in Italian. Each of these sounds has its own phonetic symbol, of course.

• Students might like to find out about the disorder known as **cleft palate**, which will give them an insight about how the palate was formed in the foetus, and might generate some concern for the problems of children with language handicap. There will be diagrams and pictures in any introduction to speech disorders (there are some in CEL, page 277).

IPE 2.2.3

palindrome (KS 3)

• This is another ancient word game, dating from around the third century BC, which was particularly popular in Latin in seventeenth-century

England. Numerical palindromes also always attract attention. At the time of writing, the newspapers were full of the fact that 19.1.91 had occurred. There was no 29.2.92, so when will the next one be? (Let the students work it out.) Moreover, palindromes haven't attracted the interest only of academics. Students may be impressed by Black Sabbath's 1983 LP, *Live Evil*. Then there's ABBA and SOS.

● Variations include both word and sentence reversals. Word palindromes include *repaper* and *reviver* – and note OXO and NOON, which look the same upside down and in a mirror. You can also have sentence palindromes where the word, rather than the letter, is the reversing unit: *Girl, bathing on Bikini, eyeing boy, finds boy eyeing bikini on bathing girl.*

EL 7

pangram (KS 3)

● Why are pangrams so difficult in English? The answer lies in the shortage of written vowels – only five, plus *w* and *y*. There are limits to what can be done.

● A reasonably sensible perfect pangram was devised in 1984: *Veldt jynx grimps waqf zho buck.* All the words are in the unabridged *Oxford English Dictionary*: the unfamiliar words are *jynx* (bird, wryneck), *grimps* (mounts), *waqf* (land given to a religious institution), *zho* (a yak/cow hybrid). It just about makes sense.

EL 7

paradox (KS 4)

● Add some famous literary paradoxes, to fuel the discussion:

War is peace. Freedom is slavery. Ignorance is strength. (Orwell, *1984*)
The child is father of the man (Wordsworth 'My heart leaps up')
For all their wars are merry ('Ballad of the White Horse')
How sour sweet music is (*Richard II*, V. 5)

● This entry should be read alongside the entry on **oxymoron**, which can be seen as a very compressed paradox.

LG 8.3

paragraph (KS 3)

● Carry out a survey of the various ways in which paragraph divisions can be signalled. There are the conventions of spacing and indentation, as mentioned in the entry, but there are also section marks (such as §), subheadings and numerals (often quite complex systems, especially in technical writing).

• More advanced students might consider how paragraphs relate to **prosody**. For example, in a short story on the radio, can they always hear the paragraph divisions? If so, what is it which leads us to them? And are there equivalents to written paragraphs in spontaneous speech?

CGEL 19.28, App III.14

paralinguistic features see **prosody**

parallelism (KS 4)

• There are two ways of approaching this topic: we can study the structures which are used in order to ensure that two constructions are parallel; and we can study the reasons for making them parallel in the first place. Note that virtually any construction can be used in a parallel way – a sequence of phrases, clauses, sentences, or some less definable part of these units. Look out for unusual word orders, which make the listener/reader expect a parallelism: *My furniture I gave to my brother. My paintings I gave to my sister.*

• Parallelism, often of a highly extended kind, is common in literature. Here's the opening of an extended example from *Richard II*:

> I'll give my jewels for a set of beads,
> My gorgeous palace for a hermitage,
> My gay apparel for an almsman's gown . . .

And another from Whitman ('Pioneers! O Pioneers!'):

> Have you your pistols? have you your sharp-edged axes?

Many examples are to be found in Anglo-Saxon verse, and in the Old Testament. Some very famous cases approach the status of proverbs, such as Pope's *To err is human; to forgive, divine (An Essay on Criticism).*

LG 4.3; CGEL 19.7

paraphrase (KS 3)

• Paraphrase is often presented as a theoretical exercise. But there are many occasions in real life where we need to paraphrase. 'Can you tell me what he's going on about?', 'What happened in *Neighbours* last night?', 'What was the film about?', 'What's this form getting at?' Students might practise paraphrasing a text with a specific audience in mind – such as rewriting a technical presentation for a popular readership.

• Some schools of literary criticism reject the possibility of paraphrase when dealing with poems and other artistic works where the close relationship of form and content is crucial to the identity of the work.

parentheses (KS 3) see **brackets**

parenthesis (KS 4)

- The entry gives plenty of examples of the use of brackets, but only one example of dashes and commas. Avoid too close an association between this term and the term **brackets** (an association which can easily be conveyed, because of the use of the plural **parentheses** to mean 'brackets'). Stress that this entry is essentially a semantic notion, not a punctuational one.

- One way of getting away from this association is to listen out for parenthetic remarks in speech. They are extremely common, especially in informal speech settings, such as conversation and sports commentary, as thought jumps about. Often a parenthesis is introduced by a specific word which tells you what's going on, such as *incidentally* or *by the way*. In speech, the prosody can be an important signal of parenthesis. As the entry mentions, the inserted speech often becomes lower, quieter and faster. Imagine how this sentence could be said, for example: *My uncle, who by the way has been out of the country recently, has just sent me a cheque*. See the entry on **comment clause** for further examples.

RG 67; SGE 15.32; CGEL 15.53–6

parody (KS 4)

- Excellent literary parodies can be found in Max Beerbohm's *A Christmas Garland* (1912). Another useful collection is D MacDonald, *Parodies: an Anthology from Chaucer to Beerbohm and After* (1960).

- Students shouldn't restrict the notion of parody to literature, as can be seen from the first paragraph of my entry. There are several TV and radio games where the participants have to say or act something in the manner of a particular author or style (*Just a Minute, Whose Line Is It Anyway?*). Similar activities are carried on in many party games. Note that genres and varieties can be parodied as well as individuals – a judge, a sermon, a sports commentator, a TV ad.

parsing (KS 4)

- This term has bad associations for many people, who remember the grammar classes of olden days with distaste. To a modern, computer-literate generation, the term has quite the opposite feeling, for it refers there to the way in which a computer might analyse ('parse') the structure of a sentence.

- The last couple of sentences in the entry are crucial. Any analysis *must* be followed by some kind of synthesis. Even if you start off with a highly motivating real-life example, it isn't enough just to analyse the bits of the sentences it contains. The exercise must be followed by an attempt to show how the analysis has helped. The 'help' might take various forms. An aspect of the meaning of a sentence may have been clarified. A previously unnoticed aspect of meaning might have been identified. Perhaps no new meanings have been encountered, but at least everyone now feels better able to talk about what is going on in the sentence. Or maybe an aspect of the author's style has been illuminated. None of this will happen, of course, if students are so bogged down in terminology that they have no energy left to interpret the analysis in relation to the language. A good example of the way in which a parsing-type analysis *can* be illuminating, and can suggest fresh ideas about the way a text is organised (in this case, about character and plot) is the Charles Dickens example cited in the notes on **direct speech**.

CEL 16

participle (KS 4)

• Participles were always one of the most boring areas of traditional English grammar, because of the way early grammarians tried to force the sophisticated Latin participial system onto English. The proliferation of terms – such as **gerund** (a noun derived from a verb) and **gerundive** (an adjective derived from a verb) – led to not a little mystification for generations of students. Modern terminology tends to be more descriptive in character (using such terms as **-ing form**), but the fact that **participle** has been around for over 2000 years gives it a certain appeal. Familiarity breeds content.

• Look out for interesting uses of the participle. Note how, in some cases, there can be a change in meaning as usage changes from verb to adjective: *James is calculating the results* vs *James is (very) calculating*. Some verbs have different participial forms for verbal and adjectival use: *He has shaved* and *He is clean shaven* or *Your pyjamas have shrunk* vs *You have shrunken pyjamas*. Some *-ed* participles change their meaning when they move from before a noun to after a noun: *the concerned people* vs *the people concerned*, *the involved questions* vs *the questions involved*.

RG 16; SGE 3.2, 7.5–6, 17.30–3; CGEL 3.2–3, 7.15–19, 17.98–103

particle (KS 4) see **multi-word verb**

partitive (KS 4) see **quantifier**

parts of speech (KS 3)

• Notice that I say 'the main parts of speech'. There were eight of these recognised in traditional English grammar (sometimes nine, if the article was allowed in), but it isn't difficult to extend the number. Remember, a part of speech is no more than a group of words which behave in the same kind of grammatical way. So, all the auxiliary verbs could be recognised as a part of speech, if you felt it was useful to do so. So could all the determiners, all the numerals, all the proper nouns, and so on. Transitive verbs could be considered as one part of speech and intransitive verbs as another. Some dictionaries do in fact label these two types of verb differently. These subdivisions are sometimes called **secondary** word classes. But it's unusual to go much beyond the basic eight or nine, which have been used in this way to talk about grammar for over 2000 years.

• Beware the **adverb**. It's an extremely heterogeneous part of speech. It subsumes words ending in *-ly* which modify verbs (*quickly*, *slowly*), words not ending in *-ly* which modify verbs (*here*, *soon*), words ending in *-ly* which don't modify verbs (*actually*, *frankly*), words not ending in *-ly* which don't modify verbs (*however*, *therefore*), and several other oddities, such as the word *not* (sometimes called a 'negative adverb'). There isn't a simple way out of this mess, which has arisen because of the looseness with which traditional grammars used the term. You have to resort to circumlocution ('*However* is a sentence-connecting adverb') or devising fresh terminology ('*not* is a particle').

SGE 2.6–7; CGEL 2.41–2

passive voice (KS 4) see **voice** (in grammar)

past tense (KS 3)

- A full classification of all the irregular past tenses in English is given in CGEL 3.13–20.

- My entry doesn't talk about the meanings of the past tense, apart from the obvious one. 'Past time' is a very large notion, though, and several types of past time can be distinguished: see the entry on **perfect** for some examples. In addition, we can use the past tense to refer to other time-scales. It can refer to present time, in such sentences as *Did you want to see me?* (which is a more polite version of *Do you want to see me?*). In *I wish I had a car like yours*, the 'hypothetical' meaning is signalled by the past tense, even though the interlocutor has the car now. In indirect speech, there's a shift of tense form, as in *How did you know I was here* (not *. . . *I am here*) (see the entry on **direct speech**).

RG 23; SGE 4.5–6; CGEL 4.11–16

pen name (KS 3) see **pseudonym**

perfect (KS 4) see **aspect**

performance see **competence**

period (KS 3) see **full stop**

periphrasis (KS 3) see **circumlocution**

person (KS 3)

- The uses given in the entry are the usual ones. Look out for the unusual uses. The first person plural, in particular, can be used in several interesting ways: to refer to the speaker/writer alone (*We shall go into this shortly* . . . – the 'editorial we'); to refer to the speaker/writer and the addressee (*We can see from this example* . . . – the 'inclusive we'); to refer to a very large number of people, such as the nation as a whole (*In World War II, we were on the side of* . . .); to refer to the addressee only (*How are we today?* – beloved of the medical profession); and to refer to a third person (Teacher leaving head's study: *We are not in a good mood today*). The 'royal we' (such as Queen Victoria's *We are not amused*) is nowadays probably found only in historical fiction. Also don't forget the colloquial first person singular uses: *Lend us your car, Let's see.*

• Note the existence of regional person forms, such as the various forms of *thou* (also used in religious contexts), *youse*, *you-all*, *y'all*, *ye*.

RG 45; SGE 6.2–12; CGEL 6.15–18

personal pronoun (KS 3) see **pronoun**

personal style (KS 4) see **impersonal style**

personification (KS 3)

• The vast majority of personifications in everyday speech are feminine. The field of computers seems to be somewhat unusual, in this respect. Animals whose sex isn't obvious, but which are attracting people's interest (pets, zoo animals), are also usually called *he* or *she* (though it isn't always clear why one person calls an orang-outan, say, *he*, and another calls it *she*).

• Examples abound in literature. Here are a couple of Shakespearean examples: *That fell sergeant, death,/ Is strict in his arrest* (*Hamlet*, V.2); *Come, civil night,/ Thou sober-suited matron, all in black* (*Romeo and Juliet*, III.2). Note also the extraordinary number of things which can be personified in children's literature (especially for very young children).

CGEL 6.8; LG 9

pharynx (KS 4)

• Students will be able to see the back part of the pharynx, immediately behind the mouth, if they look in a mirror (saying *ah*, of course). The pharynx isn't much involved in the immediate articulation of speech sounds in English; but phoneticians have begun to realise that it has an important supporting role, contributing to the resonance of consonants and vowels, and plays a significant part in the production of voice quality. You can get a sense of this by observing (or feeling) how a sore throat (which in many cases is a pharyngeal problem) immediately affects the quality of speech.

EPP 2.1; IPE 2.2.3

philology

• This term has long been used (for over 200 years) for the historical study of a language, especially for the process of working out from written records what the sound system, grammar, and vocabulary of earlier states of the language must have been. Philologists also try to reconstruct the linguistic system of languages where there are no written records. The subject is often called **comparative philology**, because of the way it compares sounds, words and structures in related languages.

CEL 50

phoneme (KS 4)

• Why St Blaise? He is reputed to have miraculously cured a young boy who was choking to death. By the sixth century he was being venerated as the patron saint of sufferers from throat diseases. The Blessing of St Blaise is still practised on his feast day in some Christian churches: two consecrated candles are placed across each other, and put against the throat of the faithful, while a blessing is said by the priest.

• This entry should be read along with the one on **minimal pair**, which is the basis of the game outlined in the first paragraph of the entry.

• The Sound Warning raises quite a tricky point, which I've largely avoided in these books. My feeling is that it's difficult enough getting students to focus on sounds rather than on letters, without confusing them with the idea that there are two types of sounds, when we study language – the physical sounds of speech and the abstract units of a sound system. I've chosen to focus their attention on the physical side, and so have used square brackets almost everywhere. It's important for you to appreciate, though, that whenever I'm talking specifically about the sounds of English, I *could* have used slant brackets. I can talk about the first consonant in *pin* either by saying 'the [p] sound in *pin*' or 'the /p/ phoneme in *pin*'. Which brackets I use depends on how I'm thinking of this unit. If I'm thinking of it as a physical sound (as a voiceless bilabial plosive, to be precise), then I must use square brackets, which show that I'm thinking of it *as a sound*. On the other hand, if I'm thinking of it as a functioning unit in the English language (distinguished from /b/ by its voicing, and from /t/ by its place of articulation, and so on), then I must use slant brackets, which show that I'm thinking of it *as a contrastive unit*. (What I mustn't do is mix up these two levels of thinking. I mustn't write 'the [p] phoneme'.) If you think that the students are up to grasping this distinction, then by all means introduce it. I have to use it myself in this entry, and also in the entry on **allophone**, as these entries address the issue directly. Equally, postpone the whole phoneme/allophone question until A level or beyond.

- If you decide to stay with it, I find that, in trying to get students to grasp the distinction between a sound and a phoneme, it helps to tell them about graphs and graphemes first. The idea of an abstract unit – what is in common to all kinds of letter *A* and what makes letter *A* recognisably different from all other letters – is much easier to demonstrate when you can see what is going on.

- This whole entry is a very good example of the uncertainty which surrounds syllabus constructors, in the early 1990s, referred to in my Introduction. What is the right age and stage to teach students about phonemes? I haven't the foggiest idea. Nor have I yet met anyone who is less foggy. To eliminate the fog, teacher feedback is crucial.

EPP 5.1; IPE 5.1–3

phonetic alphabet (KS 4)

- This entry is really in two parts: the second part is under **International Phonetic Alphabet**. That's the alphabet which is most widely used for phonetic spelling. But it's important for students to appreciate, as I say in the entry, that 'there's no single magic way' of devising a phonetic alphabet. They can invent their own, if they like – and it's a worthwhile exercise to get them to do so, because they'll learn a great deal about the (ir)regularity of the English spelling and pronunciation systems in the process. More advanced students might try to devise an alphabet which would apply equally well to all the languages they are studying.

- A quick way of seeing the differences between phonetic alphabets is to look in the front of a range of dictionaries. Some dictionaries use IPA to show the pronunciation of words. Others use a specially devised system. The consonants will be largely the same, but the vowels vary greatly.

EPP 1,3,7; IPE 4–5; CEL 27

phonetics (KS 4)

- There are two sides to practical phonetics: learning to recognise the sounds (**ear training**) and learning to make them (**performance**). I'm not sure when is the best time to work on performance in a systematic way – maybe not until after KS 4 (though some students will *want* to try to make the sounds, as they hear them). But ear training is crucial, from the earliest possible moment. Don't begin with subtleties. Very general ear training exercises, such as different types of voice quality, high vs low pitch, and stressed vs unstressed syllables, will do. If that's too easy, students can listen to the number of sounds in a word, distinguishing consonants and vowels, and listening to consonant clusters. (This is fairly easy in slow speech, but becomes increasingly difficult as normal conversational speeds are produced: in *cyclists*, for example, the [t] isn't usually pronounced.) Listening to one word at a time can build up into short phrases, and ultimately into sentences. Don't go too quickly. It's the auditory memory which has to be given time to develop, as well as phonetic awareness.

• Ear training exercises involve no more than presenting a sound, or a sequence of sounds, to students to see if they can recognise them by writing them down in phonetic symbols. You'll need to present the stimulus several times, to give them a real chance to get it right. But how *do* you present a stimulus several times? If you are confident in your own phonetic ability, you just say the sounds over and over, controlling the articulation, stress, intonation, and so on. If you aren't able to do this, the only alternative is to record the stimulus on a tape recorder and play it back. However, that can be a bore, rewinding the tape just for a couple of seconds each time. The solution is to invest in a **tape repeater**. This is a device in which two tape recorders are linked together. An extract from the first machine is recorded onto a loop of tape on the second machine, which can then be played back as many times as you like. A loop of tape which lasts for five seconds or so will be enough for short utterances. The best way of getting hold of a tape repeater is to find a tame technician, parent, or someone else who likes tinkering with these things, and get them to build one. A university phonetics department would, I am sure, be pleased to advise.

CEL 27; IPE 2–3, EPP 2, 20

phonology (KS 4)

• This entry should be read in association with the one on **phoneme**. There's more to phonology than phonemes, though. For example, phonology also studies the various aspects of a language's **prosody**, such as the intonation, rhythm, and tone of voice – but you can't easily analyse those aspects of pronunciation in terms of phonemes. (Some linguists also approach the study of phonology in ways which do not make use of the phoneme concept, but that is best left for university-level discussion.)

• Phonology only really begins to come alive when you start comparing different languages (or dialects). An excellent source-book for information about other languages is Ian Maddieson's *Patterns of Sounds* (CUP, 1984), though this is quite a specialised work. I give quite a wide range of examples of sound systems in my CEL, 28.

IPE 5; EPP 5.2

phrasal verb (KS 4) see **multi-word verb**

phrase (KS 3)

- The identification of a phrase is crucially dependent on the prior ability to identify clause elements. I haven't used the terms **subject**, **object**, etc in the entry, but these notions are implicit throughout. Beware the cases of multi-word verbs, which can sometimes cause you to make a wrong analysis: in *I switched off the light*, *switch off* is a verb phrase followed by the noun phrase *the light*. It isn't *switch* + *off the light*. Also note such sentences as *We came across the road*, which is ambiguous: *We came / across the road* means we travelled across it; *We came across / the road* means we discovered it.

- Beware the popular interpretation of the word **phrase**, in such sentences as 'I know only a few phrases of Chinese' and in the concept of a 'phrase book'. A phrase book actually contains many sentences as well as phrases.

- In these books, I've distinguished between the task of identifying phrases and the task of analysing them into their parts, handling the former at KS 3 and the latter at KS 4. If you want to anticipate some of the latter points, look at the entries on **head** and **modify**.

- Note that you can coordinate phrases within the same element of clause structure: *The cat and the dog were in the garden*. I haven't given any examples of coordination in the entry.

- A complication arises when a phrase consists of just a single word: *Cakes are expensive*. Is *cakes* a noun phrase? Linguists would say yes, because the word is closely related to such other noun phrases as *the cakes* and *the nice cakes in the shop*. If you get on to this point, the definition in the entry will need to be slightly modified: a phrase is *typically* a group of words.

RG 27; SGE 2.4; CGEL 2.25–33

pictogram see **ideogram**

pidgin (KS 4)

- Here's another example, from Cameroon Pidgin English, taken from Loreto Todd, *Modern Englishes: Pidgins and Creoles* (Blackwell, 1984). The opening words of the Apostles' Creed ('I believe in God, the Father almighty, creator of heaven and earth, and in Jesus Christ his only son, Our Lord, who was conceived by the Holy Ghost . . .'):

> A bilif fo wan God, di Fada wei i get ol trong, wei i mek heven an grong. An a bilif fo Jisas Kraist wi masa, di wan pikin fo God, wei i bon fo di Holi Gost . . .

(A literal translation: 'I believe for one God, the Father who he get all strong, who he been make heaven and ground. And I believe for Jesus Christ we Master, the one child for God, who he born for the Holy Ghost . . .')

• If you want to illustrate an aspect of the grammar of a pidgin, here's the personal pronoun system of Tok Pisin:

me	I, me
yu	you
em	he, she, it, him, her
yumi	we, us (inclusive, ie you + me)
mipela	we, us (exclusive, ie not including you)
ol	they, them

This set can be expanded to indicate the number of people:

mitupela	the two of us (but not you)
mitripela	the three of us (but not you)
yumitripela	the three of us (including you)

In this respect, pidgin grammar is actually more complex than standard English.

CEL 55

plosive (KS 4)

• There are in fact three stages involved in producing a plosive: the articulating organs come together to make an obstruction in the vocal tract (the *closing* stage); they stay together while air builds up behind the obstruction (the *compression* stage); and they separate rapidly, allowing the air to escape audibly (the *release* stage). In some contexts, though, an audible release stage doesn't happen. This is especially the case when a plosive comes at the end of a word, such as in *cup* and *road*: the release is then very gentle (we don't spit it out and say 'cu-puh' or 'roa-duh'). The same effect is found when two plosives come next to each other in a word: the first isn't usually released – as in *dropped* and *locked*. And when the plosive is followed by a nasal, as in *topmost* and *madness*, there's no release either.

• Plosives are a type of **stop** consonant, where the air flow is completely blocked off ('stopped') by the closure in the vocal tract. See the entry on **glottis**, for the notion of the 'glottal stop'.

EPP 4.3–4; 8.2

pluperfect (KS 4)

• It sometimes helps, in distinguishing the various time points, to draw a time line moving from past through present (now) to future. Mark 'then' somewhere in past time – that's the function of the past tense. Between then and now is the realm of the present perfect. Before then is the realm of the past perfect (or **past perfective**, as it's also called).

• Could the past perfect ever refer to present time? It seems unlikely, as it refers to such a distant time past. But it can, in fact: what does *I had hoped you'd stay in this evening* mean? You are hoping now – but very tentatively.

RG 24; SGE 4.9; CGEL 4.24

plural (KS 3) see **number**

polysemic (KS 4)

• There's an interesting problem which arises when you compare the entries on **polysemy** and **homonymy**. In the former case, a word has more than one meaning. In the latter case, two words with different meanings have the same shape. Let's test this difference. We feel that the *flight* of a bird and the *flight* of a ball are two meanings of the same word (polysemy). (True? Don't take my word for it. Do you *feel* it?) And we don't feel that a coat of *mail* and the arrival of the *mail* are the same word: here, we feel that they are two different words which happen to have the same shape (homonymy). (Again, true?) So, how do you decide which is which?

• When you have a clear feeling about pairs of words, there's no problem. Unfortunately, the feeling isn't always there. Is an *ear* of corn and the *ear* on your head an example of polysemy or homonymy? Most people can't say. The easy solution is to look the word up in a dictionary. But how did the lexicographer know what to do in the first place?

• Dictionaries usually base their decision on etymology. If two words have different origins, they are treated as homonyms. If they have the same origin, they are treated as polysemic. This often works quite well – but there are lots of awkward cases. We feel that a *pupil* (school) and a *pupil* (eye) are very different in meaning, though in fact they have the same origins. Conversely, we feel that *meal* (flour) and *meal* (repast) are very closely related, though etymologically they are different. This is a fascinating area, but a very difficult one to study, as there are no neat solutions. I would leave it until KS 10, or thereabouts.

CEL 17

polysyllabic, polysyllable

• This term might be useful when discussing longer words. It simply refers to a word which contains several syllables, and is a natural extension of such terms as **monosyllabic** and **disyllabic** (**monosyllable** and **disyllable**).

positive (KS 3) see **affirmative, negative**

possessive (KS 4)

- Note the use of the word *own*, which adds emphasis to the possessive: *my own car* (and, even more strongly, *my very own*). It can resolve an ambiguity: *Rajiv washes his car every weekend* could mean Rajiv's car or someone else's car, but *Rajiv washes his own car every weekend* has only the first meaning.

- English uses possessives for parts of the body (*I broke my leg*). In many other languages, the definite article would be used instead (**I broke the leg* is a common foreign error).

RG 44; SGE 6.16; CGEL 6.30

postmodify (KS 4) see **modify**

pragmatics

- This is the name of a rapidly developing branch of linguistics, and you may therefore encounter it from time to time in the 1990s. It refers to the study of language from the viewpoint of the users, especially of the choices they make, the constraints they encounter when they use language in social interaction, and the effects their use of language has on the other participants in the act of communication. It deals with such topics as the way people take turns in a conversation, the rules governing politeness and terms of address (first names? nicknames? surnames?), and the assumptions people make when they talk. Some of this is dealt with in the entries on **conversation** and **discourse**.

CEL 21

predeterminer see **noun phrase**

predicate (KS 3)

- The subject–predicate distinction isn't in fact very useful, when dealing with the grammatical analysis of a sentence. Too many disparate structures are lumped together under the heading of **predicate**. That's why I went for a semantic approach in the entry, in which the subject is seen as the element which says what the sentence is about (it's often called the **topic**), and the predicate is everything else.

• A good way of developing a sense of the complementary roles of subject and predicate is to present students with one and not the other. *Crashed into the wall* doesn't make much sense. Nor does *The drunk*. But together, magic.

SGE 2.2; CGEL 2.47

prefix (KS 3) see **affix**

premodify (KS 4) see **modify**

preposition (KS 3)

• Normally the preposition is immediately followed by a noun phrase (technically, a **prepositional complement**). But there are a few cases where this doesn't happen, such as *That's worth going to* and *The car's been paid for*. In such cases, we can't put the preposition in front of the noun phrase and say **To that's worth going* or **For the car's been paid*. On the other hand, this variation is possible in such sentences as *Which man did you give the book to?* and *To which man did you give the book?*, where there is a clear difference in formality. When a preposition is left alone like this, it is said to be **deferred** or **stranded**.

• Everyone knows about *in*, *on*, and *under*. Here are some rather unusual prepositions: *anti* (*I'm anti smoking*), *minus* (*He arrived minus his hat*), *per* (*10p per dozen*), *re* (*I've come to see you re the car*), *via* (*Go via Buxton*), *versus* (or *v*) (*Smith v Brown*). Note these regional examples: *agin* ('against'), *outwith* ('except, outside'), both common in Scots, and *while* (meaning 'till'), used for example in Yorkshire. In poetry, you might find *'tween* and *'twixt*. *Unto* is archaic, and especially biblical. *Toward* is American English (compare British *towards*).

• Some other two-word prepositions: *as for, apart from, instead of, according to, next to, prior to, together with*. Some other three-word prepositions (called **complex prepositions** by the Quirk grammars): *in aid of, in view of, in spite of, in accordance with, by dint of, by means of, on behalf of, as far as, at variance with, in relation to*.

• Point out that several prepositions can be used in more than one sense. Several have half a dozen senses. The senses of *at* include time (*See you at three o'clock*), place (*The car is at the house*), goal (*I aimed the gun at the target*), standard (*I'm thick at chemistry*), and reaction (*I was amused at her reply*). The senses of *over* include location (*The picture is over the bed*), result (*We're over the worst of it*), passage (*We climbed over the wall*), and circumstance (*Let's talk about it over dinner*).

RG 59–61; SGE 9; CGEL 9

prepositional phrase (KS 3) see **preposition**

prescription and description

• This pair of terms identifies two totally different attitudes to language study. The prescriptive approach is one which attempts to lay down rules governing the way language should be used. (The term **proscriptive** is also sometimes distinguished, referring to rules which say how language *shouldn't* be used.) Traditional English language study, dating from the latter part of the eighteenth century, has been generally prescriptive in character. By contrast, a descriptive approach aims to observe and describe the way a language is used, regardless of any social or pedagogical criteria which may exist. In this approach, all accents and dialects, whether standard or non-standard, are seen as valid linguistic systems, deserving of study. The approach used within linguistics is invariably descriptive in character. For further observations, see the entry on **grammar**.

CEL 1

present tense (KS 3)

• The present tense is also used to refer to a 'timeless' present, expressing an 'eternal truth': *Two and two are four*, *The planets move round the sun*. In the 'habitual' present, an activity occurs repeatedly: *We go to Blackpool every summer*, *Mary dances a lot*. Sentences such as *I resign* and *I apologise* reflect an 'instantaneous' use of the present (see also in the sports commentary example).

• For another use of the present tense referring to past time, see the entry on **historic present**. Another use of the present tense referring to future time occurs in the language of instructions: *You turn left at the Bank, then take the third right* . . .

RG 23; SGE 4.3–4; CGEL 4.5–10

pro-form see **antecedent**, **pronoun**

progressive or continuous (KS 3)

• We don't 'usually' say the sentences in the Word Warning, and there are other sentences like these (eg **Michael is being ready*). Because these verbs don't express the idea of an activity taking place, it's not surprising that they aren't used in the progressive. You can hardly have an activity continuing over a period of time if there isn't an activity there in the first place! But beware: all kinds of subtle meanings can arise. We don't usually say **She is resembling me*, for example, but in a special context we could say *She is resembling me more and more these days*, where the verb takes on a much more active meaning.

• An interesting exercise is to find out whether simple or progressive forms occur more frequently in different styles of English. Is it true, for example, that official letters tend to use the simple form more often than the progressive? Compare *I write to inform you . . .* and the somewhat more informal *I am writing to let you know . . .*

RG 24; SGE 4.10–11; CGEL 4.25–6

pronoun (KS 3)

• Strictly, a pronoun doesn't refer to a noun; it refers to a **noun phrase**. If it referred only to the noun, the sentence in the entry would read *The little old she in a raincoat*. It's the *whole* of the noun phrase which is replaced by the pronoun. Also, notice that the first and second person pronouns often refer directly to the outside world, and not to a noun phrase at all: in *I saw you yesterday*, the *I* refers to the speaker, and the *you* to the listener.

• There are such a wide range of pronouns that it's not possible to teach this topic sensibly all at once. To try to do so would lead to the worst kind of rote learning ('An indefinite pronoun is . . .'). Each category of pronoun needs to be studied in its own right, with full attention paid to its semantic purpose and any interesting points about its grammar and use (such as the issues discussed in the entries on **case** and **gender**). I've focused only on the semantic issues in my entry.

• Note that words like *anybody* and *something* can be analysed as pronouns, in that they stand for a whole class of noun phrases: *I saw something* means 'I saw a NOUN'.

RG 43–7; SGE 6; CGEL 6

pronunciation

• I didn't put this term into the books, because it seemed rather too basic. Students should know what it means by KS 3. However, it's worth pointing out that the term has limited value at these later stages of study, because it combines both the phonetic and the phonological aspects of language study. To say that someone has 'poor pronunciation', for example, could mean that the person has a physical difficulty with articulation (a phonetic problem) or has some kind of psychological problem causing a delay in learning the sound system of the language (a phonological problem), or of course both. It can be important to distinguish these different senses, especially in dealing with special needs.

CEL 27–8

proper noun and common noun (KS 3)

• Just because a word begins with a capital letter doesn't mean to say that it's automatically a proper noun. Some common nouns have capital letters too. For instance, we live on *the earth* – or is it *the Earth*? Some people spell it with the capital, and some don't. And if someone tells you to go to —, is it *hell* or *Hell*? It's as well not to focus too much on capital letters. Apart from anything else, they don't appear in speech.

• So, how do you know that *London* is a proper noun in speech, when you can't see the capital letter? It's partly a matter of meaning – a proper noun refers to a unique entity. And it's also a matter of grammar. Proper nouns don't have an article: we can't say **the London* or **a Bonn*. We also can't vary their number: we can't say **Londons* or **a West Indy*. Those are the rules. Now, can the students find the exceptions? Here are some. We can say *The Smiths*, meaning 'the family Smith'. We can say *I want you to bring in a Shakespeare*, meaning 'a copy of the works of Shakespeare'. *A John Smith was trying to reach you* means 'A certain person of that name whom I don't know'. And if you say *I can't see any Shakespeares in this class*, you have changed *Shakespeare* from a proper noun into a common noun.

RG 29; SGE 5.25–34; CGEL 5.60–72

prosody (KS 4)

• In phonology, the term **prosody** is usually restricted to variations in pitch, loudness, and speed of speech, and their combinatorial effect as rhythm. Other effects, such as tone of voice and voice quality, would be described under a different heading (often, as **paralinguistic features**). The term **suprasegmental** is much broader in range, covering *all* these effects, whether prosodic or not.

• This is a very general term, whose purpose is to identify an area of study. It has little practical use when students begin to describe spoken language in any detail. In such circumstances it is far better to employ the much more specific notions of **intonation**, **stress** and **rhythm** (or **metre**, in the context of poetry). There are separate entries on all these terms.

RG 75; CGEL App II; IPE 10

proverb (KS 3)

• Proverbial expressions often go under several labels: adages, maxims, precepts, saws, dictums, truisms, mottoes. Famous collections of proverbs include The Book of Proverbs in the Old Testament and *The Oxford Dictionary of English Proverbs* (OUP, 1935).

• Students should spend some time reflecting on why a proverb 'works'. It is partly grammar – the balanced and succinct syntax. It is partly semantics, with vivid images and pointed domestic allusions. It is partly phonological, with the parts linked by rhythm, rhyme and alliteration. And it is also partly cultural, with some peoples (eg in many parts of Africa) relying greatly on proverbs as a means of transmitting cultural knowledge.

CEL 11

pseudonym (KS 3)

• Other famous pseudonyms include Currer, Ellis, and Acton Bell (the Brontë sisters), Michael Angelo Titmarsh (Thackeray), George Eliot (Mary Ann Evans), Mark Twain (Samuel Clemens), Saki (H H Munro), Nicholas Blake (C Day Lewis) and Michael Innes (J I M Stewart).

• To extend the theme of this entry, relate pseudonyms to other kinds of name changes, as found in aliases or changes in a maiden name or surname (upon marriage, or simply because the name-owner doesn't like it).

• Stage names are a similar phenomenon: Fred Astaire (Frederick Austerlitz), Dirk Bogarde (Derek Gentron Gaspart Ulric van den Bogaerde), Danny Kaye (David Daniel Kaminsky), Diana Dors (Diana Fluck), Engelbert Humperdinck (Arnold Dorsey). And political names? Stalin (I V Dzhugashvili) – which means 'steel' in Russian. There are some excellent examples in Leslie Dunkling, *The Guinness Book of Names* (Guinness Superlatives, 1986, 2nd edn).

pun (KS 3)

• Puns range from the simplest and crudest of plays on words to the most sophisticated and ingenious nuances of expression. To some people they are 'the lowest and most grovelling kind of wit' (Dryden); to others they are fundamental to the creative power of language: 'In the beginning was the pun' (Samuel Beckett). Sometimes puns are very serious, as with the *Peter/rock* pun made by Jesus in the New Testament (clearer in French, where *pierre* is used for both). The Greek oracle at Delphi punned all the time. Shakespeare is full of puns: *You shall find me a grave man*, says Mercutio as he is dying (*Romeo and Juliet*. III.1). Walter Redfern's *Puns* (Blackwell, 1984) is a magnificent defence and explication of the genre. And, as a footnote, to show that puns can be a really serious matter, note the Greek term: **paronomasia**. Don't use this term, though, if you don't want to frighten away the punters.

• Students could go hunting for puns. They will find them in advertising and newspaper headlines (especially in the *Guardian* subheadings), on T-shirts, walls, and lapel badges, and in the outpourings of radio and TV comedians. Books called *1000 Jokes for Kids*, and the like, will be full of the worst of them.

CEL 11

punctuation (KS 3)

• The basic principle, in teaching punctuation, is to demonstrate contrast. Students need to see that the meaning of a sentence changes when a punctuation mark changes. If necessary, begin with the most fundamental point: why is punctuation there at all? What would language be like without it? (See the final sentence in my entry.) Develop the sense of a *hierarchy* of punctuation marks – that some are much more important, when it comes to organising meaning, than others. The word needs spaces to stand out. Sentences need capital letters and full stops to show where they begin and end. Paragraphs need space. Devise examples where the meaning alters if these graphic features aren't introduced. (There's an example under **paragraph**.) Don't get into semi-colons and the like too soon. And don't try to find rules where there are none.

• On this last point, note the amount of personal variation which exists in the use of the comma. Usage manuals tend to go for very strict rules, and try to make everyone punctuate in exactly the same way. A glance at any pair of publishing house styles, or at the manuscript works of any two authors, would show that variation is widespread. See the entry on **comma** for more on this.

● Notice that punctuation doesn't have much of a phonetic function. It's rarely used to express emotional meaning (apart from such cases as !!!), and you can't relate punctuation marks very easily to tones of voice. In particular, punctuation marks have got very little to do with the way we pause in speech. If we try to pause every time we see a comma, while reading aloud, the result will sound bizarre.

RG 76; CGEL App III; CEL 33

purism

● This term summarises the **prescriptive** attitudes of people who feel that change in language is a bad thing, causing deterioration in the language and a loss of standards. Purists feel that efforts should be made to preserve the imagined 'purity' of the language as much as possible. Earlier states of the language are recalled with nostalgia. Most aspects of language change will be attacked, from a purist point of view, especially loan words and shifts in pronunciation. Linguists regard purists as living in an unreal world, and stress the purpose, system, and inevitability of language change.

CEL 1

quantifier (KS 4)

● It's *pride*, of course. These old exam questions tended to pick on the most obscure partitive and collective expressions. It's important to realise that there are some very common everyday examples too. Some have just one associated noun: *a wink of sleep*, *a loaf of bread*. Others have several associated nouns: *a series of concerts/programmes/incidents*, *a bunch of flowers/teenagers/idiots*, *a suit of clothes/armour*, *a lump of coal/lead/sugar*. Note also the expressions of measure: *a pound/ounce/metre/kilo of . . .*

● The pronouns and determiners are an important means of expressing quantity – *the* most important means, according to logicians. In addition to the ones mentioned in the entry, there are several others, such as *half*, *several*, *enough*, *other*, *another*, and the numerals (see the entry on **indefinite pronoun** for more about these). There are also several adverbials which express quantity, such as *sufficiently*, *a bit*, *somewhat*, and *a lot* (see the entry on **intensifier** for more about these).

RG 38; SGE 5.2, 6.21–8, 8.37; CGEL 5.7–8, 6.45–63, 8.115

question (KS 3)

● It isn't a silly question to ask: why do we ask questions? People tend to underestimate how many different purposes they serve. The following is not a complete list. We use them to ask for information, of course, but there are other functions too – to request (*Would you please leave?*), offer (*Would you like some more tea?*), invite (*Will you come to dinner?*), advise (*Why don't you take a taxi?*), exclaim (*Wasn't that terrific?*), check (*You realise what you're doing?*), warn (*What on earth are you doing?*), and obtain rapport (*How are you?*). The very last type mentioned in the entry is called the **rhetorical question**, and there's a separate entry on that.

• See the entries on **echo utterance** and **tag question** in KS 4 for further types.

RG 5; SGE 11.2–14; CGEL 11.4–23

quotation marks (KS 3) see **inverted commas**

rebus (KS 3)

• The term comes from Latin, meaning 'by things', because utterances are represented by things and not words. They were common in early writing systems, such as Egyptian hieroglyphic. In Europe, they were often employed in heraldic devices, on tombstones, in shop signs, and on coins.

• Rebuses have also had a serious educational function, such as in teaching children to read, providing material for illiterate adults, and in presenting Christianity (the 'hieroglyphic Bible'). Advertisements have sometimes made use of them: for example, *DD 4 U* was a slogan for Double Diamond beer, at one point. And they can turn up in everyday speech too: *Give me an IOU*. Tony Augarde provides some nice examples in *The Oxford Guide to Word Games* (OUP, 1984).

Received Pronunciation (KS 4)

• RP isn't a single variety. In addition to a 'middle of the road' variety, there are also conservative varieties used by older people (and heard, for example, on old BBC recordings), and advanced varieties (heard, for example, in the speech of Sloane Rangers).

• It's an interesting point that far more foreigners speak RP now than do native speakers. Note also that, from an international point of view, RP is just as much a regional accent as any other: it tells the listener that the speaker is from the UK.

• An RP survey can produce some interesting results. Get the students listening to all five channels of the BBC. How far is RP used by the presenters? Which channel shows most variation? (Not Radio 3.) What is happening in Parliament? Is there more RP on the Conservative side than on the Labour side? Some domains are rather more tricky to research.

What's happening in the Church of England? How many judges with regional accents are there? (Not many.)

EL 4; IPE 6.3; EPP 1

reference

• This is a convenient term for the objects, events, and other phenomena in the external world to which language refers. The reference (or **referent**) of the word *table* is the object, a table. You will also find the term **co-reference** used, in a related sense. In the sentence *John loaned Jim his keys*, the word *his* refers to the same person as *John*: the two words are 'co-referential' – they have the same reference. On the other hand, in *John returned Jim his keys*, the co-reference is now between *Jim* and *his*.

CEL 17

reflexive pronoun (KS 4)

• The complete set of reflexives is: *myself*, *yourself*, *himself*, *herself*, *itself*, *oneself*, *ourselves*, *yourselves*, *themselves*. There is also an archaic 'royal we' form, *ourself*. 'Reflexive verbs' also exist in English, such as *behave oneself*, *perjure oneself*, and *dress oneself*.

• In addition to the function illustrated in the entry, reflexives can also be used emphatically: *He himself asked me to go*, *He asked me to go himself*. Note the way the word can move about the sentence: this isn't possible in the examples in the entry. Another interesting point is the way some constructions allow three possibilities: *Anyone but you would have resigned*, *Anyone but yourself would have resigned*, *Anyone but you yourself would have resigned*.

• Be prepared for regional variations. The reflexive is sometimes avoided in informal American English (*I'm going to get me a beer*).

RG 44; SGE 6.13–15; CGEL 6.23–8

regional dialect (KS 3) see **dialect**

register (KS 3) see **variety**

regular (KS 4) see **irregular**

relative (KS 4)

• The relative pronouns show a contrast between personal (*who*) and impersonal (*which*): see the entry on **gender** for more about this. *That* can be used with either type: *There's the book that I saw in the shop* and *There's the boy that I saw in the shop*. They also show the difference between restrictive and nonrestrictive meaning (see **restrictive**).

● There are several usage controversies surrounding the use of relative pronouns. Some people insist on using *whom* in formal English in such sentences as *'That's the man whom I saw in the park*, but not everyone shares this preference in speech (though it *is* widely adopted in writing). Also, some people don't like to use *whose* after an impersonal noun (*There's the car whose bonnet was dented*), because they feel that *whose* relates more to *who* than to *which*. However, there isn't an easy alternative: to say *There's the car the bonnet of which was dented* is extremely awkward, and **There's the car that the bonnet was damaged of* isn't acceptable at all. The only way out is to rephrase, eg *There's the car with the dented bonnet*.

● The grammar of relative clauses is quite complex, and should be left until a later stage of study. You can nonetheless keep an eye open for unusual constructions, such as the relative clause which modifies a whole sentence, rather than just a noun: *She likes polo – which surprises me*. It's not just the polo which surprises, but the girl's liking of polo – in other words, the whole sentence.

● Notice the way a sequence of relative clauses can be built up: *This is the dog that chased the cat that worried the rat that lived in the house that Jack built*.

RG 41; SGE 17.5–12; CGEL 17.9–25

relevance (KS 3)

● Be relevant. Easier said than done, because what is relevant in the mind of the speaker may not appear to be so in the mind of the listener. It's always easy to leave the listener behind, and listeners need always to be on their toes. The speaker has to *demonstrate* relevance – perhaps by spelling out the reasons for saying something. Greg's utterance could be made to appear relevant, if he then went on to say: '. . . And Fred told me of a really good way of getting from Liverpool to Newcastle.' The same points apply in principle to the written language, but of course there the writer has more time to anticipate the demands of the reader, and the reader has more time to see what is going on.

● The radio game where you have to talk for a minute on a topic without saying anything irrelevant can be usefully adapted for classroom use.

reported speech (KS 3) see **direct speech**

restrictive and nonrestrictive (KS 4)

● This distinction is so simple and obvious, when you hear it in speech, but it isn't so easy to see it in writing, and it turns out to be one of the most difficult contrasts to explain in a grammar, so don't expect students to find this entry easy-going. You'll need to read pairs of sentences aloud, to try to convey the contrast in meaning. When you say a restrictive example aloud – *My Uncle Eric who lives in Finland has just written me a letter* – remember to say the first part of the sentence in a single rhythmical unit – in a bit of a rush. Don't pause until you get to *Finland*. But when you're saying the nonrestrictive one aloud – *My Uncle Eric, who lives in Finland, has just written me a letter* – remember to pause at both commas, and drop the voice for the relative clause, as if to convey the idea that it's a parenthesis – optional information.

• Notice how, in speech, there's a strong stress on the words *red* and *green* in the penultimate example. Similarly, for a restrictive meaning of *beautiful wife*, there would have to be a strong stress on *beautiful*.

RG 41; SGE 17.3; CGEL 17.3–6

rhetoric

• This term has traditionally been used to refer to the persuasive characteristics of speech or writing, especially as practised in public oratory. It dates from classical Greek and Roman times, when several hundred types of linguistic effect ('rhetorical figures') were identified and classified. Some are presented in these books under **figure of speech**. In modern times, rhetoric continues to be studied, but with a much broader range of application. A modern course of rhetoric would look at the whole study of creative discourse, including the use of language in the mass media, and the effects of language on an audience. It now subsumes the techniques and aims of all forms of effective communication.

CEL 12

rhetorical question (KS 4)

• Notice that rhetorical questions can be either positive (all the examples in the entry) or negative (no examples in the entry). Some negative examples, therefore: *Isn't that obvious?*, *Haven't you got anything better to do, Smith?*

• A related type of question is one which is self-addressed: *Shall I apply or shan't I?* If you talk like this in company, though, be prepared for someone to chip in and tell you!

RG 5; SGE 11.12; CGEL 11.23

rhyme (KS 3)

• My entry doesn't go into rhyme in literature – it's too large a subject. Some approaches provide sophisticated classifications of the types of rhyme it is possible to have, and of the patterns of rhyme (the **rhyme**

scheme) you will find in a poem. Rhymes can be perfect repetitions of a syllable, or approximations of varying degrees of closeness (*love* vs *serve*, *love* vs *give*, *love* vs *leave*) – what are variously called **near-rhymes**, **imperfect rhymes, half rhymes** or **slant rhymes**. See the entry on **eye rhyme** for another possibility. Notice that you can have words which rhyme within a line as well as at the end of lines (**internal rhyme**).

• Rhyme is distinctive in English because it's unusual. In everyday conversation, words don't rhyme much. But why not? One reason is that the structure of the language doesn't promote it. English doesn't make much use of word endings. In a language which does (such as Latin), you could say that the words are *always* rhyming. If the grammar makes all the words in a certain role end in *-um*, for example, then poets won't find much scope for creativity.

• Why do we rhyme in poems? It is partly just for phonetic reasons: people take pleasure from the mere fact of having sounds repeated in this way, especially (as in comic verse) if the rhyme is ingenious (*Sweet little Hilary owned a distillery* . . .). It is also used for phonological reasons: it helps to organise the poem, marking a conclusion, binding lines together, sometimes even forcing words together (and thus the meanings they have). If you are reading a poem and one line ends with *blood*, you would normally (unconsciously) associate this with such notions as health and glory. If, a line or so later, you find it rhyming with *mud*, the dirty associations of this last word will carry over to *blood*, and will alter your perception of that concept. In a war poem, for example, this might be a particularly appropriate way of introducing irony.

LG 6

rhythm (KS 3)

• An interesting insight into rhythm can come from comparing the different rhythms of different languages. Compare the tum-te-tum rhythm of English, for example, with the rat-tat-tat rhythm of French. (Technically, this is the difference between **stress-timed** rhythm and **syllable-timed** rhythm.) Some varieties of English have a tendency to syllable-timed rhythm, too – such as Indian English and Jamaican English.

LG 7

riddle (KS 3)

• In Europe, riddles tend to be like those in the entry – short and humorous, and used mainly by children. In many other parts of the world, however (such as Africa, China), riddles can be long and complex, and widely used by adults. They can be cryptic statements of a poetic or philosophical character, often not cast in a question form. In this tradition, a riddle can be used in order to test a person's wisdom or judgment. The Oracle at Delphi would speak in riddles.

• In English, an important collection of riddles is in the eighth-century *Exeter Book*, written in Old English. The word comes from Old English, where it means 'opinion' or 'advice'.

CEL 11

roll (KS 4) see **trill**

root (KS 3)

• Textbooks sometimes leave students with the impression that roots are very short bits of language. Point to such cases as *elephant* to show that this is not so. Note that the root sometimes has a clear meaning (as in the case of *press* in the entry) and sometimes it doesn't. For instance, if we take the *-ous* ending away from *jealous*, we are left with *jeal-*.

• Get students to go through a piece of text (such as this entry) and identify the roots of the words. They'll need to read the entries on **affix** and **compound word** first, though.

CGEL App 1.2

rounding, rounded (KS 4)

• The rounded vowels of RP (see **Received Pronunciation**) are heard in *cot*, *caught*, *put*, and *shoe*, and rounding also turns up in certain diphthongs:

the first element in *boy* and *sure* and the second element in *go* and *how*. Notice how all rounded vowels in RP are at the back of the mouth. (In French, there are rounded vowels at the front of the mouth too.) Regional accents often have different kinds of rounded vowels – listen to the rounded vowels of Scots or Northern Irish English, for example.

• You'll sometimes see a 'spread' speech style – as when someone is speaking with a broad grin. In TV ads, you can often hear the fixed smile of the speaker in the voiceover. Listen out the next time someone says a washing powder is 'new and blue' – the [u] vowels can sound quite different.

IPE 4.4.2; EPP 2–3

RP (KS 4) see **Received Pronunciation**

rule

• This term is widely used in several different senses, so it needs to be watched. Traditionally, it refers to the prescriptions of a teaching grammar – the recommendations which need to be followed if one is to avoid criticism for using 'incorrect' language. Such a rule would be: 'Never end a sentence with a preposition.' In linguistics, the term has a broader application: here it is a statement of the formal relationship between different language elements or structures. For example, we can say that there is a rule forming the plural in English (eg 'add an *s* to a noun'), and there are various exceptions which have to be recognised. All varieties of the language have rules, in this sense, including those whose status is considered to be non-standard.

CEL 16

sarcasm (KS 4) see **irony**

schwa (shwah)

• This is the name given by phoneticians to the unstressed vowel which appears often in English, in such words as *the* and *a*, and at the end of *butter* and *sofa*. It is transcribed [ə]. Its name derives from Hebrew, where there is a similar vowel quality.

IPE 7.9; EPP 9.2

second language (KS 3) see **first language**

semantics

- This term conveniently summarises all aspects of the meaning system of a language, in particular the study of vocabulary and of the way a text's thematic structure is organised. Avoid the pejorative use of the term, when engaged in linguistic discussion, as in *That's just semantics*, where the implication is 'that's not the real issue'.

CEL 17

semi-auxiliary verb see **auxiliary verb**

semi-colon (KS 3)

- The semi-colon is the punctuation mark which signals coordination. It corresponds most closely in value to the coordinating conjunction *and*. A discussion of its functions might be introduced with reference to the associated area of grammar. Compare *Smith left his hat on the bus and Jones left his bag* and *Smith left his hat on the bus; Jones left his bag*. It is especially used when the associated constructions are long, and when commas might be in use in the vicinity. The semi-colon 'outranks' a comma, and thus gives the reader a chance to sort out 'what goes with what', as in the opening example in the entry.

- As the entry says, semi-colons are much more likely in formal writing. Check this out. How many do you find in the *Sun* or in informal letters? How many *are* there in this book, anyway?

CGEL App III.12–13

semi-vowel (KS 4) see **approximant**

sense relations

- This is a convenient term for all the types of meaning relationship which link the lexical items in a language. Chief among these are the **antonyms**, **synonyms**, and **hyponyms**, which are each given entries.

CEL 17

sentence (KS 3)

- The old definition of a sentence was 'A sentence expresses a complete thought'. The problem there, of course, is deciding when a thought is complete. Some thoughts are so complex that they take several sentences to express. And you can have a grammatical sentence where the thought is definitely incomplete, such as *Will I answer his letter, I wonder?* The other emphasis in traditional grammar was that a sentence had to have a verb in it. (This was implicit in the idea of 'completeness', too.) On this count, *SPECIAL MEETING TODAY* wouldn't be a sentence, nor would *Hello*, *Yes*, *The more, the merrier*, and thousands of other utterances. The approach I'm representing in these books recognises different types of sentence (see **major sentence** and **ellipsis**, in particular), but views them all as sentences. If you'd rather not do this, and insist on the 'verb in' criterion, fine – but you must then devise some extra terminology to describe what you see in such constructions as *SPECIAL MEETING TODAY* and *Yes*.

- It's important to point out that it's more difficult to recognise a sentence in speech. Quite often the melody and rhythm of the voice provide the clue that a sentence has come to an end. If you ask someone *What would you like to drink?* and the reply is *I'd like a cup of tea*, sounding very definite, followed by a silence, then it'll certainly sound as if the sentence has come to an end. But if the reply was *I'd like a cup of tea – and then some whisky, and maybe some milk – and after that I'd like an orange juice*, at the end of each bit you wouldn't be sure whether the person had finished. Utterances in conversation do sometimes go on and on like this. It's a good exercise to get students to listen to a tape recording of a conversation, and write it down. They'll always have difficulty deciding where to put the full stops.

- The sentence is usually seen as the highest-ranking unit of grammar, even though it can be difficult to recognise (especially in speech). (Compare the entry on **clause**, which is in fact much easier to identify.) There are nonetheless certain grammatical features which operate 'above' the sentence: see the entry on **connectivity** for more about these.

RG 1; SGE 2.2; CGEL 2.11

sequence of tenses see **direct speech**

sibilance (KS 4)

- There are many qualities of sibilance. Women often have a much sharper sound than men. Some people (of either sex) make a very tense sound, with the tongue bunched hard against the top of the mouth. Others have a very relaxed 'slushy' sound. In a lisp, where the tongue tip is used against the teeth for the production of *s*, there may be no sibilance at all.

IPE 8.4.4–5

simile (KS 3)

- It's standard practice to draw attention to the differences between a simile and a **metaphor** (which has its own entry). The essential point is that

the basis of comparison in a simile is explicitly recognised in certain words, chiefly *like* and *as*. There are a few other markers which should be noted, such as *as if*, *as though*, *akin to*, *is comparable to*, *not unlike*, *similar to*, and *resembling*.

• I've given no recognised literary examples in the entry. Five minutes in any poetry book would solve this problem. *I wandered lonely as a cloud . . .*

• An excellent source of material is Elyse Sommer and Mike Sommer, *Similes Dictionary* (Gale, 1988), which groups similes into thematic categories (affluence, age, aggression, agility, etc). It gives over 30 similes pertaining to *eyebrows*, for example, as used by a wide range of authors. There are over 100 for *smile*. If students are short on expressive ideas, they'll find plenty to stimulate their imaginations in this book. Equally, it would have to be used with caution, to avoid the copy-cat temptation.

LG 9.2.2

singular (KS 3) see **number**

slang (KS 3)

• The British lexicologist, Eric Partridge, who wrote more about slang than anyone else, gives 15 different reasons for the use of slang: for the fun of it; as an exercise in wit or ingenuity; to be different; to be picturesque; to be arresting; to escape from cliches; to enrich the language; to add concreteness to speech; to reduce seriousness; to be colloquial; for ease of social interaction; to induce intimacy; to show that one belongs; to exclude others; to be secret. Some of these functions overlap to a degree. It's the group-identifying uses which I think are the most important.

- Students could go slang hunting, using TV programmes – British police or prison slang, for example, such as *nick*, *screw* ('prison warder'), *pigs*. Programmes such as *Minder* are excellent sources. Alternatively, they could research all the slang words and phrases in a particular area, such as being drunk – *blotto, canned, smashed, paralytic* . . . A thesaurus would be a good source of examples, or a specialised slang dictionary, such as Partridge's *Dictionary of Slang and Unconventional English* (Routledge & Kegan Paul, 1961, 5th edn).

CEL 11

slogan (KS 3)

- It isn't difficult to put together a collection of slogans, using advertising sources. Note also the use of slogans in such areas as public health (*You know it makes sense*) and politics (especially at election time).

- Students should look at the linguistic structure of slogans, such as the use of rhythm, alliteration, rhyme, spelling deviance (*Beanz Meanz Heinz*), grammatical succinctness, and any other distinctive features. Geoffrey Leech, *English in Advertising* (Longman, 1966) provides a useful commentary on the properties of this variety.

sound symbolism (KS 4)

- The term **onomatopoeia** is usually found in relation to literature; **sound symbolism** is used more widely in linguistics. Another term which is often used to refer to the supposed inherent properties of sound is **phonaesthetics**.

- A good example of the purely symbolic values of sound is to be found in the Lewis Carroll poem, 'Jabberwocky': *'Twas brillig, and the slithy toves/ Did gyre and gimble in the wabe;/ All mimsy were the borogroves/ And the mome raths outgrabe*. Here there is no dictionary meaning in the content words, therefore much of the effect must come from the sounds as such (as well as from associations with real words). Not all of these nonsense words have clear sound symbolic values, of course, and this is something which you need to be cautious about. It's important not to start reading meanings into every sound. For example, if you think for long enough, you can persuade yourself that in the word *dead* you can hear the sound of the nails being banged into the coffin! Or that the word *computer* is particularly appropriate because in it you can hear the hum of the disk drive! In analysing poetry, such interpretations can have their value, but they are often idiosyncratic and controversial.

- A good example of the humorous use of sound symbolism is Douglas

Adams and John Lloyd, *The Meaning of Liff* (Pan, 1983), which finds 'appropriate' meanings for place names, based on the authors' interpretation of how they sound. For example, *Goole: The puddle on the bar into which the barman puts your change.* Another fruitful source of onomatopoeic effects: *Zap!*, *Pow!*, *Kerlunkk*, and other sound effects from comic strips.

• Other *sl-* words with a 'negative' tone include *slack*, *slag*, *slander*, *slap*, *slaughter*, *slave*, *sleazy*, *sleet*, *slosh*, *sloth*, *slovenly*, *slow*, *sludge*, *slump*, *slur*, *slurp*, *slut*. (But not all *sl-* words have such a connotation – compare *slant*, *sledge*, *sleek*, *sleep*, *slumber*.) Several other sets of onomatopoeic words seem to share common sounds: note the *-sh* ending of *smash*, *crash*, *crush*, *splash*, *slash*, *lash*, etc, or the *-k* ending of *crack*, *creak*, *click*, *cluck*, *flick*, *whack*, etc.

EL 7; CEL 30

speech marks (KS 3) see **inverted commas**

spelling reform (KS 4) see **orthography**

split infinitive see **grammar**

spondee (KS 4) see **foot**

spoonerism (KS 3) see **malapropism**

spread (KS 4) see **rounding**

standard English (KS 3)

• The best way of appreciating the power of the notion of **standard English** is to get hold of written material from various parts of the world, note the linguistic similarities, and try to find differences. Perhaps students and teachers on holiday in Canada, the USA, Australia, New Zealand, India, South Africa, the West Indies, and other places where English is spoken as a first or second language could bring back a local newspaper or magazine. Or students could ask a relative or friend in such places to send a sample. The differences, incidentally, will be largely due to vocabulary, relating to the local flora and fauna, political system, customs, and so on; but there are some grammatical and spelling differences (notably between

British and American English), and several differences of convention (such as the way we abbreviate dates: *3.4.91* is 3 April in the UK but 4 March in the USA).

• Note that the term **non-standard** is a somewhat less pejorative expression than the term **sub-standard**. Within the UK, non-standard English generally means the use of regional dialect forms, and also the use of forms which are perceived as uneducated (such as *ain't*, which is found throughout the country, regardless of regional dialect). Note that there's nothing intrinsically sub-standard about such expressions as *ain't* (which was widely used in the nineteenth century, even among upper-class speakers). It's important to get students to appreciate that the notions of standard and non-standard are not in opposition, but complement each other: the main purpose of standard English is to facilitate communication *between* groups; the main purpose of non-standard English is to provide a comfortable means of communication *within* groups – and, above all, to provide a linguistic identity for those groups. Students need to develop their ability to use both levels of communication, to see that both have a purpose, and to be proud of their ability to use both. This pride in one's local heritage is not going to be instilled if it continues to be labelled 'sub-standard', 'bad English', and the like. And to demean the student's personal variety is likely to be counter-productive when it comes to generating in students a positive attitude about language in general and standards in particular. It is this shift in perspective which characterises much of the thinking about standard English in recent years. Putting this another way: the hitherto almost exclusive attention devoted to the standard language now needs to be supplemented by a focus on non-standard language, which has its standards too. The rules governing the way a non-standard English dialect works are just as complex and intriguing as those governing the dialect we call standard English.

EL 1, 12–14; CGEL 1.23

statement (KS 3)

• The final sentence, of course. Even *Except one* is a statement, albeit an extremely elliptical one (short for *Every sentence I'm using in this entry except one is a statement*).

• Statements are used for a very wide range of functions, such as making an assertion (*Teachers are* – you finish it off), a prediction (*It's going to rain*), an apology (*I'm sorry for the delay*), an enquiry (*I'd like to know the name of the author*) – even a request (*Supper's ready*) or command (Teacher: *Johnny, there's a piece of chalk on the floor*).

RG 5; SGE 11.1; CGEL 11.1–3

stative verb see **aspect**

stem (KS 3) see **root**

stop consonant (KS 4) see **plosive**

stress (KS 4)

• When a word is said in isolation, such as *telegraph*, the prominence you hear on the syllable *tel-* is in fact a combination of loudness and pitch movement. When this happens, phoneticians often talk about the syllable being **accented**, and the effect as one of **accent** (yes, a *third* meaning for this term – sorry).

• You can see from the entry that there are two aspects to the study of stress: stress in words and stress in sentences. The latter is best handled under the headings of **prosody** and **rhythm** (which have their own entries). In relation to words, students might build up a collection of words of increasing complexity, to see just how many patterns exist. There are a lot – as any foreigner learning English knows. Errors in stress pattern are very common. So, if there are two syllables, you can have the strong stress on the first syllable (*husband*, *table*) or on the second (*antique*, *machine*). If there are three syllables, the stress can be on the first syllable (*yesterday*), the second (*important*), or the third (*understand*). If four syllables, the stress can be on the first (*caterpillar*), second (*remarkable*), third (*circulation*), or fourth (*aquamarine*). And so on. Much longer words can be investigated, such as *internationalisation*, and there are also patterns for compound words. Students will need to make use of the terms **stressed syllable** and **unstressed syllable**.

• Some words change their meaning when they change their stress (along with associated changes in the vowel): nouns become verbs, as in *'permit* vs *per'mit*, *'convict* vs *con'vict*, *'perfect* vs *per'fect*, *'record* vs *re'cord*. Note the conventional phonetic symbol for a stress mark: '.

EPP 10; CGEL 9.1–5

style (KS 3)

• This term has two quite distinct applications – an evaluative sense, presented in the first two paragraphs of the entry, and a descriptive sense, presented in the second two. Everyone has style, but only some have real *style*, in the opinion of society! A great deal of literary criticism operates with the evaluative frame of reference; a great deal of linguistic investigation (under the heading of **stylistics**) operates within a descriptive frame of reference.

• There are many contexts for stylistic study. The term appears with reference to an individual (Shakespeare's style), a level of language (formal style), an occupation (legal style), a literary genre (epic style), a period (Augustan style), and so on. It's important not to exclude any of these, as part of the study of style – for example, by allowing the study of only the 'best' uses of language, such as are encountered in literature. Apart from the intrinsic interest of studying non-literary styles (for example, to discover how journalism, advertising, or religious English 'works'), there is also the point that literary language is in a very real sense dependent on these other styles. Authors draw on the resources of the language as a whole, and this includes the whole of the language's stylistic range.

LG 1; CEL 12

subject (KS 3)

• The entry discusses the use of subjects, but doesn't say anything about their form, distribution or syntactic function. Here is a summary of the main features, therefore. Usually a subject is a noun phrase (*the Englishman said . . .*) or pronoun (*he said . . .*). It takes the subjective form of certain pronouns (*He asked the man*, not **Him asked the man*). It may also be a (nominal) clause (*What happened upset me*). It normally occurs before the verb in a declarative clause (*She is leaving*) or after the first auxiliary verb in an interrogative clause (*Is she leaving?*). A subject is obligatory in a finite clause, and is normally absent (but implied) in an imperative clause: *(You) Sit in the chair*. In finite clauses, the subject determines the number and person of the verb in the present tense (*I go, He goes, They go*). It also determines the number, person, and gender of any reflexive pronoun in the same clause (*She asked herself . . .*).

• In certain types of sentence, the first word is not always the subject. In *What is the answer?*, for example, students may think that *What* is the subject. But it is *the answer*. How do we know? Because the subject agrees with the verb in number, and we say *What are the answers* (not **What is the answers*). Similarly, by comparing *There is the cup* and *There are the cups*, it is possible to see that *there* is not the subject.

RG 9; SGE 10.7; CGEL 10.6

subjective case (KS 3) see **case**

subjunct see **adjunct**

subjunctive (KS 4)

• The subjunctive form without *-s* is often called the **mandative** subjunctive, because it expresses a demand, recommendation, proposal, intention, or the like. You can tell it's the subjunctive because there is no concord between subject and verb, and it ignores the shift between present and past tense. In the indicative, these changes take place. For example, we can say *I propose that the lady is to be elected* and *I proposed that the lady was to be elected*, with a change of tense in the indicative mood. Similarly, the verb changes if the number changes in the third person of the present tense: *I propose that the ladies are to be elected*. But if we use the subjunctive form, notice how the same form can be used regardless of the tense and number: *I propose that the lady be elected*, *I proposed that the lady be elected* and *I propose that the ladies be elected*. Other verbs which are commonly followed by a subjunctive clause are *decide*, *insist*, *order*, *prefer* and *request* (and associated nouns and adjectives, such as *advisable*, *desirable*, *decision*, and *resolution*).

- Other examples of the formulaic subjunctive: *Come what may . . .*, *Suffice it to say . . .*, *Long live the President*.

RG 21; SGE 3.23–4; CGEL 3.58–62

subordination (KS 3)

- Point out that **subordinator** is just another way of saying **subordinating conjunction** – see the entry on **conjunction** for a list of items which act in this way.

- In the entry, I talk about subordinate clauses only. The notion of subordination can also be used in relation to other aspects of sentence structure. For example, in the phrase *the big cat*, *the* and *big* are subordinate to *cat*; in *very nice*, *very* is subordinate to *nice* (see the entry on **modify**).

- Looking for subordinate clauses is always more difficult than looking for coordinate clauses. The latter are simply of the type 'A and/or/but B and/or/but C and/or/but D . . .'. The former involve the student being able to see that a clause is *inside* another clause (often called the **superordinate** clause). But, as the examples in the entry show, there are two ways in which this can happen. The subordinate clause can be *part of* the clause element in the superordinate clause – this is what happens in the *Auntie Julie* example, as I hope the layout illustrates clearly. Or, the subordinate clause can take up the *whole* of the clause element in the superordinate clause – this is what the *I said no* example illustrates. Any clause element except the verb can be expanded into a clause in this way. The subject element is expanded in *What I said was right* (where *What I said* could be replaced by *It*). The complement element is expanded in *This is what I saw* (where *what I saw* could be replaced by *true*). The adverbial element is expanded in *I left when the bell rang* (where *when the bell rang* could be replaced by *then*). And the expansion of the object element is illustrated in the entry.

RG 65; SGE 2.5, 15; CGEL 2.9, 15

sub-standard English (KS 3) see **standard English**

suffix (KS 3) see **affix**

superlative (KS 3)

• The addition of *-est* is called the **inflected** form of the superlative (see **inflection**). The use of *most* is called the **periphrastic** form. With adjectives, the choice between the two is largely determined by the length of the adjective (and the same principle governs the use of *-er* and *more*). Single-syllable adjectives usually form their comparison by inflection: *big — biggest*. (An exception is an adjective derived from the past participle of a verb: *These are the most worn shoes*, not **the wornest shoes*.) Adjectives consisting of three or more syllables take only the periphrastic form: *interesting / most interesting*, never **interestingest*. (An exception is a short adjective preceded by *un-*: *unkindest, unhappiest*.) And adjectives consisting of two syllables occur in both forms: *happiest / most happy, politest / most polite*. The situation with adverbs is different: in particular, the inflectional ending cannot be added to adverbs ending in *-ly*: *most quickly*, not **quickliest* (though these forms will sometimes be heard in non-standard English).

RG 51; SGE 7.41–5; CGEL 7.74–82

suprasegmental feature (KS 4) see **prosody**

syllable (KS 4)

• Developing a sense of syllabic weight is important. Students might try counting the syllables in their names, or beating out the number of syllables in a slogan or chant (such as a football chant).

• If students are having difficulty deciding where to make a syllable division, they will get help from a dictionary – or, at least, from certain dictionaries. One way of judging the value of a dictionary is whether it gives you information of this kind (either in the headword or in the pronunciation guide).

• Some writing systems are based on the idea of the syllable: in Japanese, for example, the *kana* writing systems represent syllables. So, there are different symbols for *ka, ke, ko*, and several dozen other syllable types in the language.

IPE 5.4–5; EPP 8.2

synchronic and diachronic

• This useful pair of terms summarises two complementary perspectives for the study of language. A diachronic study examines the development of a language through time. A synchronic study examines a state of a language at some particular point or period in time, disregarding whatever changes may be taking place. Thus, we can carry out a synchronic study of Chaucer's English, to determine its characteristics, or we can study his language diachronically, as a sample of English in the process of change from Early Middle English to Early Modern English.

CEL 65

synonyms (KS 3)

- If you define **synonymy** as two words with *exactly* the same meaning – that is, whenever word A is used, word B could be used – you won't find many examples. You may not find any. Indeed, you could argue that there wouldn't be any point in a language having two words which meant exactly the same thing. One would surely die out. What happens in practice is that the words differ in slight or subtle ways. *Autumn* and *fall* are synonyms, but the former is used in British English and the latter in American English. *A smell* and *a stink* are synonyms, but the latter is much more informal. *Politician* and *statesman* can be synonyms, but the latter is a much more highly valued term (see the entry on **connotation**). Some words are synonyms, but only in a very restricted range of contexts: both *addled* and *rancid* mean 'bad', but the former is used for eggs and brains, whereas the latter is used for bacon and butter.

- There are thousands of cases of partial overlap in meaning. Many dictionaries give you 'synonym essays' which try to tease apart the differences in meaning – for example, between *critical, captious, caviling, carping, censorious*, and *faultfinding*. A good source-book is *Webster's Dictionary of Synonyms* (Merriam, 1951), which incidentally also contains sets of antonyms and other contrasting words.

- English is rich in synonyms partly because of the way in which words came into the language over the centuries. Take *kingly, royal*, and *regal*: the first comes from Old English, the second from French, and the third from Latin. They mean more or less the same thing – majestic. But that 'more or less' is crucial. Thus we can say *royal mail* but not **kingly mail* or **regal mail*. We can say *She looked very regal*, but not **She looked very kingly*. And so on. Other examples of this kind are *brotherly* and *fraternal*, and *buy* and *purchase*.

CEL 17

syntax (KS 3)

- Look at the first sentence in the entry? If your definition of sentence is 'Begin with a capital letter and end with a full stop', the sentence runs from *No* to *sin*. Some would prefer me to have put a full stop after *No*, as I mention in the entry; but I want a continuative not an abrupt tone after *No*, so I prefer a comma. I don't want the student to 'hear' a pause in my voice between *No* and *this*. (Note the contrast with the next sentence, where I *do* want a pause after *Sorry*.)

• Syntax is *part of* grammar. It's one of the main branches of grammar. Therefore students shouldn't get into the habit of saying 'grammar and syntax'. This expression dates from a time when the subject-matter of grammar was seen as the study of word endings (as it had been in Latin). 'Word endings (morphology) and syntax' does make sense. The term **grammar** isn't used in that way any more. And in English, certainly, where there are hardly any inflectional endings, it doesn't make sense to label this minority aspect as 'grammar'.

RG 74; SGE 1.2; CGEL 2

taboo word (KS 3) see **expletive**

tag question (KS 4)

• Tagged on at the end? Almost always. But if the sentence is very long, you can use the tag earlier: *It's true, isn't it, that they'll all be wanting their money back?*

• An important (albeit obvious) feature of most tags is that the pronoun must repeat or agree with the subject of the statement: *He's ready, is he?*, not **He's ready, is she?* Note the existence of very formal negative tag questions, where the negative word is placed after the verb: *did they not?*, *should he not?* – compare *didn't they?*, *shouldn't he?* These patterns are found in some northern British dialects, too.

• Some tag questions are used regardless of the structure of the previous clause. In much regional and informal speech, for example, *in'it* ('isn't it') is used in this way (compare *n'est-ce pas* in French). Other general tags include *am I right?*, *isn't that so?*, *don't you think?*, *wouldn't you say?*, *you know?*, and the reduced tags, such as *right?*, *yeah?*, *huh?*, and *OK?*

RG 5; SGE 11.6; CGEL 11.8–11

tautology (KS 4)

• In its strictest sense, a tautology is a statement which is empty of meaning because it is self-evidently true. The kind of example which is presented in philosophy is *A woman is female* and *Venus is the evening star*. However, in general use, the term has extended to include identity of meaning between sentences, and taken on a pejorative sense, to mean *unnecessary* or *undesirable* repetition. This entry ought therefore to be read in conjunction with the one on **circumlocution**.

● Not all tautologies are to be condemned. There are times when *I myself personally* would sound all right – such as in a jocular response by a husband to his wife's surprised question 'Who did the washing up?' And all definitions are tautologies, such as *Linguistics is the science of language*. Also, some tautologies are only apparent: a deeper meaning is being signalled by the utterance. *Boys will be boys* is saying more than it seems. So is *Once I've promised, I've promised* and *When I go out drinking, I go out drinking* and *My sister is a lady*. And if someone says *I don't like that proposal*, and then *That proposal I definitely don't like*, there is an extra element of definiteness and emphasis which would be lacking if only one of the two utterances had been made.

● In literature, tautology can be used to convey something about character and attitude. A famous example is Hamlet's comment: *There's ne'er a villain dwelling in all Denmark/ But he's an arrant knave*.

LG 8.2

telegrammatic speech (KS 3)

● The examples in the entry show the word order of the sentences to be correct. This isn't always so, especially in the early stages of telegrammatic speech. Once a young scrap came up to me and said *Tickle man*. I waited. She said it again. I waited. Then she took my hand, and said *tickle man*, making it quite clear that she wanted *me* to tickle *her*. She meant: 'Man tickle.'

• Don't expect the meanings of telegrammatic sentences always to be clear. Looking at a picture of a street scene, a child said *Policeman bus*. Indeed, there were both a bus and a policeman in the picture, but what was the child saying about them? There was no way of knowing.

• The process of putting two words together into a sentence starts at around 18 months, on average. The 2-year-old in my entry is at a relatively advanced stage, as can be seen from the three-element sentences used as examples. The next step, with such a child, will be the 'filling out' of these sentences, putting in the function words (see **grammatical word**). By 2½, the telegrammatic stage should be all but over. For it to last much longer than this would suggest some kind of language delay. In severe cases of delayed language development, telegrammatic speech can continue for several years.

CEL 41

tense (KS 3)

• None of the examples in the first part of the entry are of progressive tense forms, and these should be given too (see **progressive**). Exactly the same points apply: the two tenses are *I am running* and *I was running*. Everything else involves the use of auxiliary verbs with *be*: *I have been running*, *I will be running*, etc.

• With this notion, you have to decide how to use the term. If you go for the inflectional definition, then it follows that there are only two tenses. (This is my own preference.) If you allow in a broader, semantic definition (tense = time, regardless of how it appears in the sentence), then you end up with lots of tenses, including the auxiliary verbs and time adverbials.

• This entry should be read along with the various other entries on tense. Note also the entry on **historic present**.

RG 23; SGE 4.1–6; CGEL 4.2–16

text (KS 4)

• A branch of linguistics has emerged which specialises in the properties of texts: it's called **textlinguistics**. There is still some dispute about whether this term should be restricted to the written language or should include spoken language as well. My entry very definitely goes for the broader application. I talk quite happily about 'spoken texts' and 'written texts'.

• An interesting exercise is to collect small-scale texts for analysis, such as the various kinds of ticket, programme, leaflet, label, badge, counterfoil, number-plate, logo, letterhead, certificate, passport, and so on. The aim is to try to work out the structure of the text – a grammar, if you like, which identifies its salient features. 'To be an acceptable car number-plate, the following linguistic features have to be present . . .' Even simple cases turn out to be intriguingly difficult, when you examine them. The situation with US number-plates is quite complex. And even in the UK, there are complications when you try to work out all the possibilities (the year-coding is messed up by the purchase of private plates, for instance).

CEL 20

thesaurus (KS 3)

• This is an essential piece of school equipment. Several editions of *Roget's Thesaurus* exist, and there are other products which bring related items of vocabulary together – under such names as 'word finder', for example.

• Look out for experiments in new ways of presenting lexical information. For example, the *Longman Lexicon* is an interesting cross between a thesaurus and a dictionary. You look up a word in the index at the back, and it refers you to a section where related words are grouped together – but these words (unlike in a conventional thesaurus) are given dictionary treatment.

CEL 17

tone of voice (KS 4) see **prosody**

tongue (KS 4)

• I think the only thing to be stressed here is the point about frequency: a remarkable number of sounds are made with the tongue. The importance of the tongue is reflected in the way it has come to be used as a synonym for language, in such a phrase as *mother tongue* or *the several tongues of China*.

• Get the students to work out which consonants in English do and which don't use the tongue. The only ones which don't are the ones at the lips ([p,b,f,v,m]) and anything made in the glottis (notably [h]).

• The tongue functions in three dimensions. It moves backwards and forwards, for both consonants and vowels (see the entry on **front**) and up and down (see the entry on **close vowel**), and in addition it is able to hollow the surface, to make the groove needed for **sibilant** sounds.

IPE 2.2.3.2; EPP 2.1

topic see **predicate**

topic sentence (KS 3)

• It is often difficult deciding what a topic sentence is, because a particular theme can be spread over several sentences. It's easy if the paragraph begins *John decided to go to town* or *This is how you fix a bike*, and the rest of the paragraph is devoted to developing this theme. But take the first paragraph of my entry. Which is the topic sentence there? Is it the first? Or the last? Or the fifth? In an expository style, there's a lot of re-stating, and the content of the topic sentence may appear two or three times in different guises. In such cases, it's important *not* to force a decision. If a paragraph works well, and you can't decide which is the topic sentence, don't arbitrarily choose one, on the grounds that there *has to* be one somewhere! The notion of a topic sentence comes from a particular view of what is good writing style. This view is not sacrosanct, and while it is always desirable to maintain a clear thematic organisation in a paragraph, it may not be possible to identify a single place where the theme is summarised. More important than the notion of a topic sentence are the notions of internal coherence within the paragraph and textual break between paragraphs.

• Note that as the topic sentence moves about the paragraph, in my entry, minor changes creep into it – in particular, the change to using a personal pronoun.

CGEL 19.28

traditional grammar

• This term summarises the whole set of attitudes, procedures and prescriptions which were characteristic of the prelinguistic era of language study, and especially of the European school grammars of the eighteenth and nineteenth centuries. These emphasised such matters as correctness, linguistic purism, literary excellence, the use of Latin models, and the priority of the written language over the spoken (see further, **purism**, **prescriptive**, **correctness**). Linguistic approaches, by contrast, emphasise such criteria as descriptive accuracy, appropriateness and comprehensiveness (see further, **appropriate, usage**).

CEL 1

transcription (KS 4) see **phonetic alphabet**

transformation (KS 4)

• Next door's Rotweiler hasn't been chased by our moggie out of the garden.

• An approach to grammar which focuses on this kind of structural relationship between sentences is called a **transformational grammar**. The notion of a transformation is one way of expressing the intuitive feeling of native speakers that such sentences as statements and questions, positives and negatives, actives and passives, and so on are related to each other.

The first modern transformational grammar was devised by the American linguist Noam Chomsky in the late 1950s.

CEL 16

transitive verb (KS 3)

• Other intransitive verbs include: *go, lie, die, appear, opt out, make off*. There are some verbs which can be both intransitive and transitive; grammarians sometimes say that the object is 'understood', in such cases. An example is *She's reading* and *She's reading a book*. Other such verbs are *smoke, drink, help, write, drive, walk, drop, blow down, put off*. Notice that the verb can change its meaning as it changes its status: the only way in which *kick* could be used intransitively is in the sense of 'to object'. *I made up a story* is transitive; *We were made up* ('happy') is intransitive. In such cases (and there are many of them), students should try to think of verbs as having transitive and intransitive *uses* – rather than verbs being inherently one or the other.

• Some verbs take two objects: see the entry on **direct object** for more about this. If you want to distinguish between these two possibilities, you can use the following terminology: verbs which take one object are **monotransitive**; verbs which take two are **ditransitive**.

• Note that the object can be a noun phrase (as illustrated in the entry) or a clause, whether finite or nonfinite (see **finite**). Compare the three types: *I like books; I like what you like; I like walking in the rain*.

RG 8; SGE 16.11, 14–15; CGEL 16.19, 25–7

trill (KS 4)

• The trill is a very tense sound, requiring a lot of muscular energy. To practise the tongue-tip version (the **alveolar** trill), use such words as *drive* or *tripe*, where the first sound is made at almost the same place as the [r]. You'll also hear it in dramatic style, such as verse-reading.

• A uvular trill is sometimes heard in regional accents in the north-east of England, and also in parts of Scotland.

IPE 4.3.3

triphthong (KS 4)

• You can think of triphthongs as a sequence of a diphthong plus [ə]: the diphthongs which allow this give [eɪə] as in *player*; [aɪə] as in *fire*; [ɔɪə] as in *employer*; [əʊə] as in *slower*; and [aʊə] as in *tower*. In rapidly spoken speech, however, it is common to hear this sequence of three vowel-qualities being reduced to two, and often one – as when *tower* is said [tɑː], rhyming with *tar*, in advanced RP (see **Received Pronunciation**).

EPP 3.3; IPE 7.11

trochee (KS 4) see **foot**

unaspirated (KS 4) see **aspiration**

uncountable noun (KS 4) see **count noun**

underextension (KS 3)

- This phenomenon is much more difficult to spot in children's speech than **overextension**. With overextension, such as *dog* being used to refer to a cat, the error is obvious. But if you think about the case of underextension presented in the entry, *shoes* is being used for – shoes. There would normally be no grounds for thinking that anything was wrong.
- Notice how natural an error underextension is – in the adult learning of technical terms, for example. Say you encounter a strange-looking metal rod in your lawn mower. 'What's that?', you ask an expert. 'Oh, that's a gigsprockulet,' she says. I then ask you to define *gigsprockulet*. You say: 'It's a metal rod found in a lawn mower which . . .'. If the only objects containing gigsprockulets were lawn mowers, then this definition would be fine; but if it turned out that gigsprockulets were a normal feature of several types of mechanism, then you've underextended.

CEL 42

ungrammatical (KS 3) see **grammar**

univocalic (KS 4) see **lipogram**

unstressed syllable see **stress**

upper case and lower case (KS 3)

- Upper-case letters date back to the majuscule letters of the Greek and Latin alphabets – letters which were contained within a single pair of horizontal lines. Minuscule letters had parts which extended above or below a pair of horizontal lines. The combined use of the two types (the 'dual alphabet') dates from the period of Emperor Charlemagne (742–814).

● Students might find it useful to know some of the terminology for describing parts of a printed letter. Draw a pair of horizontal lines, with an *x* between them, so that the top line runs along the top of the *x* and the bottom line runs along the bottom. The distance between the lines is called the **x-height**. Several lower-case letters are located here, such as *c*, *e*, *r*. Some letters extend above x-height, and the part which does is called the **ascender** (as in *h*, *d*). Some letters extend below x-height, and the part which does is called the **descender**. A small terminal stroke at the end of a main stroke of a letter is called a **serif** (['serif]).

CEL 32

usage (KS 3)

● This entry should be linked with those on **appropriate** and **correctness**, as it addresses the same kind of problem – how to deal with variation in language.

● Although I've focused on usage variation in my entry, it's important to realise that the study of usage doesn't deal only with variety, or with the controversial areas of language. It involves everything in language – all aspects of pronunciation, grammar, and vocabulary. The Survey of English Usage, at University College London, is as much concerned to study a sentence structure about which there is universal agreement as it is to study, say, split infinitives. It's all usage. But when you find a book called something like 'A Guide to English Usage', you'll find that it's likely to deal only with those areas which have been the source of argument – and they are very much a minority.

CGEL 1

uvula (KS 4) see **palate**

variety (KS 3)

● This is a useful term, because it subsumes everything – regional dialects, accents, literary genres, occupational dialects, social dialects, and so on. Note that not all uses of language can be easily assigned to a variety. It's often not obvious what sort of language we are dealing with. In literature, for example, the concept of 'essay' is notoriously difficult to define. To prove the point, try identifying the salient linguistic features of a literary essay?

• A fruitful task is to get students to go through two copies of a daily newspaper, cutting out each distinctive item. They then have to group the items into stylistic types. The varieties will include news reporting, letters, crossword clues, captions, editorials, sports results, and so on. Some items won't fit neatly into any category.

• A variety is a situationally distinctive use of language, but note that in any situation you can look at the language from several points of view. For example, a sermon can be viewed as a variety of religious English. From a different point of view it is an example of the variety of formal English. From another point of view it is the variety of sermon (as opposed to other varieties of religious English). And so on.

EL 6, 12; CGEL 1.19–41

velar, velum (KS 4) see **palate**

verb (KS 3)

• The old definition of a verb as a 'doing word' is, as this entry shows, hopeless. It leaves out far too many verbs.

• Pay special attention to the verb. It is the most important element in the clause, in that other elements depend largely on the verb for their occurrence and type. Whether you have an object depends on the type of verb. Whether you have a complement depends on the type of verb. Whether you have an adverbial, and what type of adverbial it is, depends on the type of verb. And the type of subject (eg whether it is animate or inanimate) is closely bound up with the type of verb.

• There are many ways of classifying verbs. One common classification is based on their syntax – whether they govern an object or not (see **transitive**). Another is based on their morphology – especially on the way their base forms, past tenses, and past participles appear. For example, some verbs change their vowel in each form (*swim/swam/swum*). Some have the same form for all three parts: *I cut it (now), I cut it (then), I have cut it*. There are seven main classes of irregular verb in English: CGEL 3.11–20 gives a full list.

RG 16; SGE 3.9–10

verb phrase (KS 3)

• The main items in a verb phrase are the **auxiliary verb** and the marker of **negation** (see separate entries on these terms). Note that in questions the first auxiliary verb comes at the very beginning of the clause, in front of the subject.

• There are major stylistic differences in English between the noun phrase and the verb phrase. In some varieties, the difference is quite noticeable. Scientific and legal English are examples, where the noun phrases can be highly complex and the verb can be as simple as *is*.

• The term **verb phrase** has a more general sense in some linguistic theories (notably, generative grammar), where it refers to the whole of a sentence structure other than the subject noun-phrase.

RG 15–26; SGE 3–4; CGEL 3–4

vocabulary (KS 3)

• Counting the words in a passage is an invaluable exercise, because it quickly brings to light the problems inherent in answering the apparently simple question 'How many words are there?' Even the apparently simple procedure of counting the word spaces (as a computer word-counting programme does) isn't fool-proof, as sometimes you can't decide whether two items are best kept separate or are to be joined by a hyphen (see **compound word** for more about this). Also, words which are variants of each other could be grouped together (see **lexeme** for more about this). For example, in the present entry, students would have to decide how to deal with the following types of problem: are *know* and *knows* counted as two or one? are *is*, *are*, *were*, and *be* counted separately, or as forms of *be*? should *do* and *doesn't* be counted separately? is *75* one word or two (*seventy-five*)?

• I counted the number of different words in the entry: the lexical **types**. The total number of words in the entry, regardless of how many times each is used, is the number of lexical **tokens**. There are 193. A useful measure of the lexical diversity of a passage is called the **Type-Token Ratio**. You work this out by dividing types by tokens. In the present case this would be 106/193 = 0.55.

• Estimates for the size of the vocabulary of English vary enormously, from around half a million to several million. Certainly, when we consider all the regional dialect differences (the world over) and all the nomenclature of natural history (to take just two areas), the larger estimates seem more realistic.

• To develop a sense of vocabulary breadth, take two large dictionaries of comparable size, find a common starting point, then compare them to see which words are in. You will be struck by the lack of correspondence.

EL 3

vocal cords (KS 4)

• Stress the remarkable number of ways in which the vocal cords are used during speech. No other vocal organ has such a diverse range of uses. Also, emphasise the importance of voicing when people make the sounds of speech, and get the entry on **voice** (in phonetics) read along with this one.

• A glottal stop is also made at the vocal cords (see **glottis**). And among the voice qualities we can make are whisper (a well-known term) and creaky voice (not so well known – listen to film-star Vincent Price when he gets really menacing).

CEL 22

vocal organs (KS 4)

• You might even argue that the brain is a vocal organ, too, in that it controls the operation of everything else!

• Find a diagram of the vocal organs in an introduction to phonetics (as in IPE 2.2, CEL 22) and get students to practise drawing it and labelling the parts.

vocative (KS 4)

• A vocative is an optional element: its presence doesn't affect the structure of the rest of the sentence. It's usually a noun phrase, and it may occur at the beginning, in the middle, or at the end of a sentence. The first and third of these are illustrated in the entry; the second is seen in *I feel, Mr Smith, that you should resign*. It's used either as a call or an address.

• Get students to classify the main types of vocatives. They may be proper names (*Mrs Bhullar*), family terms (*daddy*), titles of respect (*sir, Your Honour*), markers of status (*doctor, Mr President*), names of occupations (*waiter, nurse*), general nouns (*ladies and gentlemen*), and epithets expressing an evaluation, whether favourable (*darling, my friend*) or unfavourable (*you idiot, coward*). The pronoun *you* can be used alone as a vocative, but is strongly impolite (*Come here, you*) unless modified (*you guys, you-all*). We can use modifiers with some of these vocatives: *you silly twit, my dear chap, you with the green hat*). The use of *O* as a vocative marker is archaic. The nearest we get to this is the use of *Dear* in letter-writing.

• Note the use of vocatives in addressing inanimate objects, especially in literature: *For thy sake, Tobacco, I/ Would do anything but die* (Charles Lamb, 'A Farewell to Tobacco').

RG 13; SGE 10.31–2; CGEL 10.52–3

voice (in grammar) (KS 4)

• There are three grammatical processes which take place when you change an active sentence into a passive one: (1) the active subject becomes the passive agent, and is introduced by *by*; (2) the active object becomes the passive subject; and (3) you change the verb, by adding an auxiliary verb and putting the main verb into its participle form. So, from *The cat chased the dog* we get *The dog was chased by the cat*. (See entries on **agent**, **auxiliary verb**, **participle** and **subject**.)

• There is a widespread criticism of the passive voice. People don't like it to be overused – and some style manuals say it should never be used at all. Why? Because, they say, passive constructions are much more difficult to understand than active ones, and can lead to a very impersonal and convoluted style (see entry on **impersonal style**). There's some truth in this, but such sweeping recommendations don't tell the whole story. Certain styles need to be impersonal (such as the science example in my entry). And it's very difficult to avoid the passive, at times. Even in the books which condemn the passive, you'll find it creeping in. One such book ends with the recommendation *The passive should be avoided at all times*! You can probably see why it's so difficult to avoid. To turn that sentence into the active, the writer would have to specify a subject. Should it be *we, you, writers, speakers* . . . ? By using the passive, you don't have to choose.

• For a clause to become passive, the verb must be transitive. But not all transitive verb clauses can become passive. We can say *Carlos resembles his father* but not **His father is resembled by Carlos*. Similarly, we can't say **A large house is had by them* or **200 people are held by the cinema*. In certain cases, also, we have a passive clause which can't become active: *She was born in Holyhead, Poor John was drowned*. We can't turn these sentences around and say, for example, that *Someone drowned John*. The grammars give several other types of exception.

RG 22; SGE 3.25–6; CGEL 3.63–78

voice (in phonetics) (KS 4)

• The voiceless consonants are [p,t,k,tʃ,f,θ,s,ʃ,h].

• I've cheated a bit to get four voiced sounds in *Crystal*: the two vowels and the [l] are fair, but the [r] after the [k] is **devoiced** – part of its voicing has been lost because of its association with the preceding voiceless sound. The devoicing of consonants is very common: you'll hear it especially when a voiced consonant occurs at the end of a word, as in *cab* or *bid*. To voice these sounds fully, the words would sound something like *cab-uh* or *bid-uh*.

EPP 4.1–2; IPE 2.2

vowel (KS 4) see **consonant and vowel**

wh-question (KS 3) see **question**

word (KS 3)

• The pause criterion isn't foolproof, but it's a good start. Another test is to take a spoken sentence and ask people to put extra words in between the words which are there. They would certainly say *new washing machine* and not **washing new machine*, for example.

• The complexities of this notion become more apparent at KS 4, where I discuss the need to distinguish between **word** and **lexeme**, and the problems posed by **multi-word verbs**. Students should also consult the entry on **compound word** at KS 3.

CEL 16

word class (KS 3) see **parts of speech**

word ending see **inflection**

word games (KS 3)

• This entry simply gathers together the various entries, as examples of the genre. Students should follow them up individually. Standard reading is Tony Augarde, *The Oxford Guide to Word Games* (OUP, 1984).

• Why are word games so widely played? Possibly because they are a very democratic kind of game. They aren't like *Mastermind* and *The Krypton Factor*, where people need to have learned a great deal about a special field or be very fit or both. With word games, all native speakers are equal.

word order (KS 3)

• Other important word order changes in English include the statement/question alternation (*She is leaving – Is she leaving?*), the placement of adverbials (*Usually I go on Thursdays, I usually go on Thursdays, I go on Thursdays usually*), and the fronting of a clause element for emphasis (*Smith my name is*).

• Some of the most interesting word order variations occur in literature. Some examples:

Glad did I live and gladly die (R L Stevenson, *Underwoods*)
A man severe he was and stern to view (Goldsmith, *The Deserted Village*)
Secret was the garden; Set i' the pathless awe/ Where no star its breath can draw (Francis Thompson, 'The Mistress of Vision')
While pensive poets painful vigils keep (Pope, *The Dunciad*)

CEL 16; CGEL 2.46–59

yes-no question (KS 3) see **question**

zeugma see **coordination**

Appendix

This Appendix lists all the terms which are used in both the KS 3 and KS 4 books, grouped under several general headings. Terms in the KS 3 book are introduced by 3; terms in the KS 4 book are introduced by 4. Terms introduced by T are in the teacher's book only. Headwords are shown as in the individual entries, and cross-references are shown as they appear in the books.

General

3 body language → communication
3 communication
T competence
4 context
4 corpus
T co-text → context
T description → prescription
4 deviance, deviant
T diachronic → synchronic
3 feedback
3 first language and second language
4 informant
3 language
T level
4 lingua franca
4 linguistics
4 metalanguage, metalinguistic
3 mother tongue → first language
3 nonverbal communication → communication
T performance → competence
T philology
T pragmatics
T prescription
T purism
T rule
3 second language → first language
T synchronic
4 text
3 usage

Child Language

3 baby talk
4 expansion
4 holophrase
3 motherese
3 overextension
3 telegrammatic speech
3 underextension

Grammar

4 abstract noun and concrete noun
T accidence
T accusative
4 active voice → voice (in grammar)
3 adjective
3 adjective phrase
T adjunct
3 adverb
3 adverbial
3 adverb phrase
3 affirmative
3 affix, affixation
4 agent
3 agreement → concord
T amplifier → degree
4 anacoluthon
T anaphora
4 animate and inanimate
4 antecedent
4 apposition
3 article
4 aspect
3 auxiliary verb and main verb
3 block language
4 cardinal numeral and ordinal numeral
3 case
T cataphora → anaphora
T catenative
3 clause
3 clause analysis
4 cleft sentence
4 cohesion
4 collective noun
3 command
4 comment clause
3 common noun → noun
3 comparative
3 complement
4 complex sentence
4 compound sentence
3 compound word
3 concord
4 concrete noun → abstract noun
4 conditional clause
T conjunct → adjunct
3 conjunction
3 connectivity
T constituent
T content word → grammatical word
3 continuous → progressive
3 contraction
3 conversion
3 coordination
4 copula

3 verb
3 verb phrase
4 vocative
4 voice (in grammar)
3 *wh*-question → question
3 word
3 word class → parts of speech
3 word order
3 *yes-no* question → question

Language Variety

3 accent
3 acrostic
3 anagram
4 alliteration
4 anapaest → foot
4 aphorism
3 appropriate
3 archaism, archaic
4 argot
4 assonance
3 audience
3 back slang
3 bilingual
4 cant → argot
T code-mixing/switching → bilingual
3 colloquial speech
3 conversation
3 correctness
4 creole
4 dactyl → foot
3 dialect
3 dialogue and monologue
3 diction
T diglossia
4 discourse
3 euphemism
4 euphony, euphonious
4 expletive
4 eye rhyme
3 figure of speech
3 fluency
4 foot
4 foregrounding, foregrounded
3 formal and informal
3 genre
4 haiku
4 hyperbole
4 iambic foot → foot
4 idiolect
3 imagery
4 impersonal style
4 irony, ironic
T isogloss
3 limerick
4 lipogram
3 literal
4 litotes
3 metaphor
4 metonymy, metonym
3 metre
3 monolingual → bilingual
3 monologue → dialogue
3 multilingual → bilingual
3 non-standard English → standard English
4 onomatopoeia → sound symbolism
4 oracy
4 oxymoron
3 palindrome
3 pangram
4 paradox, paradoxical
4 parody, parodist
4 personal style → impersonal style
3 personification
4 pidgin
3 proverb
3 rebus
3 regional dialect → dialect
3 register → variety
T rhetoric
3 rhyme
3 riddle
4 sarcasm → irony
3 simile
3 slang
3 slogan
4 sound symbolism
4 spondee → foot
3 standard English
3 style
3 sub-standard English → standard English
3 taboo word
4 trochee → foot
4 univocalic
3 variety
3 word games
T zeugma → coordination

Semantics

3 abbreviation
3 acronym
3 ambiguous, ambiguity
4 analogy
3 antonyms, antonymy
3 blend
3 borrowing or loan word
3 circumlocution
3 cliche
3 clipping
4 coherence, coherent
3 coinage → neologism
4 collocation
T complementary terms → antonyms
4 concordance
4 connotation → denotation
T converse terms → antonyms
T co-reference → reference
4 denotation and connotation
T deixis
3 derivation
3 dictionary
4 emotive meaning
4 epigram or epigraph
4 epithet
3 etymology
4 focus
4 homographs → homonyms
4 homonyms
4 homophones → homonyms
4 hypernyms → hyponyms
4 hyponyms, hyponymy
3 idiom
4 incoherence → coherence
4 inference, infer
3 irrelevance → relevance
3 jargon
4 lexeme
4 lexicography → lexicology
4 lexicology
3 lexicon → vocabulary
3 loan word → borrowing
4 malapropism

3 neologism
T nonce word → neologism
3 paraphrase
4 parenthesis, parenthetic
3 pen name → pseudonym
3 periphrasis → circumlocution
4 polysemic, polysemy
3 pseudonym
3 pun
T reference
3 relevance
T semantics
T sense relations
3 spoonerism
3 synonyms, synonymous
4 tautology, tautologous
3 thesaurus
3 vocabulary

Sound System

4 affricate
4 allophone
4 alveolar
4 approximant
4 articulation, articulator
4 aspiration, aspirated
4 assimilation, assimilate
4 back → front
4 bilabial
T cardinal vowels
T central vowel → front
4 click
4 close vowel and open vowel
4 cluster
4 consonant and vowel
4 contour
T coarticulation → articulation
4 dental
T devoiced → voice (in phonetics)
4 diphthong
4 elision, elide
4 fricative
4 front and back
4 glottis, glottal
4 high vowel → close vowel
T interdental → dental
4 International Phonetic Alphabet
4 intonation
4 intrusive *r* → linking sound
4 IPA → International Phonetic Alphabet
4 labial
4 labio-dental
4 larynx
4 lateral
4 linking sound
4 low vowel → close vowel
4 mid vowel → close vowel
4 minimal pair
4 nasal
4 open vowel → close vowel
4 palate, palatal
4 pharynx, pharyngeal
4 phoneme
4 phonetic alphabet
4 phonetics, phonetician
4 phonology, phonologist
4 plosive
T polysyllabic, polysyllable
4 prosody, prosodic
T pronunciation
4 Received Pronunciation
3 rhythm
4 roll → trill
4 rounding, rounded
4 RP → Received Pronunciation
T schwa
4 semi-vowel → approximant
4 sibilance, sibilant
4 spread → rounding
4 stop consonant → plosive
4 stress
4 suprasegmental feature
4 syllable
4 tone of voice
4 tongue
4 transcription → phonetic alphabet
4 trill
4 triphthong
4 unaspirated → aspiration
T unstressed syllable → stress
4 uvula → palate
4 velar
4 velum → palate, velar
4 vocal cords
4 vocal organs
4 voice (in phonetics)
4 vowel → consonant

Writing System

3 accents
3 alphabet
3 apostrophe
T braces → brackets
3 brackets or parentheses
3 capital letter → upper case
3 colon
3 comma
3 dash
4 diacritic
4 digraph → grapheme
3 drafting
3 full stop
4 grapheme
4 graphology
3 hyphen
4 ideogram
3 illiterate → literate
3 indentation or indention
3 inverted commas
3 literate and illiterate
3 logogram
3 lower case → upper case
4 orthography
3 paragraph
3 parentheses → brackets
3 period → full stop
T pictogram → ideogram
3 punctuation
3 quotation marks → inverted commas
3 semi-colon
3 speech marks → inverted commas
4 spelling reform → orthography
3 upper case and lower case